Praise for
The Best Spiritual Writing 2010

"Outstanding . . . For thoughtfulness and literary pleasure, this instantiation may be the best yet. A beautiful collection, excellent especially for literary-minded readers of all religious persuasions; an essential purchase for most libraries." —*Library Journal* (starred review)

"Zaleski's compilation of spiritual writings restores 'best' to its rightful exceptional place. . . . It is a curious literary party at first glance, but the diverse forms, voices, topics, gradually coalesce into something bigger and more elegant, something spiritual and extraordinary."
—*Publishers Weekly* (starred review)

"[A] reliably bracing volume . . ." —*Booklist* (starred review)

"[A] luminous collection." —*Chicago Tribune*

"Like a very fine friend returned from a year's voyaging, laden with delights and treasures to share, Philip Zaleski brings us, here again, another trove of well-wrought, luminous, soul-bracing gifts."
—Thomas Lynch, author of *The Undertaking* and
Apparition & Late Fictions

"There is enough here to feed the hungry heart for years to come."
—Phyllis Tickle, author of *The Great Emergence*

The Best
Spiritual Writing
2011

Edited by

PHILIP ZALESKI

Introduction by

BILLY COLLINS

PENGUIN BOOKS

PENGUIN BOOKS
Published by the Penguin Group
Penguin Group (USA) Inc.,
375 Hudson Street, New York, New York 10014, U.S.A.
Penguin Group (Canada), 90 Eglinton Avenue East, Suite 700, Toronto,
Ontario, Canada M4P 2Y3 (a division of Pearson Penguin Canada Inc.)
Penguin Books Ltd, 80 Strand, London WC2R 0RL, England
Penguin Ireland, 25 St Stephen's Green, Dublin 2,
Ireland (a division of Penguin Books Ltd)
Penguin Group (Australia), 250 Camberwell Road, Camberwell,
Victoria 3124, Australia (a division of Pearson Australia Group Pty Ltd)
Penguin Books India Pvt Ltd, 11 Community Centre,
Panchsheel Park, New Delhi – 110 017, India
Penguin Group (NZ), 67 Apollo Drive, Rosedale, North Shore 0632,
New Zealand (a division of Pearson New Zealand Ltd)
Penguin Books (South Africa) (Pty) Ltd, 24 Sturdee Avenue,
Rosebank, Johannesburg 2196, South Africa

Penguin Books Ltd, Registered Offices:
80 Strand, London WC2R 0RL, England

First published in Penguin Books 2010

1 3 5 7 9 10 8 6 4 2

Copyright © Philip Zaleski, 2010
Introduction copyright © Billy Collins, 2010
All rights reserved

Pages 242–44 constitute an extension of this copyright page.

ISBN 978-0-14-311867-1
CIP data available

Printed in the United States of America
Set in Adobe Garamond
Designed by Elke Sigal

Contents

Foreword

IN THE SPRING OF 2009 A. N. WILSON, THE ENGLISH NOVELIST AND historian, author of contentious studies of Jesus, Tolstoy, Belloc, and C. S. Lewis, announced in the pages of the *New Statesman* that after several years as an enthusiastic atheist, he had returned to belief in God. Wilson, never afraid to bloody the page with his pen, seized the occasion to skewer several of his skeptical colleagues—and, unusually, himself as well, declaring that as a natural doubting Thomas, he should have known better than to trust the deep self-satisfaction that suffused his being when he announced to the world that God was dead. He had thoroughly enjoyed the "heady sense of being at one with the great tide of nonbelievers"; the problem was that certain irritating realizations kept getting in the way.

One was that so many of the people Wilson most admired had led a deeply spiritual life; he mentions Mohandas Gandhi and Dietrich Bonhoeffer. Another was that religion and spirituality seemed to be experiential spheres charged with meaning; might it be that those who repudiate religion are akin to those "who have no ear for music, or who have never been in love"—that is, perfectly good people with a tragic blind spot or an equally tragic lack of opportunity, who have no idea of what they are missing? It is his third observation, however, that will be of particular interest to readers of the Best Spiritual Writing series. Striking back at what he calls the "superstitious" theories of doctrinaire Darwinian evolutionists, who stake all upon natural selection and random mutation, he asks, with palpable exasperation, "do materialists really think that language just 'evolved,' like finches' beaks, or have they simply never thought about the matter rationally?" He goes on to argue that

> purely materialist "explanations" for our mysterious human existence simply won't do. . . . The phenomenon of language alone should give us pause . . . the existence of language is one of the many phenomena . . . which suggest that human beings are very much more than collections of meat. They convince me that we are spiritual beings.

Wilson's assessment fails to do justice to the Darwinian perspective; evolutionary biologists have indeed thought about the matter rationally, and their explanation for the means by which language developed, while subject to correction—as are all scientific theories—remains, for now, in place. What sends a thrill down the spine, however, is his perception that language opens into the ineluctably enigmatic, that it points toward the transcendent, that something beyond our ken is going on whenever we sound a word or write a string of letters. Every writer and reader can sense the truth of this claim. Every bit of writing, be it poetry or prose, brushes up against this mystery. We are not considering here the secrets of inspiration that lie behind a scintillating style or the discovery of *le mot juste*, but the far deeper enigma that such a thing as style—or better still, expression—or better still, meaning—exists at all. The question isn't how did language evolve, but why is there language—the articulation of good and evil, beauty and ugliness, truth and falsehood, the apprehension of mental and moral qualities and values—at all? *Why logos instead of chaos?* By what spiritual alchemy do grunts and squiggles become the Hymn to the Aten or Hamlet's soliloquy? Questions such as these lie, unvoiced, in the background of every poem or essay contained in this collection. They instill inevitably, in those with ears to hear, a sense of humbleness and wonder. I may not understand the origin of meaning, but I am impelled to bow before its numinous reality.

This intimation of the transcendental nature of language haunted our ancestors. The declaration of Genesis 1:3, "And God said, 'Let there be light,' and there was light," establishing the primacy of language as the vehicle of creation, is echoed in scripture and myth around the world: thus Vac (Sanskrit: speech), queen of gods and mother of the Vedas, the word personified, through whom all is disclosed. For many centuries, people sought for the perfect language, either the one tongue that would allow us to communicate with the divine, or—an ambition rife with hubris—the divine tongue itself with which God created heaven and earth. An early effort at identifying and deciphering these metalanguages came with the Sefer Yetzirah, a second- to fourth-century Jewish text recounting how God created the world by combining, in myriad ways, the ten Sefirot (cosmic numbers) and the twenty-two letters of the Hebrew alphabet. The quest for the perfect language became an obsession during the high and late Middle Ages and early Renaissance. Abraham Abulafia resumed the study of alphabetical permutations, finding in the juxtaposition of letters and numbers the occult wisdom of God; John Dee, through his scryer Edward Kelley, uncovered the tongue of angels and the magical infrastructure of the cosmos; Lull, Bruno, and Kircher also fell under the spell of this intoxicating search. Dante, anchored in Christian orthodoxy, contented himself with musing about it, offering in the *Commedia* and in *De vulgari eloquentia* two conflicting accounts of the origin and nature of the language of paradise.

Today we look upon all this as a colorful chapter in intellectual history. We content ourselves with natural languages, the multitudi-

nous vernaculars evolved by men and women around the world—
there are between four and eight thousand languages abroad, accord-
ing to scholarly estimates—seeking in each some means of expressing
our sense of the mystery of language and of the cosmos in which it
flourishes. This is a joyous occupation; I know a man who speaks a
dozen languages and adds a new one every two or three years. When
I ask him why he collects tongues as others collect stamps or coins,
he tenders various explanations: to be able to read, in the original,
ancient Babylonian classics or today's Icelandic newspaper; to savor
the differing flavors of this language or that, which Tolkien likens to
vintages of fine wine; to keep the mind nimble. But when I dig
deeper, he admits that the very nature of language itself draws him
on, its inexplicability, its seductive otherness, what Wilson calls in
his conversion tale "the whole grammatical mystery." It is this same
mystery, leading in one direction to metaphysics and in another to
poetry, which entrances so many modern writers, from Hopkins and
Eliot to Wittgenstein, Heidegger, and Chomsky. And it is to the
luminous enigma of language and all its conjunct enigmas—life,
death, good, evil, damnation, salvation, the "whole (choose your
own adjective) mystery"—that the Best Spiritual Writing series re-
main devoted.

My thanks to the twenty essayists and ten poets who contributed
material to this year's volume, and in particular to Billy Collins for
his splendid introduction. I notice with interest that Billy's life story
is in many ways the opposite of my own, as he found freedom in leav-
ing the Catholic Church for an independent path of "self-forgetting
and wonder," whereas I, after years of wandering in a maze of esoteric
and eastern roads, found liberation and happiness in the very same
Catholic Church. This contrast heartens me, for it confirms once
again that the Best Spiritual Writing series encompasses all who seek
God and love good writing. Perhaps this is also the place to mention

that I selected one of Billy's poems for the collection before asking him to introduce the volume. After he had said yes, I realized that his poem was too good to withdraw, on the arbitrary principle of one person, one piece, so we are fortunate to be blessed with two works by him this year. My thanks also to Carolyn Carlson of Viking Penguin; to Kim Witherspoon and David Forrer of Inkwell Management; and, as always, to Carol, John, and Andy, who have taught me how to speak the language of love.

PHILIP ZALESKI

Introduction

WHEN EXACTLY DID I STOP BELIEVING IN THE HOLY GHOST? IT MUST have been before the Catholic Church changed his name to the less spooky Holy Spirit. Surely it was his physical vagueness that caused him to be the first member of the Trinity to leave my nest of religious beliefs—even through as a child I was captivated by the image of God walking through creation with a sheet over his head. And that is pretty much how I lost my religion: one mystery and one article of faith at a time. Growing up in the Church, I began to question the long line of improbable events that make up Christian history, and the more I questioned, the more skeptical I became. Still a callow youth, I found it easy to look down on many aspects of my religion and to see religious mysteries as stories meant to dazzle, edify, and finally control the more gullible members of the faith. To be born with original sin seemed flatly unfair; and the claim of the Church to hold the only means of its erasure—baptism—struck me as monopolistic, even though I probably didn't know that word at the time. Of course, doubt is the faithful companion of belief. "A faith untested is no faith at all" was a mantra of my childhood. The truly intimate ties of faith to skepticism became clearer much later when I read Jennifer Michael Hecht's *Doubt*, an illuminating history of that connection. I remember spending many of my formative years stuck in the middle of that dichotomy, being pulled in opposite directions by my almost congenital faith and the multiplying, sirenlike voices of the secular world.

Over time, I was fitted with the full-metal jacket of Catholic education. It started with the nuns in grammar school, continued with diocesan priests in high school, and ended in college with the Jesuits. Sixteen years of it. When I began my graduate work on a sunny campus of the University of California, I had not shared a classroom with a female student since the eighth grade. My eyes would drift up from the heroic couplets of Alexander Pope to study the more engrossing hair and bare shoulders of young women. Catholicism was also very much alive and well in the home I grew up in. A cross hung on the wall above every bed, and in the kitchen there was a framed picture of the Sacred Heart of Jesus. That's the one where he is pulling open his chest to expose a bleeding heart (the organ itself!) wrapped in thorns as if to say "This is all your fault." My father's attitude toward the Church was typical of an Irish American male of the 1950s and sixties. He spent the drive home from Sunday Mass mocking the sanctimoniousness of the sermon and, if there was one, the unfairness of the "second collection," which he considered a form of extortion. Yet my mother once confided that he would never leave the house without his rosary in his pocket and, hard as it was for me to picture, that he would kneel by his bedside every night to say his prayers. My mother harbored none of my father's conflicts or antipathies. She was an unshakable believer and, if ever tested, an ardent defender of the faith. A muscular Catholic, she constantly acted on her faith through charitable donations and work in the fields of the Lord. As a member of the Legion of Mary she performed "corporal works of mercy" by delivering food and clothing to the poorer families of the parish, even knitting afghan throws to warm the residents of the local nursing home. She has been dead over a decade now, but I still write checks to the Maryknoll

Sisters, one of her many charities, just to keep the ball of her generosity rolling.

My upbringing did me a lot of good; I benefited immensely from a good classical education—plenty of Latin and Greek—and a stable family. I was a late, only child, and I got the kind of attention such a creature would expect. And one might think that such a sustained exposure to religion through teaching and example would sustain a person's faith—but that kind of thinking would not take into account the tendencies of such a regimen to backfire. I came out of high school with my faith pretty much intact. I had been an altar boy, I had sung weakly in the choir, and still within me were the same "quiet habits of obedience" that lived on in the lapsed soul of Stephen Dedalus. But at college, the theology-based curriculum seemed to want to replace my lingering faith with a methodology based on the strict application of philosophic reasoning. Why simply believe in God when you can actually prove his existence through a series of syllogisms? Why embrace the truth when you are being equipped to arrive at the truth by means of logical argumentation? The dominant brand of theology that was taught had worked its way down to us through the line of Scholasticism, beginning with Aristotle and extending to St. Thomas Aquinas and Duns Scotus, who was also hailed as a champion of the Immaculate Conception of Mary. Some progressive theologians such as Gabriel Marcel, Hans Küng (forbidden to teach because of his denial of papal infallibility), and the visionary Jesuit Teilhard de Chardin were introduced to us by some of the younger Jesuits, who had studied at the Catholic University of Louvain in Belgium. But generally, the Church fathers ruled the blackboards. The history of philosophy ended with the Middle Ages. One day in class, when questioned, an elderly Jesuit dismissed existentialism, which some of us were privately devouring, as "a bunch of chicken gunk." I dutifully recorded the words in my notebook. Heaviest emphasis was placed on apologetics, whose purpose was to train us students to argue convincingly in the defense of our faith. One of our textbooks was organized into series of philosophic questions. A section titled "Refuting the Adversaries" concluded every chapter by providing us with one- or two-sentence rebuttals of various heresies, most of them having peaked in popularity several hundred years ago. The common joke was that at graduation we would enter the world prepared to correct any Manichean or Albigensian who might attack us at a cocktail party. It would take only one or two syllogisms to show him the error of his ways and perhaps even convert him. After all, why else would we end up graduating with more credits in theology than in our majors? As I studied for examinations by memorizing pages of syllogisms, I could feel Jesus being replaced by Thomas Aquinas. Just as Flannery O'Connor ironically described herself as a "hillbilly Thomist," I was becoming a New England Thomist from the suburbs of New York. And I was stepping away from the Church in another way; the college surely did not intend to break my habit of going to Sunday Mass by forcing me to get up and attend the seven o'clock Mass every weekday morning—come rain, sleet, and frequently snow—under the threat and sometimes the application of physical punishment, but it did just that.

Other secularizing forces were also at work. My reading of Nabokov, James Purdy, Jean Genet, Mailer, Henry Miller, Camus, Beckett, and other edgy, off-the-syllabus writers of the time exposed me to social and aesthetic worlds that were dangerous, transgressive, sinful, and, of course, utterly seductive. I was moving from nagging doubts into a period of High Agnosticism. Kerouac's *On the Road* provided the novel idea that by actually leaving the Catholic Church you could become holy. *That* was new. The streets were holy; the girl stepping onto a dust-covered bus in Mexico was holy; and jazz was particularly holy. Dean Moriarity sat close to the bandstand repeating "Holy, holy, HOLY, HOLY!! . . ." And "beat" meant "beatific," as in the Blessed Virgin. Kerouac threw himself fully into the subculture of speed, drugs, and crime, but the language of his Catholicism kept bleeding through. You could abandon your doctrinal faith, but the iconography and vocabulary of the Church clung. As one lapsed Catholic paradoxically put it: "I don't believe in God, but I believe that Mary was his mother."

Kerouac was only one of many writers (there were thinkers, sociologists, scientists, and contemporary philosophers) who hinted at the possibility of a spiritual life outside of the precincts of religion. That split between religion and spirituality qualifies as one of the essential distinctions in one's maturation, right up there with Man vs. Nature. For most of us, religion comes first. The possibility of a supernatural world arrives as part of our training in a creed complete with its own rituals, liturgy, and often flamboyant history. After all, the Bible begins with a talking snake, proceeds to the torture and crucifixion of God, and concludes with the destruction of the world featuring horsemen charging through the fiery clouds and a red dragon with seven heads. In my Catholic case, the spiritual was mixed up with tabernacles, cassocks, incense, statues in alcoves, and many mysteries—glorious, joyful, and sorrowful. But gradually, through a number of influences both literary and natural, I came to sense that a spiritual realm could be accessed, not via the recommended roads of religion leading to portals guarded by priests, rabbis, imams, and religious leaders of other stripes, but instead, directly through actual daily experience.

I cannot remember a single epiphanic moment when I became liberated by that realization. The process was gradual and can be measured best by the pace of my reading. Writers were becoming my new priests, each keeping his or her grip on me only for a while before sending me into the arms of another unofficial adviser. Like most wayward and curious adolescents, I was trying on different literary voices and philosophical stances like a row of sports jackets in a men's store. In high school, I fell deeply under the spell of the Beat poets—Ginsberg, Corso, Orlovsky & Co. I began writing my own imitative poetry—inflated, near hysterical lines, in which I raged against convention, condemning the falseness of society and calling for the total liberation of man through an orgy of sex, drugs, and music. Of course, I often had to study for a quiz the next day, so I could not devote myself fully and ecstatically to the enlightenment of my fellow beings.

Reading beat literature led me naturally to Zen Buddhism, which was being busily imported to Western readers by interpreters such as Alan Watts, D. T. Suzuki, and Gary Snyder. And Robert de Ropp's *The Master Game* provided a simplifying perspective on the whole scene by seeing human activities as a set of games, each with its own goal. The object of the Mammon game was wealth. The object of a game called Cock on the Dunghill was fame. The object of the Religion game was salvation. And the object of the Master game—whose many manifestations included sitting meditation, dervish dancing, and psychedelic adventuring—was enlightenment. Enlightenment—not a reward for good behavior handed to you after you die, but an opening of consciousness to be experienced now.

I was an English major, too. And later a professor of English, and along the way in my teaching and reading of poetry, I discovered little apertures into something larger. I sensed that these discoveries were "spiritual" if only by default; that is, I had no other word for them. Early on, I remember being stopped in my reading tracks by an Emily Dickinson poem, in which church and state were separated with calm authority:

> *Some keep the Sabbath going to church;*
> *I keep it staying at home,*
> *With a bobolink for a chorister,*
> *And an orchard for a dome.*

Some keep the Sabbath in surplice;
I just wear my wings,
And instead of tolling the bell for church,
Our little sexton sings.

God preaches,—a noted clergyman,—
And the sermon is never long;
So instead of getting to heaven at last,
I'm going all along!

Here, the open natural world of the poet's backyard is preferred over the enclosed rituals of mid-nineteenth-century New England Protestantism. Instead of church, choir, vestments, bells, and sermons, Dickinson surrounds herself with birds, trees, and God himself, "a noted clergyman" indeed. That the outdoors itself could be a kind of church was later reinforced when I read Thoreau and Emerson, who wrote that the "happiest man is he who learns from nature the lesson of worship."

In reading poems, I often found myself falling through a little hole into something more extensive than the words around it. This happened often in Wordsworth, particularly in *The Prelude,* and in many of Coleridge's so-called conversation poems. *The Prelude,* Wordsworth's oxymoronic "autobiographical epic," chronicles a lifetime marked by veil-dropping moments of insight "into the life of things" beginning in childhood. There are dramatic moments such as the sudden appearance of the moon as the poet is climbing Mount Snowdon when "a light upon the turf / Fell like a flash; and lo! as I looked up, / The Moon hung naked in the firmament / Of azure without cloud, and at my feet / Rested a silent sea of hoary frost." But more striking to me were less sublime passages whose lines seemed to open little doors. Before the boy Wordsworth experiences guilt by stealing a boat, he describes it as

> *A skiff that to a willow tree was tied*
> *With a rocky cave, its usual home.*

Such a simple but perfectly rendered image (the iambic rhythm is a steadying force) pulled me into a kind of second reality, or reality to the second power. Even this image from Coleridge—

> *. . . and though now the bat*
> *Wheels silent by, and not a swallow twitters,*
> *Yet still the solitary humble bee*
> *Sings in the bean-flower!*

suggested a little world within, a moment opening up into a vastness.

Such moments of sudden insight providing peeks into a world both beyond and within are common to haiku, which is measured not only in seventeen syllables but in its ability to turn a small observation, usually of the natural world, into a penetration of the surface of things. Blake thought eternity could be held in an hour, but in haiku a second is all it takes. Compressed into Basho's famous "Old pond— a frog jumps in—the sound of water" are three senses of time: the old pond, the relatively young frog, and the vanishing moment of his leap and splash. In many haiku, two events happen at once. "The trout leaps up— / and below him in a stream / clouds float by" (Onitsura) or "Summer coolness— / lantern out, / the sound of water." (Shiki) The simple point of these little poems is that the poet was present to witness these double or triple sensations. The poems are declarations of the poets' existence as much as they are observations of nature. And just as the riddles known as koans are designed to throw us out of our minds by confounding logic, some haiku move us into another zone through optical illusion—"The nurseryman / left behind / a butter-fly" (Ryota) and bewildering statements of the obvious—"Walking the dog / you meet / lots of dogs" (Soshi). Like much lyric poetry, haiku is the expression of a moment of focusing, a heightening of attention to the world around us. In such moments, a fusion occurs between inner and outer worlds; consciousness and its worldly environment are reattached. The poem becomes a bit of amber in which a fleeting moment is trapped. If the latent power in atomic particles, which are the building blocks of matter, can be released by smashing them in a cyclotron, then the power latent in moments of experience, which are the building blocks of time, can be released through the sheer power of attentiveness.

The tradition of Christian mysticism extending from the desert anchorites of Egypt and Irish monks in their beehive huts to the reclusive religious orders of today is marked by such moments of ecstatic wakening. For the majority of its followers, religion is less of an experience than it is a set of beliefs, a moral code, and a picture of the hereafter. But spiritual experience—at least the kind I am discussing—is indeed an *experience,* usually marked by a sense of sudden entry into another dimension. This spiritual life is one of surprising glimpses, which often resist verbal description, as distinct from a sustained set of theological beliefs and doctrines, which can be explained to anyone, as any proselytizer knows. Wordsworth's phrase "spots of time" neatly captures the size of such intense moments of insight in which time is pierced and an eternity is revealed.

"Never be ashamed of staring," Flannery O'Conner once advised writers, "there is nothing that does not require . . . attention." The practice of looking carefully *is* a practice and one can get better at it. Annie Dillard reminds us that natural observation involves a bit of luck. Nature is a "now-you-see-it-now-you-don't experience," she writes, suggesting that patience plays a part in our ability to see what is really happening around us. Gary Snyder has speculated that the origins of meditation may lie in early hunting practices when men without projectiles would have to sit still outdoors for long periods of time waiting for an animal to come close enough to clobber. If they waited long enough, they would likely fall into a trance. But simply looking closely and unselfishly is a way to create a place in the spirit, to wear a groove that can be revisited. Wordsworth writes in his little "daffodil" poem "I gazed—and gazed—but little thought / What wealth the show to me had brought." That second gazing, set off by dashes, is a significant moment in the history of staring, a looking so intense that it can lead to self-forgetting and wonder.

At this point in my life, the spiritual arrives sporadically in momentary perceptions, reminders of a dimension greater than the one bounded by time and space, the world we walk through with our egos pointed forward. I don't think such moments can be hunted down or willed. Perhaps the only possible way to invite such experiences is Wordsworth's "wise passivity," which rests on the faith that the receptive mind will be rewarded by an influx of the kind of phenomenon we are used to blocking out. These special times of awareness offer an intimate contemplation that can fill us with the kind of gratitude that is a form of prayer—not a prayer for eternal salvation, but a prayer of thanksgiving, and perhaps a supplication for another glimpse, another tap of profundity.

Any reader new to this series will be struck immediately by editor Philip Zaleski's broad interpretation of the word "spiritual." I, for one, was surprised to learn last year that he detected something spiritual in a poem I had written about an albino gorilla that I came upon in a book about Barcelona. Well, if someone thinks that poem is spiritual, *then it's spiritual*, I thought, as I happily signed the permissions form. This year's selection is a further demonstration of Zaleski's imaginative sense of what constitutes spiritual writing. Quite a few poems are included: in one, Coleman Barks is led smoothly from Ted Hughes's letters back to Gregory of Nyssa and Plotinus; Philip Levine revisits a magic knife from 1934; Islam, Greek mythology, and Christianity are gathered under the heading of the contemplative life by

Marilyn Nelson; and C. K. Williams dances exuberantly through the history of religion and poetry. Jesse Kellerman's "Let My People Go to the Buffet" is a bit of irreverent shtick that is just as funny as its title. Joel Cohen finds similarities between the apples of poetry and the oranges of mathematics. As if to balance Robert D. Kaplan's chronicle of the clash between Sri Lanka's Buddhist and Hindu factions, Seyyed Hossein Nasr brings into focus many common features of Christianity and Islam, two "channels of grace" that may lead to sanctity and illumination. Barry Lopez adds to his inspiring oeuvre with a sampler from his world travels in which he longs for and experiences an intimate connection with the physical earth. Terry Teachout points out the Catholic underpinnings to Flannery O'Connor's fiction, and Anita Sullivan, a piano tuner, makes brilliant connections between styles of tuning for the violin and a seventeenth-century religious composition. Many other facets of the transcendent await the lucky reader of this year's collection; and Philip Zaleski deserves our applause for once again expanding and enhancing our understanding of the spiritual.

BILLY COLLINS
Winter Park, Florida

The Best
Spiritual Writing

2011

COLEMAN BARKS

Starting Out from Ted Hughes's Letters

FROM *The Georgia Review*

He would have his children make lists of similes'
    and reward them thruppence each for the good ones.
So & so is *like* so & so.

This list rose up in me when I read that.
A pot is like a possibility.
A beef stew is like a pile of leaves with children hiding in it.
The end of a love affair is like the rest of my life.
A pair of glasses set out on the desk is like forgetting your name.
A rainy late afternoon playing the board game Sorry
with two grandsons, Tuck (11) and Woody (7),
and my son Benjamin (45) is like
the peach basket James Naismith nailed ten feet up
at Springfield College in Massachusetts, December 1891,
trying to keep his delinquent students active but noncombatant,
indoors during the winter. They used a soccer ball.
The joy of being side by side touching shoulders with someone
so loved and so different from one's own self is like a simile.
Being wonderfully full of oneself is like
feeling mean and forgetting your heart.

Surely something will survive this
self-destructing love that pulls us along.

Gregory of Nyssa says there is a sort of watchful sleep
where one is neither awake nor not-awake,
not caught in either opposite but fusing both
in a place where mind has gone out of itself
but is not yet under the control of what we might call a creative
     imagination,
a giving-in to some sovereign, wider intelligence—
the source of simile and metaphor, say.

Gregory of Nyssa writing subtle comments
in whatever language he used in the wilds of fourth-century
     Cappadocia,
on whatever surface he wrote on with whatever he wrote with,
his notes on the nature of awareness as it floats
between more nameable conditions is *like*
driving a car and talking into the rearview mirror,
to someone in a far-off bed, as one does with the new OnStar
     technology.
You touch the mirror in a certain place, the bottom left,
to hang up. Or it is like Thoreau's concept of economy,
what he went out to Walden Pond to explore.
He wanted to be careful how he spent the spirit's energy,
his vitality. Like me talking about *that*,
one April Thursday in 1981 to a class of sleepy sophomores,
who rouse to the idea only when I confess
that I never buy shaving cream, but rather collect those
     elusive bits
of hand soap from all around the house and save them in a cup,
and stir that with a cheap shaving brush for lather.

Then I ask them their secrets for saving a bit here, a bit there.
What I mostly get are ways of ripping off vending machines.
Warm water poured in the coin slot, the two quarters on a
    string trick,
and a *very* elaborate bill-folding Scotch tape caper.

And never pay the toll road tolls, just make a gesture of throwing
and drive through leaving them whirring, clanging, and flashing
    in your wake.
Nobody ever comes after you, or if they do, say the change
is on the ground back there, and there always is some.

Where are these clever petty-cash schemes leading
and what are they like? Like something decided-on,
a cleared-off campsite on the forest floor,
a starting-out place, and Plotinus.

Because that master said in Greek in the bright sun of
    Alexandria,
or maybe Rome, *playing*. The power of growth
in plants, in the ground itself, and surely in us,
is a form of *play*. All motion, even the movement of this
    sentence,
leads us playfully toward contemplation,
those quadrants of sky the soul aspires to.

And what is this *contemplation*
Plotinus says we are all in the midst of becoming?
Inner opening into emptiness,
where everything and nothing are no longer *alike*,
but boundary-less play inside a single point, the one
where I have gotten enough sleep,

where I feel calm and ready behind-my-eyes,
settled and potentially hilarious in nervous system and brain,
waiting for the beckoning cabin-call of how we *begin*
to watch a movie, read a novel, listen to new music.

In the front yard lives the oldest thing around, a white oak
that I used to say is my love for the world,
that I now would just call love as it is,
belonging to nobody, no metaphor, the very.

Letters of Ted Hughes selected and edited by Christopher Reid (New York: Farrar, Straus and Giroux, 2007), 312–13. In a letter to his children, Frieda and Nicholas, 26 April 1971, he lists various ways for them "to earn some cash." Method 4 is "Similes—For every good one, threepence. Make lists. We look forward to the weekend. Love, Dad."

Gregory of Nyssa: Martin Laird, over a number of years of wandering study, has written a book about this magnificent mystic, *Gregory of Nyssa and the Grasp of Faith* (Oxford: Oxford University Press, 2004). In Homily Seven on Ecclesiastes, Gregory says, "Having nothing it can grab . . . our mind . . . slipping . . . in dizziness and confusion . . . returns again to what is natural to it" (page 52). In the early 1990s I was traveling in Cappadocia with my son Cole. I had wandered off by myself when I heard a voice calling my name. I looked up into the sheer overhanging rock. Nothing. Then I saw Cole's face smiling from a tiny head-shaped oval in the stone directly above me. He had climbed up a passageway hollowed out by the monks to give me my own moment of dizzy return to what was natural, my fear and my love for him. *Please get down from there.*

Plotinus (204–270 CE), Ennead III, 8, 1—"Then are we now contemplating as we play? Yes, we and all who play, are doing this, or at any rate, this is what they aspire to as they play." From the A. H. Armstrong translation in the Loeb Classical Library (1966–74), page 361.

Plotinus, Ennead III, page 363—"Every action is a serious effort toward contemplation." Copied into a 1981 notebook of mine.

RICK BASS

The Return

FROM *Orion*

ALL THROUGH THE WINTER, THE DEER HAVE TRAVELED THE SAME
paths over and over, packing the deep snow, their sharp hoofs down-
cutting to form lanes, and then nearly tunnels, through the soft drifts.
They keep these trails so packed down that the snow in them gets
compressed into some kind of super-dense, cobalt- or galena-colored
substance, more slippery than mercury, more dense than lead—and
paradoxically, or so it seems at first, these trails, which once marked
where the snow had been worn down to its thinnest margins, are
now the last remaining threads of winter: fifteen feet of snow super-
compressed to a height of only a few inches, so that even in the re-
turning warmth of May, these luminous ice trails linger long after all
the snow has melted; and having no need to use these trails, which are
slippery now, the deer avoid them. Instead, the deer step carefully
across the spongy dark duff—surely they must feel spritely, unen-
cumbered at long last—and in this yin-and-yang inversion, white
snow to black earth, they shed their winter coats, leaving their hol-
low hair in tufts and clumps all over the woods, the braided, winding
rivers of it running now at cross-angles to the old paths of hoof-
matted ice.

The hair glints in the newer, sharper light of springtime, looking
like spilled straw, or silver needles—trails of it leading all through the

woods—and this shift in the riverine sentences that echo the deer's passages—a shift even more pronounced than the reversal of a tide—is for me, as with the coming of the first trillium, one of the most visual markers of the season, the true and irreconcilable end of winter. Though the mud and forest puddles will dry out, and the winds will soon enough scatter those concentrated rivers of hair to a more democratic and widespread distribution, in May it is still all clumps and patches, the deer shedding great wads of hair against any rough surface: the bark of a hemlock, the stub of branch on a fallen lodgepole. And all throughout the forest, too, are the whitened, ribby spars of winter-killed deer, appearing like so many ships stranded by the white tide's great withdrawal; and in caves and hollows too, beneath the fronds of great cedar trees, entire mattress nests of deer hair can be found where a mountain lion has fed all winter long: dragging one deer after another to his or her favorite cache and gnawing on them until the bones stack upon one another like a little corral and the disintegrating hides shed their fur. After the end of winter, in such places, the ground may be half a foot deep in white belly hair—the snow-tide pulling back from the lion's lair, retreating horizontally, with new life poised at the leaping edge of vertical green roar . . .

May is a wonderful time to see the eagles, both bald and golden, the former returning with the opening of the river ice; and during this period they feast gluttonously on the moraine of an entire winter's worth of road-killed deer. Nearly every morning on the drive to school in early May, my daughters, Mary Katherine and Lowry, and I will pass at least one such eagle banquet, with two or three bald eagles—both the mature adults and the adolescents, which are just as large but don't yet have the white head—accompanied often by a golden eagle or two, and when the eagles see a car or truck approaching, they abandon their roadside feast and on great wide wings flap, wheeling in all directions to their various sentinel perches like children who had been roughhousing while their teacher stepped away from the classroom scrambling back to their seats upon whispered news of the teacher's return. Fur from the deer carcasses loosened by the eagles' talons swirls in the air, glinting like pins and needles, deer hair stirred on the currents of the eagles' departure and by the passage of our truck.

Time and time again I am astounded by the regularity and repetition of form in this valley and elsewhere in wild nature: basic patterns, sculpted by time and the land, appearing everywhere I look. The twisted branches in the forest that look so much like the forked antlers of the deer and elk. The way the glacier-polished hillside boulders look like the muscular, rounded bodies of the animals—deer, bear— that pass among those boulders like living ghosts. The way the swirling deer hair is the exact shape and size of the larch and pine needles the deer hair lies upon once it is torn loose from the carcass and comes to rest on the forest floor. As if everything up here is leaning in the same direction, shaped by the same hands, or the same mind: not always agreeing or in harmony, but attentive always to the same rules of logic; and in the playing-out, again and again, of the infinite variations of specificity arising from that one shaping system of logic an incredible sense of community develops—a kind of unconscious community, rarely noticed, if at all, but deeply felt.

Felt at night when you stand beneath the stars and see the shapes and designs of bears and hunters in the sky; felt deep in the cathedral of an old forest, when you stare up at the tops of the swaying giants; felt when you take off your boots and socks and wade across the river, sensing each polished, mossy river stone with your cold bare feet. Felt when you stand at the edge of the marsh and listen to the choral uproar of the frogs, and surrender to their shouting, and allow yourself, too, like those pine needles and that deer hair, like those branches and those antlers, to be remade, refashioned into the shape and the pattern and the rhythm of the land. Surrounded, and then embraced, by a logic so much more powerful and overarching than anything that a man or woman could create or even imagine that all you can do is marvel and laugh at it, and feel compelled to give, in one form or another, thanks and celebration for it, without even really knowing why . . .

Each morning in May I feast hungrily on the sight of the eagles pulling loose with their beaks and talons the tufts of deer hair that are so much like the shape of the larch and pine needles upon which the carcass rests, and into which the remnants of the carcass will soon be dissolving, the trees and bushes then growing up out of that deer-enriched soil to sprout branches that are the same shape as the antlers had been. One story. Many parts, but only one story, and the rhythm of each month carrying us along, beneath, or within that one chorus.

It seems extraordinary to me to see such a sight on the way to school nearly every morning, in the awakening days of May, and I like to consider how such images—in both their singular beauty as well as in the braided rhythm that is created by their accumulation—help to comprise the fabric of the girls' childhood, days of wild green regularity so incomparable to and unquestioned by any other experience that such sights seem "normal" to them, though even in the dailiness of it, the wonder of May, and of all the months here, I try to explain to the girls to not take such things for granted—saying this even as I am fully aware that there is a part of me that most wants them to take such sights for granted; to accept such bounty as their unquestioned due, to perceive it as regular and familiar—and no less beautiful in that familiarity.

In a way that I haven't yet figured out how to fully articulate, I believe that children who get to see bald eagles, coyotes, deer, moose, grouse, and other similar sights each morning will have a certain kind of matrix or fabric or foundation of childhood, the nature and quality of which will be increasingly rare and valuable as time goes on, and which will be cherished into adulthood, as well as becoming— and this is a leap of faith by me—a source of strength and knowledge to them somehow. That the daily witnessing of the natural wonders is a kind of education of logic and assurance that cannot be duplicated by any other means, or in other places: unique, and significant, and, by God, still somehow relevant, even now, in the twenty-first century.

For as long as possible, I want my girls to keep believing that beauty, though not quite commonplace and never to pass unobserved or unappreciated, is nonetheless easily witnessed on any day, in any given moment, around any forthcoming bend. And that the wild world still has a lovely order and pattern and logic, even in the shouting, disorderly chaos of breaking-apart May and reassembling May. That if there can be a logic and order even in May, then there can be in all seasons and all things.

JOSEPH BOTTUM

Words of Nectar and Cyanide

FROM *First Things*

YOU CAN TRACE, THROUGH THE HISTORY OF PHILOSOPHY, A LINE OF aphorism—that odd, somewhat disreputable method of doing philosophy as a kind of bastard poetry. Maybe even as a kind of magic: truth as something to be summoned by careful incantation and the weird precision of a witch's spell.

It starts with Heraclitus, of course, and the deliberately obscure metaphysical assertions that either began as aphorisms or, left as fragments from his lost essays, ended up that way: *Time is a child moving counters in a game,* and *The way up and the way down are one,* and *We both step and do not step in the same rivers.* Epicurus, perhaps, did philosophy in this epigrammatical way. Diogenes and Marcus Aurelius certainly did. And then there are all the half-lost Greeks: Sophists, Epicureans, Atomists, Cynics, Skeptics, and Stoics, together with occasional Presocratics and random Neoplatonists and stray Peripatetics—the long parade of ancients whose words survive only in the scraps and slivers that make them sound like maddened masters of philosophical concision.

Revived in the Renaissance, this method of doing philosophy by dictum and adage would flower particularly among the French: the civilized Montaigne, the polished La Rochefoucauld, the God-haunted Pascal. Spinoza did a little of it, from time to time. Nietzsche's aphorisms would raise the method to a high art form in the nineteenth century, and Wittgenstein's *Zettel* would return it in the twentieth century to the pure philosophical density with which it began in Heraclitus.

Interestingly, you can also trace a line of pessimism through the history of philosophy, and it would weave in and out to touch this line of aphorists at a surprising number of points. Perhaps none of them quite reach the grim perfection of Samuel Beckett's image of existence as the brief fall from a bloody womb to a splattered death—of human life as a woman giving birth while she squats astride an open grave. But it's there, often enough, in the senseless physical universe perceived by the ancient Cynics and Skeptics and even some of the Stoics. It's there among the Epicureans, too, for all that they demand the pursuit of pleasure: "From the heart of the fountain of delight," as Lucretius points out, "there rises a jet of bitterness that tortures us among the flowers."

Strip out the passages on grace, and you can find as bleak a vision—in fact, a bleaker vision—in Christian philosophy, from St. Augustine on. "Imagine a number of men in chains, all under the sentence of death, some of whom are each day butchered in the sight of the others," Pascal would write. "This is the image of the human condition."

And what is much of nineteenth-century philosophical pessimism but Christianity without the possibility of redemption? "Against the palpably sophistical proofs of Leibniz that this is the best of all possible worlds," Schopenhauer insisted, "we may oppose seriously and honestly the proof that it is the *worst* of all possible worlds."

Here's the curious thing, however: Both these lines, the aphoristic and the pessimistic, reach something like their pinnacle, their unsurpassable peak, in the works of a Romanian-born French writer named Emil Mihai Cioran. He was the greatest genius of aphorism in the history of philosophy, and he was the greatest monster of despair.

In the decades before his death in 1995 at age eighty-four, Cioran was often grouped among the French existentialists. The fit was never all that good; his first and in many ways most revealing book, *On the Heights of Despair,* was published in Romanian in 1934, when he was only twenty-three—before he could have been influenced by, say, Albert Camus. Besides, as a school of philosophy, existentialism is about as dead these days as such things can get. Who still reads Jean-Paul Sartre and Gabriel Marcel? They are names without content, the half-remembered authors of the dusty bestsellers on our parents' shelves.

Cioran, however, still lives, in his grim, dark way. All of his works are in print in good translations, together with several biographical studies, and to read the man today is to realize that he makes most of his contemporaries look like children at play on a beach while an ocean looms unnoticed beyond them. It is, in fact, only in our own time, with the distraction of French existentialism finally out of the way, that E. M. Cioran comes into his own as an author—the creator of a set of reflections that refuse to be subsumed: One end of the fabric of human thought, the darkest edge, pinned firmly and forever down.

Certain themes spread like cancers through his work. That truncated Christian worldview, for instance: a sort of Augustinianism without Christ. Without hell, too—but, then, whenever pessimism is pushed far enough, damnation always begins to seem unnecessary, with this fallen world itself a kind of inferno. "Man started out on the wrong foot," as Cioran once observed. "The misadventure in paradise was the first consequence. The rest had to follow."

Death, too, is the constant topic, an insistence that we not flinch from the skeleton that leers at us every time we look in the mirror. Many of Cioran's best-known aphorisms begin and end with that reflection: "It is not worth the bother of killing yourself, since you always kill yourself too late," for instance, and "I live only because it is in my power to die whenever I want; without the idea of suicide I would have killed myself a long time ago."

Both inclination and principle kept him from creating a system. What coherent structure could be built from such deadly aphorisms, anyway? But insofar as he could be systematic, he set out to reject systematically every form of consolation. If he would not allow himself the complex submission of the Christian mystics he simultaneously admired and despised, he certainly would not indulge the simplistic surrender of, say, Richard Rorty's desire "to josh" the citizens of democracies out of their mere "habit" of wanting metaphysical foundations. "A marvel that has nothing to offer, democracy is at once a nation's paradise and its tomb," he sneered.

This clarity about our modern lack of metaphysical foundations may be a key to his work. Cioran was bombastic, some of the time: "If I had children, I would strangle them immediately." He was self-obsessed, nearly all of the time: "I long to be free—desperately free. Free as the stillborn are free." He could be brightly clever: "Progress is the injustice each generation commits with regard to its predecessors." And he could be annoyingly opaque: "We die in proportion to the words we fling around us."

But always he understood what the modern absence of foundations does to us: "I do not forgive myself for being born. It is as if creeping into this world, I had profaned a mystery, betrayed some momentous pledge, committed a fault of nameless gravity." And he could never find satisfaction in the easy self-congratulation of being a rebellious doubter of other human beings' claims to truth. "Skepticism," he observed, "is the sadism of embittered souls."

Cioran had a distinctive look, a compact man with the swept-back swoosh of long Einsteinian hair and an enormous, deep-crinkled forehead. The eyebrows, however, are what everyone remembers: huge, expressive things, like woolly caterpillars, that seemed to have a life of their own—a livelier, more active life, in truth, than the rest of his melancholy face.

The son of an Orthodox priest, Cioran was born in 1911 in the small village of Rășinari, high in the Romanian mountains. An insomniac most of his life, he found as a student something like a community in the university nightlife of Bucharest, where he was perceived as the most promising member of the new generation of Romanian intellectuals that included the playwright Eugène Ionesco, the essayist Mircea Eliade, and the philosopher Constantin Noica. Together as young men, many of them—including Cioran—fell under the spell of Nae Ionescu, their philosophy professor, who preached that a local application of Fascism would create a modern Romania from the train wreck of the Austro-Hungarian empire.

The much cosseted young student, promoted as the great hope of the new Romania, won the Royal Foundation's Young Writers Prize in 1934 for his first book, *On the Heights of Despair,* and, after finishing his thesis on the philosophy of Henri Bergson, was awarded a major scholarship to the University of Berlin.

That was perhaps the worst place for someone of his age and training, and it quickly led him into praise of the Nazis in Germany, the Fascists in Italy, and the Iron Guard in Romania. After his second collection of aphorisms, the 1935 *Book of Delusions,* he attempted to take up some of these nationalistic themes with his third volume, *The Transfiguration of Romania,* in 1936.

Actually thinking his way through the topic, however, Cioran came to heterodox conclusions, and the book was promptly denounced by the Fascist press, which read it as an attack on the "spirit of Romania." In many ways, that experience of rejection by the Fascists immunized him against the Fascist temptation—and it is common to explain away his flirtation with National Socialism as merely the error of a young thinker still finding his feet.

The fall of Communism in the 1990s, however, made available more information about Cioran's years in Romania: his 1940 radio broadcast, for instance, in praise of Corneliu Zelea Codreanu, the leader of the Iron Guard who had, Cioran declared, "given Romanians a purpose." Marta Petreu's 2005 *An Infamous Past: E. M. Cioran and the Rise of Fascism in Romania* chronicles those lost early years, and Ilinca Zarifopol-Johnston's new *Searching for Cioran* attempts to explain how the young Romanian philosophy student dropped his political interests to become the later French writer.

Certainly, he came to see the necessary disaster of his kind of youthful enthusiasm: In 1968, while watching the student revolts in Paris, he wrote a friend, "The only thing I can tell you about the recent events in my neighborhood is that they reminded me of the 'heroic' age of the Iron Guard. . . . Nothing will come of it." And certainly, he knew that he had erred: "The writer who has done some stupid things in his youth, upon his debut, is like a woman with a shameful past. Never forgiven, never forgotten," he wrote in 1979. But his response was not to mention any actual facts about his early years, letting the closed borders of Communist Romania keep his secrets. Open admission and open repentance would have served him better.

With the publication in 1937 of *Tears and Saints,* his reflections on reading the mystics, he received a scholarship from the French Institute of Bucharest and left for Paris, which would remain his home for the rest of his life. In 1945 he published *The Passionate Handbook,* his last book written in his native language, and in 1949, after abandoning an attempt to translate Mallarmé into Romanian, he published *A Short History of Decay,* the first of his works to be written in French.

The book was a minor sensation in its era, a time of early public acclaim for existentialism. Published by Gallimard, it won the Rivarol Prize (the last prize Cioran would accept), and, on the proceeds, he moved into a small apartment in Paris, a genuine garret, where he lived the rest of his life.

At that point, the facts of his biography seem almost to cease, as though he had withdrawn from the world except for his writing. Eight more slim volumes of aphorisms and essays followed: *All Gall Is Divided* (1952), *The Temptation to Exist* (1956), *History and Utopia* (1960), *The Fall Into Time* (1964), *The New Gods* (1969), *The Trouble with Being Born* (1973), *Drawn and Quartered* (1979), and *Anathemas and Admirations* (1986). His fame would decline slowly but steadily through the 1980s, only to revive a little before his death in 1995—although, in truth, he was lauded late in life less as a thinker and more as a mere survivor: the last of his generation still around.

That's not the way to appreciate him—if "appreciate" is a word that can be used for Emil Cioran. The more one reads him, the more morbid he proves. The consciousness of death, he wrote in *On the Heights of Despair*, is "not the luminous drunkenness of ecstasy, in which paradisal visions conquer you with their splendor and you rise to a purity that sublimates into immateriality, but a mad, dangerous, ruinous, and tormented black drunkenness, in which death appears with the awful seduction of nightmarish snake eyes."

Cioran's dance with death is unmatched in the history of philosophy. Even Pascal, in comparison, appears amateurish. And yet, the case of Pascal offers some insight into what, exactly, Cioran aimed at.

Consider this: One way to take Pascal is as an author who asks, in essence, whether it is possible to live with the awareness of death. And he notices immediately our "diversions," the ways we invent to forget that death is imminent. But such diversions can have only a temporary effect, for they merely cover what is boiling under the surface of existence. Death becomes all the more painful when we create "attachments" to life, to things, to people—to everything we know under the name of life.

Pascal saw attachment not merely as a link to earthly life but as a sign of corruption. Human beings, unable to find certainty, desperately attach themselves to what is fleeting and doomed to perish. "When I see the blind and wretched state of man, when I survey the whole universe in its dumbness and man left to himself with no light, as though lost in this corner of the universe," he wrote in the *Pensées*, "I am moved to terror. Then these lost and wretched creatures look around and find some attractive objects to which they become addicted and attached. For my part I have never been able to form such attachments."

Cioran seized this Pascalian insight with a kind of gloomy glee. In *The Trouble with Being Born,* he notes, "If attachment is evil, we must look for its cause in the scandal of birth, for to be born is to be attached. Detachment then should apply itself to getting rid of the traces of this scandal, the most serious and intolerable of all." Not that the alternative is much prettier: "To claim you are more detached, more alien to everything than anyone, and to be merely a fanatic of indifference!"

Perhaps, of all philosophers, Pascal most deserves this title of "a fanatic of indifference." And yet, however grace-stingy Pascal's Jansenist God may be—for that matter, however morbid Pascal's reflections seem—Cioran nonetheless reads Pascal as a Christian optimist: a proclaimer of grace and a believer that life ultimately triumphs over death, as meaning triumphs over senselessness and good triumphs over evil.

The difference between Pascal and Cioran cannot be reduced to a question of rhetoric, outbidding each other on whose thought allows the greater suffering and thereby shows more clearly the core of existence. Cioran remains Pascal's greatest reader, and he strives throughout his work to *account* for Pascal—in a way that is possible only for someone whose sensibility is fundamentally religious, despite his antireligious demeanor. Cioran's quarrel with Christianity is not that it is false but that it attempts to cancel the fear of death by the "abstract construct" of salvation.

Still, he admired Christian religion for at least recognizing the abyss. Much worse is philosophy, which is, he wrote, "the art of masking inner torment." Death is particular to each of us, and the philosophers are wrong when they think that anyone can teach someone else how to die. "The irrevocability of agony is experienced by each individual alone, through infinite and intense suffering. . . . Only such moments of agony bring about important existential revelations in consciousness. . . . Most people are unaware of the slow agony within themselves. . . . Since agony unfolds in time, temporality is a condition not only of creativity but also for death." Even if all philosophical questions were answered, we would still experience anxiety: "Nobody in despair suffers from 'problems,' but from his inner torment and fire."

In *The Trouble with Being Born,* Cioran writes, "If I bump into my birth, into my obsession, it is because I cannot grapple with the first moment of time." Perhaps this accounts for his lifelong interest in the Christian mystics who, in the ecstatic state, are taken out of time: merged in the timeless vision of God, where there is no past or present or future. He developed the thought in "Dealing with the Mystics," an essay in his 1956 *The Temptation to Exist,* where, curiously, he declares that mystical experience is not false.

His quarrel with the mystics is not that they lie but that they see death as an obstacle to be overcome. He quotes St. Teresa of Avila, who argued that the soul, aspiring only to its creator, nonetheless "sees at the same time that it is impossible to possess its creator if it does not die; and since it is impossible for the soul to put itself to death, it dies of the desire to die, until it is actually in the danger of death." Cioran replies: "Always this need to make death into an accident or a means to reduce it to disappearance instead of regarding it as a presence—always this need to dispossess death. And if religions have made of it only a pretext or a scarecrow—a weapon of propaganda—it is the duty of the unbelievers to see that justice is done, to reestablish death and to restore all its rights."

Here is the half-Augustinianism in which Cioran often dwelt. However un-Christian and areligious he sounds, his sensibility is religious through and through. In *The Temptation to Exist* he speaks of being "emotionally" attached to Christianity and insists that his history is the history of Christianity. It makes sense, I suppose. Who among unbelievers can discern just how deep the darkness goes? His call to unbelievers is a voice crying in the wilderness.

Consider this aphorism from *The Trouble with Being Born:* "Though we may prefer ourselves to the universe, we nonetheless loathe ourselves more than we suspect." In phrasing, it belongs more in the mocking line of La Rochefoucauld than in the desperate line of Pascal, but the aphorism continues with the full awareness of self-hatred and the Pascalian worldview: "If the wise man is so rare a phenomenon, it is because he seems unshaken by the aversion which, like all beings, he must feel for himself." Of course, Pascal's man can feel an aversion to himself because of his corrupt nature: The existence of the divine provides a measure. But how is it possible for Cioran's man to have a similar feeling?

The caustic cynicism of La Rochefoucauld provided the answer: All our problems are nonproblems, and our pursuit of social distinction and comfort is ridiculous in comparison even with itself. "I know that my birth is fortuitous, a laughable accident," Cioran observes, "and yet as soon as I forget myself, I behave as if it were a capital event, indispensable to the progress and equilibrium of the world."

The French existentialists did not listen to Cioran for the simple reason that his work cannot lead to the social or political programs that they all eventually came to desire. Cioran's thought is a philosophy of nonparticipation, of non-ambition. In the end, "we are all humbugs: The problem is how to survive."

The brilliance of the prose is what makes all this readable—what makes it bearable, even, and thus, in a sense, runs cross-grained against its author's own themes. There's no doubt that Cioran could write. His similes and metaphors are always striking and oddly perfect. The Hungarian language, he once observed, is both beautiful and monstrous, like "words of nectar and cyanide." The Balkans, he noted, have a simultaneous taste for clutter and devastation, "for a universe like a brothel on fire."

Nietzsche is often cited as the source for Cioran's philosophical thought and aphoristic method, although, as a grown-up pessimist and writer of aphorisms, Cioran would note, "Thanks to the maturity of our cynicism, we have ventured further than he." Curiously, his final word on Nietzsche, in the late collection *Drawn and Quartered,* is a criticism of the rhythms of the German's prose: "a panting excess in the writing, the absence of rests."

That may point to the deepest stylistic influences on Cioran: not Nietzsche, but the French aphorists. Take this line: "Vices wait for us in the course of life as hosts with whom one has to be housed in succession; and I doubt that experience would make us avoid them if we were permitted to follow the same road twice."

And compare it to this: "It is easier to get on with vices than with virtues. The vices, accommodating by nature, help each other, are full of mutual indulgence, whereas the jealous virtues combat and annihilate each other, showing in everything their incompatibility and their intolerance."

The first is from La Rochefoucauld, and the second from Cioran, but one would be hard-pressed to tell the difference. Cioran is the best forger La Rochefoucauld ever bad. And yet, there remains an enormous gap between Cioran and his French masters. Cioran may have insisted on cynicism, but the polished libertine La Rochefoucauld was, in fact, the true demon of cynicism: saturnine, satanic, and sleek. In comparison, Emil Cioran seems more like a saint: an idealist of despair, an innocent of cynicism.

La Rochefoucauld wanted to be clever, while Cioran wanted to be wise—and "wanting to be wise" is what the word "philosophy" means, even if, to undertake it, Cioran had to attack the idea of philosophy itself: "What a pity that 'nothingness' has been devalued by an abuse of it made by philosophers unworthy of it!"

Dozens of marvelous lines appear in his writing:

- "Anyone can escape into sleep, we are all geniuses when we dream, the butcher is the poet's equal there."
- "Great persecutors are recruited among martyrs whose heads haven't been cut off."
- "My mission is to kill time, and time's to kill me in its turn. How comfortable one is among murderers."
- "True moral elegance consists in the art of disguising one's victories as defeats."

And yet, even taken all together—even assembled as a grand denial of grand systems—they do not add up to enough. They are not all for which the wanting of wisdom hungers, and a limit exists here, somewhere: a place beyond which the aphoristic method cannot go, a human reality it cannot express. In the end, as Cioran himself admitted, aphorism is a "fire without flames. Understandable that no one tries to warm himself at it."

Still, the bastard poetry of aphorism, its weird, compressed magic, remains a necessary corrective. Philosophy must have this kind of thing, if only to understand why philosophy itself is important. "I seem to myself, among civilized men, an intruder," Cioran once wrote of his life, "a troglodyte enamored of decrepitude, plunged into subversive prayers."

And so he was. But until we recognize the darkness, we cannot see the light; philosophy's candle matters only if we realize that genuine shadows lurk beyond reason's small illuminated circle. "There is no limit to suffering," E. M. Cioran insists we remember, and so he posted himself like a sentry on the edge of reason, refusing to turn away from the night.

ALICE LOK CAHANA

Words Are Not Enough

FROM *Portland*

I WANT TO TELL YOU THE MIRACLES THAT HAPPENED IN AUSCHWITZ. And the people who despised the Nazis and how they turned around from despising.

Here is one story. I met a man in Israel who told me: I was fourteen years old when the Nazis came into my house, and we had prayer exactly at that moment, and my father said: *Take the Torah and put it around your body and go out from the room.* And the boy went and did exactly what his father said. And he arrived to Auschwitz. In Auschwitz, first they undress you, he went up to one of the Polish people and he said, I cannot undress, I am carrying a Torah, the Torah is the most sacred book we have. The Polish man got scared and he went around saying the boy has a Torah on him, we cannot let him into the crematorium. Soon everyone surrounded the young man. They said to him, you cannot undress; pretend that you are finding some work in the clothing. Because people undress, they left their clothes on the ground, and then into the crematorium they go. The young SS soldier who was waiting outside the crematorium, he said to them, you must tell me what you are hiding, because all of you will die anyhow. And the young SS soldier found out that this little boy was carrying a Torah, and he went to the boy and said: Listen, I know what you are doing. Listen, every morning you come to me I will help you get food and you don't go to work. And guess what happened? This young man survived and the Torah survived, and it is in Jerusalem. The moment I heard that story I decided to create scrolls. I don't know how to do it but I want to celebrate the scrolls. The sanctity has to go with us no matter where we are. And so I made scrolls, and each one has a name, and I made one with that boy's name.

Here is another story. When I was in Auschwitz, I kept asking, why am I here, what did I do wrong? What did my grandfather do wrong? What did my father do wrong? And I decided I knew what we did wrong: *We read the letters backwards*, that was our mistake. The letters that always revived me! They killed us because we read the letters backwards! But after Auschwitz, when I read the Torah, the letters revive me again and again, so that could not be it. That could not be. And a young American man, he put me in the right knowledge. You didn't do nothing wrong, he said, the world did something wrong, terribly wrong. This young man, he went to Budapest in the beginning of it all, and he saved Jews, he gave out passports of Sweden, and because the Hungarians didn't know how to read Swedish, this was how my father was saved. And thousands of others too, with these pieces of paper. I am here to tell you that one man can make a difference, and that man can be you, any of you. Your task is to better the world.

I made a painting that has holes in it. Why is there holes? Because God says to us, I cannot do all. I can create you, but I cannot do it all. You have to help Me fix the holes and put everything together. This is the learning from the Holocaust. That each of us is here to fix the holes. My little brother, they put him in the crematorium. What did my mother, undressing in front of strangers, holding this little boy by the hand, what did she say to him? What? No one knows. *There* is a hole.

You know everything was terrible in Auschwitz. There was no food, there was no water, there was cold, you didn't know whether your father or mother lives. I worked in a factory in Auschwitz. One day in the factory, it was almost Christmas, and the snow that fell was like a table set for guests, it was so beautiful, it was so white. And of course we had to work inside, starting at five o'clock in the morning and finishing at five o'clock at night, and not having food or anything we need. The foreman watching us every minute making sure we are making every ammunition supposed to be made. And the foreman looked at me and called me over. I was sure I was to be punished because all the way walking there the SS man is whipping his whip. You don't work fast and you don't do the work like it is supposed to, they beat you. I was fifteen years old and my legs are shaking. I am trying to tell him please just don't hurt me. Please I will work faster. And the foreman says bend down bend down bend down and I feel that he is about to be beating me he says take that white bread, put it under your coat, and go out fast. That was my Christmas. What an incredible man. The SS man was behind him. He bet his life to give a child a chance. You know what a slice of white bread meant? Could you imagine that I am starving? Instead of beating me he gave me bread I could share with my sister. So you see, everywhere there are good people, everywhere.

I don't know how much you know about the Holocaust. What is your interest in it? What do you want to do with your life, where do you want to go? What is hurting in you? What are your holes to fix? What is now important in my life, and in your life also, is that after the Holocaust, we shaking hands with each other, that we are nobody lesser than the other. That we understand the real meaning of what God created us for. You have the task. You have the task to better this world. There are holes in people also but those we create and we can fix with love. God wants us whole. We should fix the hole and make a good human being. Use all of your hands. One time I gave a painting to the pope, Pope Benedict. He said to me come, come!, and he held my hands. I tell him the painting is us arriving to Auschwitz, we were so frightened, and the first thing they did, they took away your name, so that you are not a person, you are a number. When you don't have name, you are nobody. The pope asks why is yellow in the painting and I tell him that is the yellow stain, that is the odor in Auschwitz, that odor never left me. That wonderful man had tears in his eyes. He held my hands for nineteen minutes. Then they put my painting by the Sistine Chapel.

My grandfather was a wonderful person and he said about the Nazis, it cannot happen in Hungary, maybe in Poland, maybe they didn't know, maybe, maybe, maybe, and we had all kind of maybes, you understand, and we didn't want to believe. Because just like you are sitting here, you would not believe. What, Germany? Germany is wonderful, they wouldn't do that. When I arrive to Auschwitz, I say to my sister, you know, somebody made a mistake. Very soon they will come and apologize. Somebody will apologize; we don't belong here. People running around in pajamas, what is this? Insane asylum, what is this? It cannot happen. We did not believe like you would not believe, you would not believe that it can happen in your town. We didn't believe. And unfortunately because we didn't believe, this is where we got.

In Auschwitz, there is a thousand people in a barrack, can you imagine that? In the barrack there is a bunk and six people are on it, nothing, no pillow, no cover, no nothing. Just one little piece of cloth, and if any of us wanted to turn on our side, the others had to turn to that side also. It was so cold, unbelievably cold. In the beginning, you know what I did? I gave away my bread. I say, I will not eat this, this is terrible bread! I got shiny brown shoes on me then, and somebody said they give sometimes a little margarine here, I said, margarine? We never had margarine, we ate butter, you know. And I put the margarine on my shoes, until I realize this is our food. So you slowly adapted yourself to something so horrendous that you cannot believe the human being can be like that, or do that to each other. So this is what we have to do, beautiful people, this is what we have to do: not to hate, not to hate, not ever.

Now you cannot imagine what it means to go out to freedom after Auschwitz. How do you go to freedom? How should I enter freedom? I did not even have a dress. I was sent to Sweden and someone invited me to Passover. Someone gave me a blue dress. I went to the door and I could not enter. I walked around in the flowers. Finally I went and opened the door, and it was beautiful halls and beautiful tables and people, you know, and the lady who invited me, she says, there is a little room there, why don't you just go and change? Ha, I didn't have anything to change into! But I went to the little room and saw a calendar and I said to myself, I will learn the days in English, and so I learned all the days until all the guests arrived. Finally everybody sat down, and they started to talk, and guess what they talked about? The price of the gold on the international market. And I thought, my god, this is how you celebrate the Passover? You know how many people were put in the crematorium a day? So very quietly I took my coat and walked down into Stockholm until I had no tears. I thought, what will I do with my freedom? Will I be quiet or will I scream? But it cannot happen again! At that time, I decided, I will not be silent. But of course my art is very silent, because some of the things you want to say, words are not enough, and only the art can talk.

I was very embarrassed what I did, very embarrassed. I thought if my mother would be alive she would never permit me to get up from any table and leave the house. And when I met my husband I said I have only one wish, take me back to Sweden so I can apologize this family for being so rude and leaving them, and my husband said, I do it for you. We went to Sweden back and I went to the same house and the lady say to me, I don't remember you. And my husband holding the flowers and I'm crying. So life is very interesting. Because you cannot expect everything. I had the task to tell you my story, and now I am eighty years old and it's very hard, because I am crying every day. Where is my brother, where is my mother, what happened to them? And so I have the task, nobody else. I have the task, no matter how hard it is, to come here, and tell you my story. I will tell you one more story: Steven Spielberg in his film about five of us who survived [*The Last Days*], did something colossal for me. I told him I will do what he asked me to do, go back to Auschwitz, but he has to do me one thing, he has to help me find my sister, this is fifty-six years after she dies. And guess what happens? The German person who was in charge of who died and who was alive opened the books, and here is my sister's name. And so after fifty-six years, I found my sister. My husband and I put down a stone for her and there she is under a tree and leaves cover the tree.

You know why I give the pope the painting? Because the first thing he did, when he became a pope, he went to Auschwitz and he kneeled and prayed and asked how could this happen? When I read that in the paper I thought to myself, this is it, I have to thank him somehow, because after all these years he could easily do nothing and be quiet. But he didn't.

How did I deal with God in Auschwitz? This a very strange story. My sister Edith and I decided that we would pray every Friday for the Sabbath. But they didn't let us pray, they didn't let us speak. We had to be quiet. We had to be nothing. So one Friday night I say, why don't we pray inside the latrine? So we went to a corner in the latrine and started to pray, and the Hebrew songs, you know, are almost universal, and more children came, from all over the world it was people there, and the children heard us praying in Hebrew and singing, and for a moment, a moment, God was with us there, and we all prayed, and every week, more and more people prayed. We discovered that the SS would not go into this filthy place. So this is where we prayed. And it is also very beautiful thing of Steven Spielberg, when I went back to Auschwitz, I saw the latrine still there, and I started to scream, and he says what are you talking about? So I told him the story, and he got some Jewish boys to sing the same songs in the latrine, if you listen carefully you will hear them, young children singing. The song they sang means, *Angels who come here, bless these children, bless them and bless the world.*

Here is one more story. When they took us from our home they put us in a cattle train and there was two buckets there, one with water for drinking and the other for sanitary use. There were eighty people in the train, men and women and a woman who was pregnant. Edith and I could not bear to use the bucket in the corner. So when we got to the border there was a young soldier who opened the door for fresh air. I said to him, please please let me go down for a minute under the wheels, my sister and I cannot bear to going to the bathroom in the bucket. And he understood and let me down. Wasn't it a miracle?

JOEL E. COHEN

A Mindful Beauty

FROM *The American Scholar*

MY GRADE SCHOOL EDUCATION IN MATHEMATICS INCLUDED A STRICT prohibition against mixing apples and oranges. As an adult buying fruit, I often find it convenient to mix the two. If the price of each is the same, the arithmetic works out well. The added thrill of doing something forbidden, like eating dessert first, comes free. In any case, the prohibition against combining apples and oranges falls away as soon as we care about what two subjects, different in some respects, have in common.

I want to mix apples and oranges by insisting on the important features shared by poetry and applied mathematics. Poetry and applied mathematics both mix apples and oranges by aspiring to combine multiple meanings and beauty using symbols. These symbols point to things outside themselves, and create internal structures that aim for beauty. In addition to meanings conveyed by patterned symbols, poetry and applied mathematics have in common both economy and mystery. A few symbols convey a great deal. The symbols' full meanings and their effectiveness in creating meanings and beauty remain inexhaustible.

Consider the following examples, which involve a beautiful poem of A. E. Housman (1859–1936) and some applied mathematics from my own recent research.

In August 1893, Housman wrote:

> *With rue my heart is laden*
> *For golden friends I had,*
> *For many a rose-lipt maiden*
> *And many a lightfoot lad.*

> *By brooks too broad for leaping*
> *The lightfoot boys are laid;*
> *The rose-lipt girls are sleeping*
> *In fields where roses fade.*

The surface meaning is simple: I regret that my friends, once young, have died. At that level of sophistication, the surface meaning of *The Odyssey* is equally simple: Odysseus has trouble getting home. Below the surface of Housman's poem, though, multiple meanings (social, personal, and allusive) interact.

The poem's social meanings arise from its time and place. The 63 poems in the collection *A Shropshire Lad* (of which this is number 54) describe the nostalgia of a country boy who moved to the big city. The poems, published in 1896, resonated widely in English society, where the population was rapidly urbanizing. By 1900, England would become the first country in the world to have most of its people living in cities.

The poem also had personal meanings for Housman. The scholar Archie Burnett's 2003 essay "Silence and Allusion in Housman" showed that many of his poems were "for Housman a means of finding a voice for the love that dare not speak its name, a way of breaking silence, a veil for disclosure, at once catering to reticence and facilitating expression." In May 1895, Oscar Wilde was sentenced for the crime of "gross indecency" (homosexuality but not buggery) to two years' imprisonment with hard labor. Housman's *Shropshire 54* seems benignly neutral about boys and girls, maidens and lads, and Housman went to great lengths from his youth onward to conceal his homosexuality. But his passionate objection to society's treatment of homosexuals, including Wilde, is clear in several poems in *A Shropshire Lad* and in his later writings, as the critic and scholar Christopher Ricks demonstrated in his essay "A. E. Housman and 'the colour of his hair'" in 1997. Among the personal meanings of "With rue my heart is laden" is what Housman dared not say.

This poem also has allusive meanings for those who read it with the literary background that Housman brought to writing it. In *Cymbeline* (act 4, scene 2), Shakespeare wrote a beautiful song of mourning for a boy, Fidele, thought to have died (but only drugged in a deep sleep):

> *Golden lads and girls all must,*
> *As chimney-sweepers, come to dust.*

Here are Housman's "golden" "lads" and "girls." John Sparrow in 1934 noted echoes of Shakespeare's dirge in this and two other poems of Housman's. Beyond the specific words, Housman echoes Shakespeare's point that mortality masters all. But there is more to this allusion, as the poet and critic Rosanna Warren has pointed out. Fidele is in fact a young woman, Imogen, in boy's clothing. In Shakespeare's time, the female role of Imogen would have been played by a boy or young man, giving the audience a male actor playing a female (Imogen) pretending to be a male (Fidele). Given what is now clear about Housman's sexual orientation, it seems plausible that Housman, consciously or not, identified with the doubly cross-dressing Imogen/Fidele, and nurtured a hope that his poems, if not he, would live.

The economy of the poem is evident in the many images compressed into eight lines and in the questions left unanswered. As the poem opens, the narrator speaks of his rue-laden heart, raising the question: Why is he sad? The second line explains why: his friends are gone. Where have they gone? Wait till the second stanza. Who were the rose-lipt maidens (echo of *Othello*, act 4, scene 2, as noted in Archie Burnett's 1997 edition of Housman's poems) and lightfoot lads in lines 3 and 4, and what were his relations with them? What happened in those friendships? The narrator never says. Instead he speaks of brooks too broad for leaping, evoking not slender streams easily leaped but a broader, slower descent to the sea in the fullness of time. Only in the last three lines, where the boys and girls are laid in death, in fields where roses fade, do we finally learn that his friends are gone not only as a result of migration (possibly) but also as a result of mortality. Additional questions remain. Why is the narrator's mourning plural and anonymous? (*The Oxford English Dictionary* does not support any sexual interpretation of "laid" at the end of line 6, as the earliest sexual use of "lay" or "laid" dates from 1932.)

Turning from meanings to patterns, we face another mystery. How do the combined patterns of the symbols, on the page or spoken, evoke so much beauty? The patterns in these eight lines interweave meter, rhyme, ending accent, internal repetition, play on the letters *r* and *l*, alliteration, du-bi-du consonants, and two layers of chiasmus, within two symmetrical stanzas. Each line is written in iambic trimeter, and each set of four lines constitutes a quatrain.

> *With rue | my heart | is laden*
> *For gold | en friends | I had,*
> *For man | y a rose | -lipt maiden*
> *And man | y a light | foot lad.*
>
> *By brooks | too broad | for leaping*
> *The light | foot boys | are laid;*
> *The rose | -lipt girls | are sleeping*
> *In fields | where ros | es fade.*

The irregularity of the anapests in lines 3 and 4 relieves the repetitious symmetry of the other lines. The rhyme scheme is equally simple: *abab*. The ending accent alternates feminine ("laden," "leaping") and masculine ("had," "fade"). There is an extraordinary amount of internal repetition. The first syllable of "laden" reappears in "laid" and, with a slight change in vowel, in "lad." The second syllable of "laden" reappears in "golden" and "maiden." Lines 3 and 4 repeat "many a" exactly. The phoneme "rōz" in "rose-lipt" and "roses" appears in lines 3, 7, and 8. "Lightfoot" appears in lines 4 and 6. Every even-numbered line ends with *d* (the initial consonant of "death," a word that does not appear in the poem), preceded by one or another variant of the vowel-sounds that the letter *a* can exhibit. The poem uses two liquid consonants: *r* 10 times and *l* 12 times. Alliteration crosses lines: "many," "maiden," "many"; "lipt," "lightfoot," "lad," "leaping," "lightfoot," "laid," "lipt," "(s)leeping"; "friends," "fields," "fade"; "brooks," "broad," "boys." Another pattern, for which I do not know a technical name, I have called du-bi-du consonants. It is the pattern illustrated by the consonants in its name, du-bi-du: "lightfoot lad" (*l-f-l*), "brooks too broad" (*b-t-b*), "lightfoot boys are laid" (*l-b-l*), "fields where roses fade" (*f-r-f*).

The pattern of chiasmus is central to this example of the connection I want to make between poetry and applied mathematics. In poetry, chiasmus refers to the statement of two words or ideas and then their restatement in reverse order. A subtle example of chiasmus is the appearance of maiden and lad (female, male in elevated language) in lines 3 and 4 followed by boys and girls (male, female in demotic language) in lines 6 and 7. The change in language from elevated to demotic suggests that even the highborn are brought to earth, and the reversal of order suggests that even any precedence in life ("ladies first," maidens before lads) may be undone in death. The second stanza gives another example of chiasmus. Line 5 tells where (by brooks too broad for leaping), and line 6 tells who (the lightfoot boys). Line 7 tells who (the rose-lipt girls) followed by line 8, which tells where (in fields where roses fade). Again the pattern conveys a meaning: the brooks (line 5) and fields (line 8) enclose the boys and girls (lines 6 and 7) as a coffin contains its cadaver. The patterns of the symbols and the messages of the poem are inextricable.

In mathematics (pure or applied), a strict definition would limit "chiasmus" to the exact repetition of two symbols (a, b) in reverse order (b, a). A more inclusive definition includes any repetition of a sequence of symbols in a permuted order.

Like poetry, applied mathematics combines multiple meanings, economy, pattern, and mystery. In its scientific or practical applications, applied mathematics points to something external. It also alludes to prior mathematics. Its few symbols convey a lot. Its use of symbols often involves internal repetition, symmetry, and chiasmus. It is replete with unexpected truths, unexpected applications, and diverse proofs that illuminate different aspects of a single truth.

My example from applied mathematics comes from work I did with two outstanding colleagues, Johannes H. B. Kemperman, retired from Rutgers University, and Gheorghe Zbăganu, University of Bucharest. In 2000, Zbăganu published a fact new to mathematics:

If n is a positive integer (a counting number like 1, 2, 3, . . .), and $a_1, a_2, \ldots a_n$ and $b_1, b_2, \ldots b_n$ are any nonnegative real numbers (any fractional or whole number larger than or equal to zero, such as 17 or 0.333333 . . . or 3.14159 . . .), then

$$\sum_{i,j} \min((a_i \times a_j), (b_i \times b_j)) \leq \sum_{i,j} \min((a_i \times b_j), (b_i \times a_j))$$

No understanding of the meanings of this beautiful formula is necessary to appreciate that it is an intricately patterned array of symbols. Whatever it means, the formula has a left lobe $\sum_{i,j} \min((a_i \times a_j), (b_i \times b_j))$ and a right lobe $\sum_{i,j} \min((a_i \times b_j), (b_i \times a_j))$ mediated by $\leq$. The symbols in the left lobe are exactly the same as the symbols in the right lobe but the letters a and b appear in different order; this is chiasmus in the broad sense. In the right lobe, (a, b, b, a) is an example of chiasmus in the strict sense as the sequence (a, b) is repeated in reverse order (b, a). That is about as far as one can go without having any idea of the meanings of the symbols.

Understanding the formula's meanings only enhances one's sense of its beauty, economy, and mystery. The connective $\leq$ between the two lobes means that the quantity on the left is less than or equal to the quantity on the right. The expression $\sum_{i,j}$ means sum (add) for all pairs i, j, where i and j are positive whole numbers from 1 to n. Finally, $\min((a_i \times b_j), (b_i \times a_j))$ means the minimum (smaller) of $a_i \times b_j$ and $b_i \times a_j$, and similarly for $\min((a_i \times a_j), (b_i \times b_j))$.

The words "If n is a positive integer, and $a_1, a_2, \ldots, a_n$ and $b_1, b_2, \ldots, b_n$ are any nonnegative real numbers, then," which precede the formula, declare that the inequality holds for any such numbers. Therein lies the immense and surprising power of Zbăganu's inequality. A numerical example illustrates its economy of expression. If $n = 2$ and if $a_1 = 2, a_2 = 5, b_1 = 4, b_2 = 3$, then the expression on the left side of the inequality equals $\min (2 \times 2, 4 \times 4) + \min (2 \times 5, 4 \times 3) + \min (5 \times 2, 3 \times 4) + \min (5 \times 5, 3 \times 3) = 4 + 10 + 10 + 9 = 33$, while the expression on the right side equals $\min (2 \times 4, 4 \times 2) + \min(2 \times 3, 4 \times 5) + \min(5 \times 4, 3 \times 2) + \min (5 \times 3, 3 \times 5) = 8 + 6 + 6 + 15 = 35$. As the formula predicts, $33 < 35$. Zbăganu's inequality asserts that, no matter what natural number n you may pick, and no matter what nonnegative real numbers $a_1, a_2, \ldots, a_n$ and $b_1, b_2, \ldots, b_n$ you may pick, the value of the left side will be less than or equal to the value of the right side.

Zbăganu's inequality has social or referential meanings because it answers a question Zbăganu was considering in the mathematical theory of information systems: If one of two messages must be sent over a channel with only two input symbols, A and B, and with n

output symbols, $1, \ldots, n$, is the chance of error in transmission smaller if the first message is sent as AA and the second message as BB, or if the first message is sent as AB and the second message as BA?

The left lobe of Zbăganu's inequality represents the probability of an error in transmission if the first message sent is AA and the second is BB, while the right lobe represents the probability of error in the alternative. Hence the inequality says that coding the two messages by AA and BB gives a lower risk that the wrong message will be received than coding by AB and BA. (The tongue-in-cheek message for teachers might be: If you're trying to teach your students one of two messages, it's better to convey the message twice in the same way than to convey it once in each of two different ways. But don't take this interpretation too seriously; some students have memories, unlike the communication channels in this theory.)

Nothing prevents us from playing formally with Zbăganu's inequality as long as we remember that such formal play yields only questions, not answers. For example, if we exchange multiplication and addition, we get another formula:

$$\prod_{i,j} (\min[(a_i + a_j), (b_i + b_j)]) \leq \prod_{i,j} (\min[(a_i + b_j), (b_i + a_j)]).$$

Is this formula always true if n is a positive integer, and a_1, $a_2, \ldots, a_n$ and $b_1, b_2, \ldots, b_n$ are any nonnegative real numbers?

Pushing the same idea further, we produced 64 possible generalizations of Zbăganu's inequality by replacing each occurrence of addition or summation, minimum, and multiplication by each of four operations: addition, multiplication, minimum, and maximum, then looking for a direction of the inequality $\leq$ or $\geq$ that would make the statement true whenever n is a positive integer and $a_1, a_2, \ldots, a_n$ and $b_1, b_2, \ldots, b_n$ are any nonnegative real numbers. Zbăganu's inequality is one of these 64. We produced another 32 formal generalizations of Zbăganu's inequality by swapping in other mathematical functions (for cognoscenti, the spectral radius of a square nonnegative matrix, and quadratic forms). The mathematical question for us became: are these other 95 inequalities besides Zbăganu's inequality always true or true under some interesting conditions?

Here are a few examples of the resulting generalizations of Zbăganu's inequality, which we proved to be true under appropriate conditions:

$$\sum_{i,j} \max((a_i + a_j), (b_i + b_j)) \geq \sum_{i,j} \max((a_i + b_j), (b_i + a_j)),$$

$$\prod_{i,j} \min(\max(a_i, a_j), \max(b_i, b_j)) \leq \prod_{i,j} \min(\max(a_i, b_j), \max(b_i, a_j)),$$

$$\sum_{i,j} \min((a_i a_j), (b_i b_j)) x_i x_j \leq \sum_{i,j} \min((a_i b_j), (b_i a_j)) x_i x_j,$$

$$\rho(\min((a_i a_j), (b_i b_j))) \leq \rho(\min((a_i b_j), (b_i a_j))),$$

$$\int\int \log[(f(x) + f(y))(g(x) + g(y))] d\mu(x) d\mu(y)$$

$$\leq \int\int \log[(f(x) + g(y))(g(x) + f(y))]\, d\mu(x) d\mu(y)$$

You are supposed to be saying, or at least thinking, ooooooh, aaaaaaaaah, how beautiful these formulas are.

Every mathematician knows, and every student of elementary mathematics has to learn, that swapping the operations of addition, multiplication, minimum, and maximum does not generally produce true formulas.

But after a few years of hard, exciting work, Zbăganu, Kemperman, and I were astonished to find that when $n = 2$, all 96 formulas we had invented by purely formal manipulations are true. When $n > 2$, 62 of our first 64 generalizations are true but two are false in general. Some of the inequalities involving the spectral radius and quadratic forms are false in general, some are true. We were able to distill several of our inequalities into a more abstract so-called matrix-norm inequality that is valid for any one of the four operations of addition, multiplication, maximum, and minimum—the kind of mathematical discovery that brings joy to the hearts of applied mathematicians (or at least to the hearts of the three of us).

Our inequalities have meanings both referential and allusive. I described earlier Zbăganu's construction of his inequality in the context of information theory. Among our other inequalities, several have interpretations in operations research with potential applications for scheduling transportation and manufacturing. In addition, our inequalities allude by similarity of form to a beautiful inequality by Augustin-Louis Cauchy (1789–1857):

If n is a positive integer, and $a_1, a_2, \ldots, a_n$ and $b_1, b_2, \ldots, b_n$ are any nonnegative real numbers, then

$$[a_1^2 + \ldots + a_n^2]\,[b_1^2 + \ldots + b_n^2] \geq [a_1 b_1 + \ldots + a_n b_n]^2.$$

Equality holds if and only if for some real constants λ and μ with $\lambda^2 + \mu^2 > 0$ we have $\lambda a_j + \mu b_j = 0$ for $j = 1, \ldots, n$.

In 2004 the mathematician Michael Steele called Cauchy's inequality "one of the most widely used and most important inequalities in all of mathematics." The opening words and symbols are identical to those of Zbăganu's original inequality except that Zbăganu's restriction to nonnegative numbers is absent from Cauchy's inequality. Here the letters a and b which appear in the left lobe in the order (a, a, b, b) appear in the right lobe in the order (a, b, a, b), whereas in Zbăganu's inequality they appear in the right lobe in the order (a, b, b, a). For readers with the requisite mathematical background, Zbăganu's inequality alludes to Cauchy's inequality no less clearly than Housman's verse alludes to Shakespeare's.

A deeper and more substantial connection lies beneath the similarity in the pattern of the symbols. After Zbăganu's inequality appeared in 2000, Ravi Boppana of New York University proved it in a new way. In 2006, Titu Andreescu of the University of Texas at Dallas and Gabriel Dospinescu of Lycée Louis-le-Grand, in Paris, found new proofs that strengthen Boppana's intermediate result on the path to Zbăganu's inequality. Some of these proofs depend on the Cauchy-Schwarz inequality, a generalization of Cauchy's inequality. So among the lines of logical genealogy that lead to Zbăganu's inequality are lines that pass through Cauchy's inequality.

In applied mathematics, as in poetry, at the end of the analysis, things not yet understood remain. Why are so many of our formulas true? They were generated by a formal process that any mathematician, pure or applied, regards with total disbelief. In the first group of 64 putative inequalities, why are the two particular failed inequalities false when $n > 2$? Why are the proofs of the true inequalities so extraordinarily diverse? Why can't we find a unifying approach that separates the sheep from the goats, the true from the false? Perhaps most mysteriously, why do several of our formulas have meanings for potential practical applications?

The critic and scholar Helen Vendler has shown me a precedent for the mixing of poetry and applied mathematics in *Seven Types of Ambiguity*, written by William Empson (1906–1984) at the age of 22 and published when he was 24. At Cambridge, Empson won firsts in mathematics and English. His book repeatedly cites the commonalities of poetry and math. For example, Empson quotes from George Herbert's book *The Temple* (1633) the eight-line poem "Hope," which alternates lines of iambic pentameter and iambic trimeter. Empson wrote:

One can accept the poem without plunging deeply into its meaning, because of the bump with which the short lines, giving the flat, poor, surprising answer of reality, break the momentum of the long hopeful lines in which a new effort has been made; the movement is so impeccable as to be almost independent of the meaning of the symbols.

And, indeed, the symbols themselves seem almost to be used in a way familiar to the mathematician; as when a set of letters may stand for any numbers of a certain sort, and you are not curious to know which numbers are meant because you are only interested in the relations between them.

As apples do differ from oranges, poetry does differ from applied mathematics, despite their commonalities. For example, in poetry but not mathematics, sound and "mouthfeel" (Galway Kinnell) matter. In applied mathematics, unlike poetry, calculation and shared scientific concepts and data, rather than intimate experience, lend conviction. Examples of differences could be multiplied. They do not undermine the significance of the similarities.

Poetry and applied mathematics, with mysterious success, both use symbols for beautiful, economical pointing and patterning. Pointing establishes a relation between symbols and a world beyond the domain of symbols. Patterning establishes a relation between symbols and other symbols in the same domain. Poetry and applied mathematics fall along a continuum between pointing and patterning.

The pointing of symbols to something else is most important.

Formal prose	Numerical data collection
Poetry	Engineering
Songs with words, program music	Applied mathematics
Abstract music	Pure mathematics

The patterning of symbols themselves is most important.

The same continuum runs in the visual arts from journalistic photography at the extreme of pointing to purely abstract art at the extreme of patterning. Between those extremes lies most of the world of art, mixing apples and oranges, mixing meanings and patterns, along with poetry and applied mathematics.

The differences between poetry and applied mathematics coexist with shared strategies for symbolizing experiences. Understanding those commonalities makes poetry a point of entry into understanding the heart of applied mathematics, and makes applied mathematics a point of entry into understanding the heart of poetry. With this understanding, both poetry and applied mathematics become points of entry into understanding others and ourselves as animals who make and use symbols.

The author wishes to thank Helen Vendler and Rosanna Warren for their helpful comments on prior drafts of this article.

BILLY COLLINS

Grave

FROM *The Atlantic*

What do you think of my new glasses
I asked as I stood under a shade tree
before the joined grave of my parents,

and what followed was a long silence
that descended on the rows of the dead
and on the fields and the woods beyond,

one of the one hundred kinds of silence
according to the Chinese belief,
each one distinct from the others,

but the differences being so faint
that only a few special monks
were able to tell one from another.

They make you look very scholarly,
I heard my mother say
once I lay down on the ground

and pressed an ear into the soft grass.
Then I rolled over and pressed
my other ear to the ground,

the ear my father likes to speak into,
but he would say nothing,
and I could not find a silence

among the one hundred Chinese silences
that would fit the one that he created
even though I was the one
who had just made up the business
of the one hundred Chinese silences—
the Silence of the Night Boat,
and the Silence of the Lotus,
cousin to the Silence of the Temple Bell
only deeper and softer, like petals, at its farthest edges.

ROBERT CORDING

Czeslaw Milosz's Glasses

FROM *The Southern Review*

I

Shortly after his death, they came to me
in a blue velvet Sailor fountain pen case,

a gift from a poet-friend who found Milosz
had left his glasses behind at a poetry festival.

By the time she reached him, he had
already bought a new pair. He's wearing

them in a photograph on the back cover
of *Second Space*; he's writing a poem,

or pretending to be for the photograph.
I like to think he's listening to the daimonion

he sometimes heard, writing down what it said—
faithfully. Yet he scoured every poem

for the disguises he knew were his, and unavoidable,
no matter how carefully he tried to listen.

II

His glasses fit my wide head. I like to
put them on, but when I look through them,

the spruce tree outside my window is no longer
a spruce tree, hardly a tree at all; his glasses

make my head hurt. Which is meet and right,
as the prayer book says, no one knowing

better than he how the eyes are a temptation.
So much evil in believing that others see

the world just as we do. He knew words
could never navigate the roundness of things,

and yet knew, too, his work was to catch
the complexity of all in one unwritable sentence

he tried to write again and again.
Such a long journey to describe things

as they are. Sunlit depths of rivers. A wooden
table set with plates for dinner. The roundness

of pears. The shape of a woman's breasts under
a summer dress. And also: a Nazi putting out

a cigarette on a Jewish child's arm. A pregnant
woman lying in a Warsaw street, being kicked,

begging for the blows to end. Families taken away,
wherever they were herded to, a nowhere.

III

I met him once. He read his poems, and after
we had dinner with some others. I never said

how much I admired him, the poems.
We talked about the Psalms, their thirst for justice,

and he said that man's instinctual sense of
what ought to be was precisely (and "perversely,"

he added) what lay behind the appeal
of propaganda in the modern era, lies

always more alluring and comforting
than reality. He drank too much and, rising

from the table with his cane, stumbled
and fell—something I tell only because

I feel he, who knew his faults better than anyone,
would have wanted me to. As he approached

his ninetieth year, he wrote that his former lives
were like "ships departing," that the countries, cities

and gardens he'd known all this time, were "ready now
to be described better than they were before"—

as if he'd just received a new prescription,
and could see, at least for the time being,

more clearly through his newest glasses.
I keep his old glasses in my desk drawer,

and take them out at times when I begin
a poem. Not for inspiration, but for correction.

PAUL J. GRIFFITHS

Turning Points

FROM *The Christian Century*

CHANGES OF MIND AREN'T SUPERFICIAL OR EASY THINGS. MINE HAVE usually come as forced exits from the comfort of myself to somewhere more painful. I have had to learn to be beside myself.

In the late autumn of 1976, in the ground-floor reading room of the University of Oxford's New Bodleian Library, I decide that I need to be baptized. I'm twenty. It's a sunny day, I've just had my morning coffee in the King's Arms across the street, and I've been reading Athanasius in preparation for a tutorial on the Arian heresy. The tableau—the sun across the blond wood reading tables, the soft smells of damp wool and old paper, the feel of sandals on my feet as I walk up and down beside the tall stacks of shelves—is clear to me still. Baptism is one decision among several: I also decide which languages I need to learn to read, or to read better (French, German, Latin, Greek), and which thinkers I need more intimate acquaintance with (Augustine, Heidegger, Wittgenstein).

I go, a few days later, to speak with my college chaplain, Trevor Williams, about being baptized. He treats me with kindness and undertakes to instruct me in preparation for baptism the following Easter. He is Anglican, and so I am baptized into the Anglican Communion. I consider no other. I am English, after all, and this is Oxford. I am hazily aware that there are other churches, other communions; but I give almost no consideration to their differences, and likewise none to Anglican specificities. I think, with some justice, that I already know more theology than most Anglicans, and that what I need is simply the sacrament. Six months later or so, at Easter in 1977 at the Church of St. Mary Magdalen in Oxford, I am baptized and subsequently become a regular communicant and occasional petitioner of God for this and that.

I was then—it seems to me now, more than three decades later— as profoundly self-centered as most people of that age. And the reception of the sacraments had no transformative effect upon the fabric of my experience or upon my intellectual passions—none, at least, then discernible to me. I would not have wanted them to. But in fact, I now think, the reception of the sacraments was efficacious: it began gradually to set me aside, to place me beside myself, and, equally slowly, to make of my studies less an instrument for self-gratification and the domination of others and more an ecstasy of response to God.

Five years after my baptism, in the late spring of 1982, on a cold, bright day by Lake Mendota in Madison, Wisconsin, I find myself again beside myself, this time with anger and frustration. I am twenty-six. I have been for some time studying Indian Buddhist thought and am at the moment receiving instruction from Geshe Lhundub Sopa in the technicalities of Buddhist metaphysics. He is a monk and a scholastic, then perhaps in his fifties, trained in the systematic thought of the Tibetan Gelug school. He is teaching a graduate seminar at the University of Wisconsin in Madison, where I am a student in a doctoral program in Buddhist studies. He is my adviser and has been teaching me for close on a year, especially in the *Abhidharmakosa*, a fourth-century Sanskritic summa of Buddhist thought; but I am angry with his teaching methods and with him and want to find a way out.

• • •

There is a long distance between Oxford and Madison and, in a different way, between the study of theology in the former place and that of Buddhist metaphysics in the latter. I have traversed those distances theologically. My Oxford studies and my baptism have raised for me the theological question of what Christians should think and teach about long-lived traditions of religious thought and practice other than their own. I had decided, with the absurd confidence of youth and still as an Oxford undergraduate, that I would answer this question, and that in order to do so I must gain substantive expertise in an alien tradition by learning to speak it as a second first language—to handle its lexicon and syntax as if I were a native speaker. I chose, for local and contingent reasons, to do this with Indian Buddhism, which involves the study of Sanskrit and, eventually, Tibetan, and after beginning those studies at Oxford I moved to Wisconsin to pursue them in greater depth. That is what has led me to the study of the *Abhidharmakosa* under the tutelage of Geshe Sopa.

Sopa teaches as a scholastic and as one thoroughly textualized. He has memorized the texts from which he teaches—the Tibetans like to say that if you have your learning in a book on the shelf at home, then of course you don't really have it; it needs to be in your head, ready to go—and he teaches and thinks in deep conversation with his texts. Each class begins with a chant of the verses memorized for that day and proceeds to oral exposition of the text. Sopa has no interest in the questions that concern me—questions about textual transmission, about versions, about whether there are good reasons to think that the central claims of the texts he expounds are true, and about the relations between Buddhism and Christianity; he simply teaches, calmly. If he does not find a question interesting or thinks it irrelevant to the matter at hand, he smiles mad nods and leaves it aside by returning to the text. He embodies his text and gives voice to it.

I want other things. I want to be given the skills that will provide me an academic career. I want my questions answered. I want him to argue with me. I do not want to submit to his text, and certainly not to him. My anger is about all those things. I vent it, take another adviser, finish my work with dispatch—a six-hundred-page dissertation on Indian Buddhist meditation-theory, arduously typed and retyped—find a job at the University of Chicago and begin, with rapidity and ambition, to claw my way up the academic ladder.

Geshe Sopa placed me beside myself with anger. He also showed me, though I was not then remotely ready to see it, what it might be like to set oneself aside in favor of a textual tradition, to permit oneself to be overwritten by it and made its creature. His lessons in this I can now see for what they were, and I am grateful for them. I learned from him what I had not learned from my Christian teachers, which is how to read. It took me a decade or so to begin to make sense of the lesson and to begin to use it as a reader of the Christian text. That is a practice in which I am still engaged and will be until death and beyond.

Spring at the University of Notre Dame in Indiana is a gorgeous time: the campus is especially beautiful. Mary, golden atop the dome that can be seen from almost everywhere on campus, smiles, and the world is as it should be. But in the spring of 1988, five years after I've received my doctorate, I find myself angry once again, angry enough that I am ready to resign from an academic career then in its early stages. I am thirty-two. The occasion for this anger is a seminar I have recently attended, given by a colleague from the anthropology department (I am teaching in theology) on the subject of Christian-Muslim relations. I have raised with him the question of whether, in his view, it is ever appropriate to argue with Muslims about the adequacy of their understanding of God in light of Christian Trinitarian conviction. He replies, calmly and reasonably, that this is never appropriate, that we are surely past that outdated and harmful emphasis on apologetics and mission. Isn't understanding what we need to seek?

I argue, too polemically and too angrily and without subtlety, that he is selling the idea of truth short and that being a Christian means, among other things, having deep convictions about the crucial significance of Jesus Christ for the entire cosmos and thus understanding the Christian narrative as capable of embracing all others just as Christ was eager to embrace everyone, Muslims included. I convince him of nothing and spend the next few days stewing over the event.

It gradually assumes symbolic significance for me. I come to see it as representative of all that is bad about the academic life. If what the academy does to Christians is make them incapable of seeing the importance of the gospel's truth, then why am I in it? Am I not a Christian? Am I not supposed to be preaching the gospel? How can I bear to spend a career immured in this hell? I convince myself that I can't. After several days of discussion with long-suffering faculty colleagues—Joseph Wawrykow acts a saintly part here—and an even longer-suffering and supportive spouse, I decide to resign my position effective at the end of the academic year and write a letter formally saying so to my chair and dean. That dean, Nathan Hatch, now president of Wake Forest University, is humane and perceptive. He tells me that he will sit on my resignation letter for six weeks, and if at the end of that time I still want to resign, he will accept it. If not, he will tear it up.

For the next few weeks I am, again, beside myself. There is, I am sure, something importantly right in my judgments about the academic enterprise; but it is equally obvious to me that there is something wrong with the passion and vehemence with which my own sense of being right is suffused. I become increasingly aware, too, that I have real and nonnegotiable practical responsibilities to my wife and two small children (then one and four years old). I back down and withdraw my resignation and am graciously received back into the academic community at Notre Dame—much more graciously than I deserve.

I was learning something. The most important thing, I now think, was the lesson that, yes, Jesus does trump the university, and that, yes, my primary loyalty is to him. I had, for the previous five years, been trying hard to forget Geshe Sopa's lessons in reading and to dry out my baptismal soaking of eleven years before in the harsh fires of academic ambition. What Augustine likes to call the *libido dominandi* had assumed an excessive importance: I had published my first book; a second was on the way; I was publishing essays and articles; and I had my eye on early tenure. Everything was in place, but my affections—my loves—were misweighted and that out-of-jointness was in part corrected, or at least moved in the direction of correction, by this incident.

This lesson began to bear fruit in ways that even I could see. I found a renewed delight in my sacramental life as an Episcopalian; I sought my local bishop's permission to preach, which he gave, and for a number of years I preached, off and on, in pulpits in the Episcopal Diocese of Northern Indiana; and I began to write more explicitly theological work, combining my historical and exegetical work on Buddhism with Christian-theological analyses of and responses to that tradition and writing some books and essays on how Christians should respond to the facts of religious diversity. I began to read widely and with passion in contemporary theology—George Lindbeck and Alasdair MacIntyre were important here, as later was John Milbank; I discovered Hans Urs von Balthasar; I read the early encyclicals of John Paul II and as a result began to read almost everything that appeared above his name. These men, of course, do not agree about everything; what I liked in them was the primacy that each of them gave to the Christian claim and the intellectual confidence with which they expounded that primacy.

Anger is, among the seven deadly sins, the most ambiguous. It is the least clearly sinful and the most possibly fruitful. For me, it has often accompanied the ecstasy of being drawn away from myself, set beside myself and thereby closer to God.

American Independence Day 1996, in Chennai (once Madras), South India. A hot day, like all July days there. The sweat runs between my shoulder blades as I pace the roof. I am forty. I am spending the summer in a Jesuit-run ashram called Aikiya Alayam, on the edge of the city. I am teaching now at the University of Chicago Divinity School and working on a book called *Religious Reading: The Place of Reading in the Practice of Religion*. I am in India to read and write, and for a breathing space. The work is going well, and I can see the shape of the book before me. I am Anglican still: I am going to the nearest congregation of the Church of South India on Sundays and attending daily mass with the Jesuits during the week. After a week or so and some considerable conferring among themselves, they invite me to participate fully in their daily mass, and I happily do so: I've not much notion of the doctrine and discipline of the Catholic Church on these matters and so am not fully sensible of the complexities of this position. I am, however, grateful for the hospitality shown me.

The sisters who prepare food and run the place had surprised me the week before by bringing me a special cake on the 29th of June. They assumed that I would know why, but I don't. They laughed, and although we have little language in common, they eventually got it across to me that this day is the Solemnity of SS. Peter and Paul and therefore my name day, my saint's day, a proper occasion for celebration. They know that I am not Catholic, and I think they were amused by the depth of my Protestant ignorance about things that matter. I was moved almost to tears by the unexpectedness of the gesture and by the vistas opened to me by it: a world in which the communion of saints is an everyday matter. This was the beginning of another derailment, another progressive setting aside of myself.

It deepens a few days later. I'm walking past the Catholic cathedral in Chennai, pondering whether to go in, when a large crowd of people makes a noisy exit. They gather behind a decrepit but beribboned and garlanded flatbed truck, and as it moves slowly away, they walk behind it, singing. More and more people join them as the truck makes a slow pilgrimage through the city. Bad (to my ear) and very loud recorded music blares from speakers on the truck. People begin to dance and sing. I follow, wondering what is going on. I manage to ask and to understand some part of the answers given me. I learn that an image of St. Thomas the Apostle is being paraded through the city as part of the celebration of that saint's feast day on July 3. I have long known that Thomas was supposed to have brought Christianity to India, and this piece of knowledge now comes alive. I learn that his relics are enshrined in the cathedral and that there is great local devotion to him. By now there are thousands of people following the truck-borne image, and I, along with them, am transported.

The next day, American Independence Day, I walk the roof of the ashram in the heat of the afternoon (mad dogs and Englishmen: everyone else is sleeping), restless and still ecstatic. I contrast the deep and direct devotional passions I've seen the day before with the staid and oddly English worship I've been experiencing in the Church of South India. I think of the Jesuits and their mass, celebrated early in the morning with the cool breeze blowing through the portico, the sweet smells of flowering trees whose names I do not know, and the soft mixture of Tamil and Latin caressing my ears. I meditate upon the sisters who knew my name day when I did not and gave me the ability to celebrate it. I think of John Paul II's witness and work.

It is suddenly and strikingly obvious that I should seek full unity with the bishop of Rome. I've long known that there are no theological or other conceptual difficulties for me in that move; and I have occasionally toyed with the thought of what it would be like to be Catholic. But it had remained a thought, and now it is a conviction. Five months later, on the third Sunday of Advent in 1996, I am received into the Catholic Church at the parish church of St. Thomas the Apostle on the South Side of Chicago.

It's a bright, cool day in Durham, North Carolina. I'm fifty-three. I'm writing the account you are reading not in an ecstasy of self-forgetfulness and not in anger, but with some puzzlement at the difficulty of doing such a thing. I've written it in vignettes rather than as a connected, sequential account because that is how it appears to me. I am deeply opaque to myself in the present and even more so as the present recedes into the past. My Oxford self of 1976 is almost completely gone, and my later selves in Wisconsin, Notre Dame, and Chennai are not much more available. What stands out, in bright relief, are tableaus: short sequences of events whose details are vivid and whose power remains strong. But the connections that would string those vignettes into a narrative are mostly dark; to supply them would require an act of imagination at present beyond me, and were I to attempt it now the result would be a fiction, a figment, a phantasm.

What remains is gratitude for the God-given gift of time, of thought, and of the companionship of the saints, living and dead. Two among the dead—John Henry Newman and Aurelius Augustinus—have been my constant companions since even before my Oxford days. They showed me, before I had any hope of understanding it (I still have not much), the scope and flexibility and fascination of the gospel's challenge to thought. An ever-present thread in my intellectual life (how hard it is to use that phrase without pomposity) has been this sense, inchoate and undeveloped, of gratitude for the gift of tools with which to think. My Anglican teachers gave me Christian language and a first acquaintance with the work of those who had used it before me. My Buddhist teachers showed me what it is to submit, joyfully and with intellectual energy, to a tradition of thought and practice and how, therefore, to read.

And my more than twelve years in the warmly embracing arms of the Catholic Church have given me the whole of the tradition, a vastly expanded range of authorities and teachers with whom to think, and a cloud of witnesses, living and dead, to chide me and support me and take me further from this burdensome self, whose spectacular inner theater it is the business of Christians gradually to transform into an outer-directed voice, a small note in the chorus of praise to the God who is not a being among beings, but rather the giver of being itself. As Augustine writes: *non solum non peccemus adorando, sed peccemus non adorando,* which is to say that adoration of God is both necessary and sufficient for the avoidance of sin. I have not changed my mind about that, but I have come to see its meaning more clearly.

Sesshin with Sasaki Roshi

FROM *Shambhala Sun*

"YOU MAY HEAR BURSTS OF GUNFIRE OR EXPLOSIONS DURING THIS sesshin," the sign read. That gave me pause. Formal Rinzai Zen practice with Joshu Roshi was always intense, but gunplay had never before been part of the equation. As I read on, I realized that a movie was being shot in the neighborhood. It figured. Here in LA, reality and illusion mingle effortlessly.

I had come to Rinzai-ji, the home temple of Kyozan Joshu Sasaki Roshi's network of Zen centers and monasteries, to participate in a seven-day *sesshin* marking the forty-sixth anniversary of his arrival in the U.S. Forty students were converging from as far away as Austria to practice with the 101-year-old teacher.

Although he has taught thousands, Joshu Roshi remains an enigma in the West. He has published little of his teaching, and he seldom speaks in public, apart from the *teisho*, the talks he delivers during his sesshins. Because he regards encounters with journalists (and everyone else, for that matter) primarily as teaching opportunities, in interviews he seldom talks about himself, preferring to keep the focus on Zen practice. None of this appears to concern him. He was firming up his teaching schedule for the rest of the year. "I have no plan [for retirement]," he tells me. "Of course, I have no plan, period. There is no word 'retirement,' as far as I'm concerned." Lately, though, he has been saying he will live to be 128.

Sesshin, which in Japanese literally means "gathering the mind," is a staple of Zen practice. It is a physically and mentally demanding period of intense *zazen* (sitting Zen meditation) coupled with regular meetings with the teacher. Joshu Roshi continues to lead eighteen or more sesshins a year, a pace that challenges even his most dedicated students.

"He has no dharma successor and he lives to teach," says Seiju Bob Mammoser, the priest who was serving as the administrator for this sesshin. "It's like if you have a child and you see he's suffering because he's caught on some foolish thing, and you want him to change. Roshi sees we're suffering a lot, needlessly, and he's trying to help us understand that."

As we arrived for the Sunday-afternoon chanting session that would kick the sesshin off, I greeted old friends and introduced myself to people I hadn't met before. The setting was pure Southern California. The *zendo* was an eighty-year-old building modeled on a Spanish mission church, with whitewashed masonry walls and a high ceiling made of massive exposed wood beams. The surrounding streets were lined with stately hundred-foot palm trees, and a subtle floral fragrance wafted on the placid breeze.

I'd never sat a sesshin at Rinzai-ji, but I knew more or less what to expect. We would rise at 3:00 A.M. for chanting, followed by four twenty-five-minute periods of zazen as students went one by one to *sanzen*, a private interview with the teacher. After a formal breakfast, Roshi would deliver an hour-long teisho, followed by more zazen and sanzen. Another round of chanting, zazen, and sanzen would follow in the afternoon and again in the evening before we retired, sometime after 9:00 P.M. We would do this for seven days in a row, not speaking the entire time.

Although he is well south of five feet tall and only appears in public once a day for teisho, everyone always feels Roshi's indomitable presence during sesshin. Photos from when he first came to the States portray a powerful bulldog of a man, and the tales of his fierceness back then are legion. He's much gentler now that he must conserve his energy, but his determination to practice with every ounce of his remaining strength inspires great devotion among his students.

"I consider Roshi to be the *kancho* [abbot] of Zen worldwide," says Oscar Moreno, a retired computer science professor from Puerto Rico who sat next to me for the week. He has studied with Joshu Roshi since 1975 and estimates that he has sat close to three hundred sesshins with him. "Roshi is at the top of Buddhism, and that's why he has not certified anyone as a successor," Moreno says. "Unless they know what he knows and realize what he has realized, he won't be satisfied."

Everyone in the zendo wore black. Seated by a bronze gong at the altar, the chant leader's low, unearthly moan morphed into "Myoho renge kyo," the first line of Lotus Sutra. Everyone joined in, chanting phonetically in Sino-Japanese as an assistant drummed, speeding up the rhythm until we were rolling along at a kinetic clip. The Heart Sutra followed, then a series of other sutras.

Roshi hobbled into the zendo, his gait slowed by age and a bad case of sciatica. Wearing his fierce, implacable practice face, he sat in a chair while a list of those participating in the sesshin was read aloud. The members included priests, monks, nuns, and lay students ranging from a nineteen-year-old college freshman to several people in their sixties. The formalities concluded and, the evening meal approaching, Roshi shuffled out of the zendo.

Joshu Roshi was born in 1907 to a farming family near Sendai in Japan's Miyagi Prefecture. At fourteen, he became a novice under Joten Soko Miura Roshi at Zuiryu-ji in the northern island of Hokkaido. Later, he trained for twenty years at Myoshin-ji in Kyoto, receiving teaching authority in 1947. In 1953 he took over as abbot of Shoju-an, where the teacher of Zen master Hakuin Ekaku had once presided. Nine years later, when a group of Americans wrote to Myoshin-ji asking to have a monk come teach in the States, the head priests there decided to send Joshu Roshi.

He arrived at LAX on the morning of July 21, 1962, carrying a Japanese-English dictionary and an English-Japanese dictionary. John F. Kennedy was president. Telstar, the world's first communications satellite, had just been launched, and the Beatles were an up-and-coming band from Liverpool. Joshu Roshi managed to make himself at home in this new land, living for a while in a garage behind a student's house.

His timing was perfect. Young people exploring alternative spirituality soon came to sit with him. He ordained his first American monk in 1964, and four years later he and his students bought Rinzai-ji, a 1920s-era residence in South Central Los Angeles. In 1971 he opened a monastery in an old Boy Scouts camp on Mount Baldy in California's San Gabriel range, and the next year he established Bodhi Manda Zen Center in Jemez Springs, New Mexico. Since then, his priests and monks have started centers throughout North America and Europe.

Early Monday we were startled awake as someone swept into the dorm ringing a bell and flipping on the lights. Settling onto my cushion a few minutes later, I could hear a few sleepy birds chirping as Lucy, the black-and-white temple cat, nonchalantly strolled through the zendo. The assistants served hot green tea, and then it was down to business. For the day's first period of zazen, the zendo's head monk used the wooden *keisaku* (sometimes called "the encouragement stick") to give two stinging, energizing blows on each shoulder of any student who was slouching or falling asleep.

It was still not light out when the administrator rang the bell, summoning students to sanzen. The zendo erupted as a handful of people leapt from their seats and raced for the exit, jostling one another to be first in to see the teacher.

My turn came and I bowed into the sanzen room. Roshi was sitting in a low chair, surrounded by vases of fresh flowers, a hanging scroll, and some statues. I approached him and performed another deep bow, then I knelt.

"Hai. Koan," Roshi said in his low, gravelly voice, a cue to tell him what koan I had been working on since the last sesshin—koans being the puzzling riddles that students of Rinzai Zen contemplate as part of their training. I announced my koan in a loud voice, since Roshi had grown hard of hearing in recent years. He cupped his hand to his ear and I repeated it. What followed was all too familiar. He posed some questions, which I failed miserably to respond to. He said a few more things in his heavily accented English, but one phrase came through loud and clear: "Still thinking."

Yup, he had that right. It often takes me a couple of days at the start of sesshin to get my head clear, and Roshi always has an uncanny ability to tell when I'm lost in the realm of conceptual thought. In Zen Buddhism we practice directly realizing the nature of reality, dropping our ordinary discursive thinking to see things freshly—as they really are. But that is surprisingly hard to do, and Zen teachers constantly look for ways to shake students up, jostling them out of conventional, conditioned mind. Joshu Roshi is particularly good at this; many of his students tell similar stories of sanzen encounters in which he was so attuned to their state of awareness that he seemed to be reading their minds.

He picked up his little brass bell and rang me out. Chagrined, I made a thank-you bow and returned to the zendo.

Joshu Roshi does not confine himself to the classical canon of Chinese koans passed down through Japanese Zen. He often uses koans of his own devising that he feels are suitable for Americans. He might ask a student, for example, "When you see the flower, where is God?" He changes or rewords koans frequently, which tends to keep the student off balance. Rather than strive for a momentary experience of enlightenment, he wants his students to learn to consistently manifest (his word) true love—a poetic expression for unification or nonduality.

Oscar Moreno says that Joshu Roshi nurtures in his students a slow process of ripening that naturally leads them deeper and deeper. "The maturation, the wisdom, happens slowly and I find it very deep," Moreno says. "All the time he leads you through a contradictory process, where you say, 'Oh, now I know what enlightenment is.' But then he shows you the other side."

After a brisk formal breakfast in the zendo, we returned to the dorms for a few minutes of personal time, during which students catnapped, brushed their teeth, or showered. Many stretched to relieve stiff backs and legs. The first few days of a sesshin are when you remember just how hard it is, and you may ask why you're putting yourself through it. Thankfully, the mood usually passes.

One of my companions in the dorm was George Bowman, a respected Zen teacher in his own right whose original teacher, the late Korean Zen master Seung Sahn Soen Sa Nim, first encouraged him to sit a sesshin with Joshu Roshi in the late 1970s. "It was a really life-changing experience," Bowman says, having sat several sesshins a year with Joshu Roshi ever since. Describing what he laughingly calls a "love-dread relationship," Bowman says that working with Joshu Roshi keeps him humble and honest: "It's always digging deeper, climbing to the top, getting knocked down, and starting over."

The next morning Roshi entered and, with help from his attendants, he slowly climbed to the high seat, where he read the opening section of the subject of this week's teisho: "Hyakujo's Fox" from the *Mumonkan*. At first he barely mentioned the familiar koan. Instead he spoke of God, something that would surprise people who think of Buddhism as nontheistic. Buddhism doesn't deny God, Roshi told us, but it doesn't personify God the way other religions do. Like everything else, he said, even God must obey the law of impermanence and cannot be a fixed entity.

Anicca, the Buddhist principle of impermanence, plays a key role in Joshu Roshi's teaching, a model in which two equal and mutually opposing activities endlessly meet and separate. The instant in which they unify is variously described as true love, equality, zero, or emptiness. It is the unification of subject and object. But when these two activities separate, the objective world—the world of self and other—appears. Joshu Roshi uses a variety of synonyms for these two opposing activities, referring to them as expansion and contraction, plus and minus, mother and father, or male and female. Joshu Roshi calls his style of teaching Tathāgata Zen, Tathāgata being one of the names for the Buddha. While the teaching may sound abstract, Roshi wants his students to manifest it in their zazen and, whatever else it may be, it is a very sophisticated guide to meditation.

An hour into teisho, the administrator rang a bell. We hadn't heard much yet about Hyakujo or the fox. "I'm not feeling well," Roshi said. "I feel a little woozy." But later, after a period of hot, sleepy zazen, we found ourselves filing off to sanzen.

Already on this first day, some people were so sleepy they forgot to bow when entering the zendo, or they moved when they weren't supposed to. Groggy myself, I would relax into my breathing, only to drift involuntarily into microsleep. Catching myself, I'd sit bolt upright and straighten my back. But the sleepiness returned and the cycle would repeat itself. A fresh breeze cooled things off in the evening, and as the sun faded, a police helicopter circled overhead and a passing ice cream truck played "Für Elise." No gunfire, though. Soon enough we were back in our dorms.

The next morning, one of the priests opened the first period of zazen by hitting the first six monks—including me—with the kei-saku. Good morning! This is sometimes done to set a more rigorous, energetic tone in the zendo. I found the blows relaxed the tense muscles in my shoulders and upper back.

Roshi talked in teisho about plus and minus, mother and father, birth and death, fluidly shifting from one to the next, and in sanzen he assigned me a new koan, which I would wrestle with for the remainder of the week. After breakfast, I noticed the kitchen staff had brewed coffee. A small blessing.

Another ice cream truck came by after dinner, blaring a repetitive ditty. As it happened, we were doing a practice that involved walking slowly around the zendo, chanting one syllable from the Heart Sutra with each step. This wholehearted chanting in unison was creating a powerful sound that filled the zendo and drowned out the extraneous—random thoughts and ice cream trucks included.

I was coping with a familiar pain beneath my right shoulder blade, an ache that intensified until it felt like someone was twisting a knife in my back. I knew it was arising from mental tension and prolonged sitting in a fixed posture. The genius of sesshin, I reflected, is that it offers many different ways to squeeze you and make you uncomfortable. You're stuck in a hot, sweaty,, aching body with no escape: what do you do? I've learned that the only thing that works is to unify with the discomfort. And one way or another, unification is what Roshi always teaches.

In sanzen the next morning Roshi sized up my response. "Ego," he spat, and rang the bell. Later, in teisho, he talked about the old man in the koan who approached Hyakujo and begged to be released from a particular error he had made, which had caused him to be reborn five hundred times as a fox. The old man in the story was a "monster," Roshi said, because he couldn't manifest unity with his students. I was feeling a bit monstrous myself.

On Thursday we reached the sesshin's halfway point, and fewer and fewer people were making enthusiastic sprints for the door at the start of sanzen. Maybe I wasn't the only one confounded by my koan. More than once, the head monk had to bark, "Sanzen!" to get people to leave the zendo. Stuck though I was, in afternoon sanzen that day something I did seemed to resonate with Roshi; at last I felt I was moving in the right direction.

Things changed on Friday, as newcomers joined us for the final three days of sesshin. Among them was Paul Karsten, a student of Roshi's since 1973 and the president of a Seattle acupuncture school. Karsten sees his study with Joshu Roshi as the practice of making relationship with others. "My studies have made me a more effective health care practitioner," he says. "I've trusted Roshi to help point me to what's important."

Roshi took a long time with people in sanzen that evening, and I felt I was having a more freewheeling encounter with him, letting go of some of myself. I felt energized as we left the zendo that evening, and for a while, sleep wouldn't come.

Despite getting no more than four hours of sleep, I felt pretty good on Saturday, day six. The city around us was quiet, and it occurred to me that people were thinking about going to the beach. During teisho, Roshi told the famous story of how, as he grew old, Hyakujo's students stole his gardening tools so he'd have to rest from his labors around the monastery, and how Hyakujo stopped eating in protest. A good bit older than Hyakujo himself, Roshi told us he'd been suffering from sciatica for twelve years. "Now, if I sit for more than fifteen minutes, it hurts," he said. And yet, I reflected, he spends an hour a day in teisho and at least six hours a day sitting in sanzen. That tremendous effort in the face of pain inspired me.

Two days after sesshin ends, a translator and I would sit down for an interview with Roshi in his apartment. Wearing a white kimono and reclining in an upholstered chair, Roshi was in a relaxed mood. At one point he teasingly pinched the translator's earlobe to make a point.

"How are you this morning?"

"Tired," he says. "After sesshins I need two days of rest. I used to not need anything. One day is not good enough—I need two days. By the third day I become vital again."

"You call your teaching Tathāgata Zen. Where did the teaching of Tathāgata Zen originate?"

"Chinese Zen defined *tathāgata* and *tathā-āgata*. One is 'Thus coming,' and the other is 'Thus-going.' It originated in India— Indian Buddhism already had this concept. It's a moving activity, so it is 'Thus-coming, Thus-going.' Even we contemporary people are asked how we define this moving activity. It is a very essential thing.

"This moving activity never stops. And then, all the time it's smoothly proceeding. Though it is moving all the time, when it proceeds forward, it's the activity of forward moving, and when it comes back, it demonstrates the activity of coming back. Here, we have to understand the concept of difference or discrimination. What is the concept of difference or discrimination? That is called *kyo* and *rai*. *Kyo* is 'to leave.' *Rai* is 'to come.'"

"Will Roshi find American successors?" I ask.

"I don't know about that," he says. "It's not in my consideration. It does not help me to know who it would be. Some might say, 'I have received your Tathāgata Zen teaching, and I will continue your activity,' but that can be a lie. If someone comes around saying, 'I'm going to throw my whole body into continuing your activity of Tathāgata Zen,' then I would say, 'Oh, is that so?'"

The seventh day dawned clear and cool, and I enjoyed spacious sitting in the zendo. Late in the afternoon, it was announced that we would end a little early and then go to see Roshi for a final interview—a formal good-bye.

It was then that I finally got what Roshi had been driving at all week. It had literally been staring me in the face all along. Roshi smiled and rang the bell.

EDWARD HOAGLAND

Barley and Yaks

FROM *Orion*

CHINA USED TO BE A WORD FOR CROCKERY IN THE WEST, BUT NOW has become at once our banker, our competitor and yet supplier, and, as a dynamo, incipiently our cloud-befouler. Sixteen of the world's twenty worst cities for air pollution smoke there, and the Gobi's winds do blow. When you land at Beijing's airport you may cough claustrophobically and think you need cataract surgery, the vistas appear so milky. Then the landscape unrolls as you're traveling—continuously huffing and puffing, steaming and smelting—with people, people, hurrying and laboring minutely at extracting or earthmoving, but without the tapestry of liberties and spiritualities you'll see in India. Fearing the ideological somersaults of the past, they live in the present, a bit robotically. Echoes are discouraged, memories dropped. On the other hand, a nation bursting at the seams with what is approaching one-fourth of humanity, of course, cannot be categorically disliked— all those live-wire youngsters, spooning lovers, hobbling oldsters— and Sun Yat-sen's portrait had replaced Chairman Mao's in presiding over Tiananmen Square during the 2007 Golden Week spring holiday when I visited. The police presence was not oppressive and rumor had it that his visage might someday adorn some of the currency, as China's concept of the context in which Mao's 1949 revolution occurred evolves and broadens.

The country didn't nearly implode, like Russia did at first, in moving from forced collectivization toward a market economy, or need its natural resources to rescue it, as Russia did its oil fields. Instead, a dialectic flexibility, broiled through decades of Hundred Flowers cultural purges or Great Leap Forward convulsions and doctrinal flip-flops, punctuated by horrendous famine (all telescoped into half the time the Soviets had employed for their experiments), helped goose its phenomenal recent growth. Greed became admired rather than a capital offense. Yet these switchbacks have fostered a more prudently unironic attitude among middle-aged Chinese than characterizes any other dictatorship I've been in. Having watched not only dissenters, but advocates who, devastated after the next course correction, opted out, most Chinese have accepted being noncommittal as the normal mode, even when this neutrality is expressed through a hectoring tone—since hectoring has remained the method of discourse throughout the past half century. I dropped in on a World Trade Organization conference at my hotel and noticed how distinctly forcefully China's delegates spoke, no matter how little objection could be raised to whatever they were saying.

The past has been erased, the present is mistrusted, and the future feared, as the cliché goes. Indeed, for example, many of the Buddhist temples that were razed in earlier sociopolitical tempests or during the 1959 conquest of Tibet have been reconstructed for purposes of tourism—yet without dormitories for the monks, who otherwise might be able to bring their actual religious spirit to life. Building cranes, enormously angular, loomed above Beijing, and cement factories fumed on any road or rail route I took out of this great boomtown. In the park adjoining the Forbidden City, each trash can had been assigned by the police to a particular homeless person to wrangle a living from. The man my friend Tenzing and I talked to was thirty-six, looked fifty-six, a yak herder from faraway Gansu Province, who said the local police there had disabled one of his hands with a knife during a false-arrest scuffle—which broke up his marriage and his livelihood—and then granted him no redress. After journeying to Beijing to appeal his case, he'd been refused a pension but permitted the right to recycle the bottles and cans from this one garbage barrel for his sustenance, and to sleep, winter and summer, under a nearby bridge. Couldn't I, he asked, find him a job herding yaks in the United States?

It's hard to find a translator because, although the Chinese study English in school, most of their teachers, too, have never spoken to a foreigner, or at least not an "Ocean Person," the slang term for somebody who isn't Asian. To do so during the Marxist years could have prompted an arrest, in the unlikely event such a chance even arose. So from embarrassment or vestigial caution, educated folk don't regularly initiate conversations or volunteer their help in the manner common when one is traveling elsewhere. Religious input—whether of the Taoist, Buddhist, Confucian, Christian, or Muslim variety—was also consciously scrubbed out of the body politic decades ago, as well as the ethic of simple help for victims of injustice or privation, as counterintuitive to survival. Therefore displays of hospitality or kindness are rare; and I understood why a college student of mine in the U.S.—though majoring in the language—had returned from a summer trip to China saying it had been awful; he was "a slave" for a while in a village where he'd run out of money, and worked with his hands for a businesswoman for only rice for his belly, until a European couple happened to pass through and rescue him.

Thus for a combination of reasons the best translators, apart from a few professionals, tend to be outlaw Tibetans who learned their English illegally in India while attending the Dalai Lama's schools—having accomplished the perilous crossing of the Himalayas on foot for a couple of weeks, while hunted by detachments of the Chinese army, into Nepal. The return journey, years later—whooshing across a jungle river, harnessed to a hidden cable and equipped with false papers, then maybe smuggled farther underneath the packages in a mail truck—would be scary also. People not shot but captured, of either sex or any age, are kicked like a human football by the soldiers in a concrete room until they bleed from every orifice, and then starved to skin and bones for six months in prison in the "re-education" process.

In any case, the experience is transforming. A brown bear rises on her haunches for a gander at the little band of escapees sneaking across the shoulder of her snowy mountain, then wading hand in hand through the terrifyingly neck-deep braided channels of the Brahmaputra River. After trading some of their clothes to nomadic Nepali herdsmen for food during the final stretch of the hike toward a bus ride to the storied freedoms of Kathmandu, they reach New Delhi, and Dharamsala, or Bangalore. Tenzing is a generic name I am employing for various Tibetans who assisted me, including one who finally did break through after being caught the first time and beaten within an inch of his life, then jam-packed in a cell for months with a university student who had been turned in by his own professor, who'd walked into his dorm room unannounced and spotted a book by the Dalai Lama on the table. Both boys could scarcely walk when they were released.

So, you wind up with pickup translators who speak English like an Indian and are living in a ten-dollar-a-day Beijing hotel, or on two dollars a day in Chengdu, the capital of the province of Sichuan—to which I now caught a sleeper from one of Beijing's wonderfully efficient old train stations, though my compartment mates—a mother, her small daughter, and the grandmother (this family the dependents of a Xerox company district manager)—were harassed by the railroad police because the little girl was now one meter tall and didn't yet have a separate internal passport. The deluxe train, like Beijing's subway, its central boulevards of banks or ministries, its zoo and main amusement park, was like a cleaned-up version of the Western standard. But with no fallow patches of real estate outside, cotton or truck gardens were planted wherever colorless blocks of bare-bones cement housing didn't adjoin another spuming surge of industry.

We chugged up into the Min Mountains, crossing several of the Yangtze's feeder headwater valleys—the Jialing and Jiaojiang river watersheds—a lonely, lovely, severely grudging, bristly, Colorado-style, hardscrabble ranching country of cul-de-sacs short on grass but rich in rock pitched toward the sky. Soon, however, each budding watercourse was being dredged along the downslope for factory sand or roadbed gravel, as we descended to the mining pits, refinery furnaces, brickyards, and power plants of another busy city. Wheat and apple trees grew on the terraces, till rice and sugarcane, soybeans, corn, sorghum, tobacco, and pig and fish farms replaced them in the lowlands, with water buffalo at work, and mimosa, cypress, and banyan trees or cotton fields interspersed by housing blocks for the dense labor force, but much more regimentedly than in an Indian landscape.

Chengdu, in Sichuan Province, a leading, upbeat little city, was never conquered by the Japanese during World War II, nor its amenities subsequently leveled by Red Guard gangs. In the Tibetan quarter, I ate yak dumplings and drank buttered tea in an upstairs restaurant where heretical thoughts could be muttered—an ocher-clad monk was eating there. Tibetan salt, herbs, and hides used to be carried the two hundred fifty miles south to Chengdu by middlemen, who traded Chinese rice, sugar, and tea for them at the end of a yak trail out of the mountains near Jiuzhaigou; and I heard stories about the Chinese conquest of Tibet during the 1950s. Doomed clan chieftains had ridden out of their villages with a couple dozen cavalry, waving their swords and bolas against the machine guns. Or, equipped perhaps with muzzleloaders and defending a defile so narrow that the invading tanks couldn't clank through, Tibetan snipers had picked off the Chinese infantry while their women and children huddled safely in a pocket notch behind them. But never having seen an air-craft (there are still Tibetans who have not), they'd left air power out of their calculations, whereupon MiGs or helicopter gunships swept in and strafed their families, sheep, and yak herds catastrophically. The last holdout patriarch martyred himself and his two sons when their bullets ran out while besieged in a cave among the crags. But one son did survive, so his proud descendants are somehow marked with the same scar his father's shot had left.

My informants, Tenzings all (that common Tibetan name has become more famous in its Sherpa incarnation in Nepal, the Sherpas being a people of Tibetan language and culture who are said to have originated in and migrated from the Min Shans some centuries ago), sat chatting on a bench by a goldfish pool while I visited a historical museum with life-size statuary of ancient Chinese war-lords, each hugely mustachioed and ostentatiously well fed. When I asked whether the Chinese soldiers raped the Tibetan girls they captured trying to cross the border into Nepal, the Tenzings told me no, they were only whipped, but that the Nepalese soldiers on the other side might grab and rape them before turning them loose. They said their own families in the mountains still had muzzleloaders, however, bought from Muslim gunsmiths whose families had forged them from time immemorial, and who knew how to make nothing else. The Uygurs of Xinjiang Autonomous Region—adjoining Tibet, but also over against Tajikistan, Kyrgyzstan, and Kazakhstan—have a current rebellion simmering against the Chinese regime because they enjoy the advantages of resupply from neighboring sympathetic core-ligionists with Kalashnikovs.

The Chinese periodically lighten up on the Tibetans, however, allowing them three children per family, for instance, instead of only one, as with the ethnic Han, who comprise 90 percent of the nation's population. LESS CHILDREN, LESS PROBLEM, says a ubiquitous bill-board. But another admonishment sounds more urgent: CHILDREN

ARE NOT A TOURIST ATTRACTION—lest the toxin of child prostitution spread from nearby countries like Thailand and Cambodia, which are blighted by it. Even so, a woman who is officially summoned to the district hospital to have her tubes tied after bearing her quota, but then loses a child, may want to raise the money to visit a distant clinic sub rosa and try to get her fertility restored. Families believe that an infant can die if a spirit, and not necessarily a malign one, merely passes too quickly through the room: that its vulnerably un-seated soul may be swept along.

A subway was under construction through Chengdu, but the breezy parks and college campuses, pedestrian nooks and refurbished temple architecture (though skeletally manned), and quirky shops and restaurants would probably hold their own. Leaving Chengdu's fertile plain, we drove north through Dujiangyan, Wenchuan, Ma-oxian, Zhenjiangguan, and Songpan, mostly above the gorges of the Min River, which was being industrially stripped of its bed to manu-facture concrete and dammed for more hydroelectricity, pluming ab-solute thunderclouds of dust from a sequence of emptied agricultural riverine communities. Jackhammers, bulldozers, and earthmovers were operating around the countless tunnels under construction, with one lane left for traffic. The uprooted villagers had staged sev-eral spontaneous demonstrations that had blocked this road until they were smothered by army troops, the driver told me: because in a People's Republic any public protest can be construed as mounted against, not a corporate project, but the interests of the country's entire populace, and therefore the dissenters deserve to be regarded as treasonous.

As we mounted past the hundred miles of denuded blast zones and hair-raising hairpin turns with ten-ton lorries rounding them, toward thinner watercourses and an alpine climate, the industrial possibilities diminished, and we began seeing fruit or walnut or-chards, flocks of sheep and goats, and, by the walled trading center of Songpan, gnarly roofed Tibetan villages with yaks moseying shaggily in the meadows. North from the Huanglong highlands, we could glimpse snow-tufted mountains and the kind of passes between them that legends sprout in. Spirits—beneficent, indifferent, or malicious—inhabit all such regions, and the passes are thoroughfares for them as well as for people. But certain passes are so heavily and swiftly trafficked during the night that a human traveler or herdsman caught halfway through by a storm or bad planning, who falls asleep, may lose his life's spark—which can be blown out like a candle flame by the wind of the spirit's passing. He'll be found in daylight, unbruised, unfrozen.

And despite the venerable yak-train trail going by, where Tibet's salt, sheep's wool, and mountainside medicinal herbs and furs were bartered for Chinese rice, sugar, wheat, and tea in Songpan, it was barley, which grows in the Tibetans' own harsh climate, that was their staff of life. Still is, my Tenzings said. They harvest the barley kernels into yak-skin sacks, then store as much as a five-year stockpile in great log caches almost the size of their houses against hard times. To grind a two-month supply into flour, each family—using in turn the village's water wheel—first pours a quantity into a large dry frying pan lined with sand, which is later strained off and can be employed again. After three minutes on the flames, the grains begin to pop into floral form like mini-popcorn and leap up toward your face as you stir the batch with a bamboo whisk; and it is these you grind, daylong, in shifts at the water wheel. The flour alone, stored dry, will keep for about a year, or maybe fermented for three months into a wine—in nine, into a kind of brandy or whiskey, which, if aged for another nine years, reaches a peak.

Barley, lacking gluten, bakes as an unleavened flatbread, soured with yak milk, but mainly is eaten as porridge, together with other staples like cheese, or with turnips, beans, cabbages, potatoes, or onions, grown in season and stewed or sautéed along with meat once a day. To prepare the meal of porridge, or *tsampa*, whether at home or while camped after scrambling across the steppe with a hundred browsing yaks, you fill your big wooden bowl halfway with hot tea, then add half a handful of yak butter to melt in it, and crumble in another half handful of cheese. Meanwhile three handfuls of barley flour have been gently boiling and now are kneaded into a richly moist mixture to create an edible warm dough that you nibble in small pieces with more buttered tea as a beverage. Calves have gotten the skim milk and bean stems—or the goats and pigs have, if a family's youngsters feel like chasing them, because the nearest escarpment can be a three hours' hike straight up. Yaks, by contrast, may be as tame and slow as the water buffalo domesticated by the Han Chinese at lower elevations, and worth four hundred dollars apiece if broken to ride and plow with—ten times a sheep's value, plus possessing the added advantage of furnishing eight times as much meat. This is important to Tibetans, who are not vegetarians but leery of the actual act of killing, which they believe people will answer for in a difficult, hallucinatory death. Thus having fewer scenes of slaughter to remember is better. The brother of one of my guides had just sold his entire herd of sheep in order to be free of the burden of slaughtering them for income, and not to a butcher but to another shepherd for less money.

Tibetans didn't hunt a lot or pursue predators for fun or eat waterfowl or fish, as a rule, and so when the Chinese conquered Tibet in their 1959 blitzkrieg, resettling countless lowland Han in its territories to dilute the traditions, religion, and character of the region, it was like a paradise at first of duck shooting and fishing for the newcomers. In many villages the work inevitably was no longer focused upon herding yaks and growing barley but skewed toward logging the forests or commerce. When I asked, in a community of ethnic Han that has been superimposed among the Tibetans in the

Saba Valley, if the senior members could recall where they'd been transplanted from, their friendly faces suddenly went blank.

"We don't remember."

They kept 108 penned pigs, however, the same number as there are beads on a proper Buddhist prayer string. Numbers are important. Any cluster of Tibetan villages will boast a fortune-teller schooled in reading not only the stars' basic alignments but the permutations into which dice fall when repeatedly questioned. Up a notch, perhaps, from the dice thrower will be the local shaman, who has learned the properties of a whole arsenal of herbs, and where to search each of them out, plus the alchemy of spells: how to cast them or break them. Individuals train and apprentice for both of these vocations, and may be tempted into venality or malice in the matter of spells, for instance. But there is also the rarer phenomenon of men who are genuine healers—inspired—born with the gift—who can't be hired, like some of the shamans, to practice, for example, blacker arts. They simply try to heal people, blowing drops of water on them from their palms, or flicking it with a finger or a quill, to make them well. If that doesn't work, after keeping a patient for about a week in his compound, the healer will probably refer him to a government hospital. (A fortune-teller may have originally influenced the family's decision to try the healer first.)

The wood dove is the Tibetans' Virtuous Bird, not to be killed. Nor should the cuckoo, which is called God's Bird because it brings the summer. A different species, called the Cuckoo's Wife, arrives even a little sooner; it was pointed out to me by one of my Tenzings, fluttering like an ouzel around the Pearl Shoals waterfalls in Jiuzhaigou National Park. A certain rare antelope, the takin, is the Virtuous Animal (though its preciousness to Tibetans doesn't prevent the Chinese from shooting it), while up at timberline grows the Tree of the Gods, furnishing firewood to herders, who at that altitude will gratefully wave a spiral of smoke scented with yak butter and barley flour as a thank-you gesture to them.

Gods have generally undergone an earlier human phase, and some hubristic miscue may tumble them down into human form again, or lower, into an animal incarnation, or even one of the eighteen circles of Hell. Some spirit mountains have historically been frightening just for the wraiths and apparitions inhabiting them, who might jostle whomever they considered an intruder off a cliff. But others were deliberately left untrodden as sanctuaries for the animals living there, where wolves, leopards, bears, pandas, dholes, or eagles could den or nest undisturbed. And still other mountains have been perceived as protectors of the villages located beneath—from flood or drought, lightning, hail, earthquake, or fire—and the grazing and hay-cutting rights to their slopes inherited only by certain clans. Even before Tibetans knew about germs, they usually boiled the water they drank, as if for tea, rather than swallowing it "live" or cold from a stream. But children are not sheltered unduly from household or dooryard dirt, lest they turn sickly later on; and because their mothers work up on the sloping shingled roofs a lot, both summer and winter— whether drying foodstuffs in the sun, or freezing meat, or sweeping off the night's snowfall—many kids roll over the edge at least once or twice and break a limb, which is regarded as toughening them. To my North American eyes, my Tibetan friends had features like Eskimos, but I heard Han Chinese mistake them for Mongolians.

In the old days, freelance Bön or Buddhist holy men went off to meditate in the mouth of a cave under a notable peak for a dozen years or so, and then returned to marry and father children like anybody else, yet were available for soothsaying or simple consultation, drawing on perspectives they'd accumulated. The cave might have been visible for quite a distance because of the circle of birds perching or whirling around the entrance hole, perhaps fed by the anchorite, but lending him clairvoyance. Bön beliefs, preceding Buddhism in the Himalayas and still not wholly absorbed, are more animist and shaman centered—surviving in spotty but potent form in isolated villages, along with the burly, "four-eyed" breed of watchdog Tibetans kept to ward off bandits, leopards, wolves: so called because of its black tuft of fur over each regular eye. Families kept a cat, as well, to guard the barley stores, and a horse for prompter errands than the yaks they rode might perform.

When I asked whether yetis still roam the spirit mountains, my friends demurred, but described the females' breasts as being so long you could run downhill to escape them because they'd trip on their teats and fall. Uphill, they threw the things over their shoulders and might catch up with you. One man had not been killed when grabbed. Instead, he'd been imprisoned inside a cave for the purpose of impregnating his captor, with a stone rolled across the front that he couldn't budge. Yet once the baby was born, so much time had elapsed, she, beginning to trust him, grew careless about the placement of the stone. He made a break for it, downhill toward the river, because yetis can't swim. And her dangling breasts, as well as the child in her arms, did indeed slow her up. So when he'd swum safely across, she yelled at him, holding their infant by the legs, ordering him to return. When he shook his head, she raised it up and ripped it in half, throwing a leg, an arm, and half of the rib cage over the water to him.

Between the rocks above timberline a wild sort of tobacco grows that herders can dry to put in their pipes, with an aroma like incense, that makes them feel young again as they clamber about after their animals. For nomads on the Tibetan Plateau, stretching north from the Min Shan toward Mongolia, the most lucrative occupation may not be yak shepherding anymore, but herb gathering on the steppes for the medicinal trade. In particular, they'll search every May and June for a plant whose magical properties are epitomized and enhanced by its spending half of its life as an animal. Only a sharpster, gazing low as the sunrise strikes across the grasslands, can be sure to spot the twin hornlike blades before they wilt amid thicker, taller, ordinary vegetation in the midday heat. Inconspicuous as these are, yet sorcerously crossing between kingdoms—plant to animal—during the arc of the year, the organism's leaves when powdered, or the roots and stems when soaked in whiskey for a week, often bring Tibetans relief from pain or other ills. And now they're widely wanted for holistic rejuvenation, pinches being cooked, as "caterpillar fungus," into the menus of the fanciest restaurants, such as the one that slowly rotates on top of the roof of Beijing's International Hotel. A grass in the summer, a worm in the winter, between each pair of leaves, my Tenzings said, two eyes and a mouth gradually appear.

China launched a space satellite into orbit from its experimental facility in Sichuan Province while I was there. And meanwhile the inoffensive, harlequin-colored giant panda prowled remote, selected bamboo forests for shoots to loll and chew on, a remarkable recent symbol the country has chosen to represent itself. Tibetan monks and nuns have been beaten to death for talking to tourists as my Tenzings were speaking to me, if it was recorded in a way that could be retrieved, so they and I were antsy not to be overheard. Yet one of them was occasionally talking on a cell phone to his dad, who was driving seventy yaks to their summer pasturage hundreds of miles away. Relentless logging and roadbuilding were altering the region, and the following spring, the Sichuan earthquakes would wreak far more terrible avalanche damage than might have been the case if all those earthmovers and bulldozers hadn't been chiseling the valleys for more than a decade. But you can still encounter five-colored pools sinuously connected by rivulets wriggling through reed beds bursting with wildflower blossoms, warblers, butterflies—enough space and salience for solitude, or a fugitive moment of empathy with a porcupine wandering across a rockslide wipeout up in the sidehill woods.

In China's cities no punctuation occurs in the daylight rush of human beings. Mopeds, pedicabs, motor scooters, bikes, and pedestrians interweave with hordes of autos, vans, buses, and dump trucks in the kind of democracy which Communism did bequeath, where citizens, although now quite unequal in wealth, have the same right to the road. Even afoot, they'll step out into traffic like comrades, not peons. The street markets are ebullient, the railroad stations seethe like India's with every condition of person—nuzzly couples courting, children dashing, families glued to one another as they thread the crowds between an avenue's overpass and the terminal's maw, where beggars of all ages and both sexes sprawl.

Without killing family ties, revolutionary atheism did nevertheless put a crimp into the charitable imperative that all organized religions stipulate, substituting work-to-eat strictures that become all the more severe in a country where spirituality has long been under siege. There are few mosque or temple or cathedral plazas within which souls in need may appeal for help beyond the scrutiny of civil authorities. The whims of secularism and a robotic military reign supreme. You see it not just among the police but in the train crews and street cleaners; and the cell-phone epidemic places ordinary people from whom charity might be asked at a still further remove, since, when they are text messaging or self-absorbedly conversing with distant relatives, they are not where they appear to be. India is as crowded, and yet marbled with age-old moral contexts, Jain or Hindu, Gandhian or Gurkha.

In underpasses beneath Beijing's avenues I met blind lutenists and Tibetan silversmiths—huskers and peddlers beyond the supervision of surface constables. My guide now was a Sanskrit scholar who, even without crossing the Himalayas to worship with the Dalai Lama in Dharamsala, could have been loyal to him, since no one knew what he was reading. Nonetheless, he had braved the snows, lived on forged papers, evaded the Kalashnikov patrols. On the other hand, he'd never been in the capital before or flown on an airplane (as we did from Chengdu; I showed him how to stop his ears from hurting), ridden a subway, or hailed a taxi. He was skeptical of the economic-powerhouse model when no backstop of ethics was provided. His Tibetan secondary school had been closed by the government for its forbidden curriculum, and the studies he had completed as a fugitive in India would have sent him to prison if they had been known. Seeing me off at Beijing Airport was scary for him because when my bags were searched, if his Tibetan face had aroused sufficient suspicion for my notebooks to be looked at, he could have been seized and starved for years in jail. But all that happened was that the customs inspector yelled at me because, without Tenzing to help at the last, I was slow to follow his instructions, issued in Chinese.

Over the Pacific on the twelve-hour flight, I missed these Tenzings, now back in their precipitous valleys, milking yaks and boiling barley, or possibly employed in minor jobs where credentials aren't called for. China's strictures on freedom exact a great cost. And the panda's camouflaged face, whose black-and-white pattern is familiar worldwide, looks tear stained, much as the cheetah's does in Africa: Tear-blotched cheetahs and pandas—whose habitats, which created their furry camouflage, have been skinned. The highway on which I drove north from Chengdu, landslide damaged during the earthquakes of 2008, has been repaired. But China's pell-mell secularization has not, foretelling perpetual cultural avalanches far worse than the physical ones.

NANCY HONICKER

Taking the Veil

FROM *Portland*

AT THE HEART OF CHRISTIANITY ARE THE WORDS SPOKEN BY JESUS
to his disciples in an upper room in Jerusalem, a few days before his
death: *I am the way, the truth, and the life: no man cometh unto the
Father, but by me.*

For Muslims there is also only the one God, but Mohammed is
His Prophet. In Islam, any mingling of the divine and the human,
any hint of the Word made flesh, the very essence of Christianity,
is sin. Can these two mutually exclusive positions be reconciled in a
shared love of God and humankind?

I am a professor in a French university in Saint-Denis, just north
of Paris, in the heart of those dangerous suburbs where violence
erupted in November of 2005. Until 1789, Saint-Denis, with its mag-
nificent basilica, was the seat of the spiritual authority of the French
monarchy. Today its churches are almost empty, the number of con-
versions to Islam is on the rise, and Saint-Denis is the center of a large
Muslim community. In front of the Tawhid Cultural Center, a few
steps from the basilica, clusters of men gather at all hours of the day.
The street is crowded and traffic jammed at the hours of the five daily
Muslim prayers. Many of the men wear the *kamis*, a tunic that de-
scends to mid-calf, in imitation of the dress of the Prophet. All women

are veiled, a white band covering that part of their foreheads left uncovered by the veil.

To understand the appeal of Islam here, one must first understand that religious practice in France, Catholicism in particular, is considered *ringard*—both old-fashioned and stale. Though France has an excellent Catholic daily newspaper, *La Croix*, and a very active and innovative Catholic press, religious practice is mostly desultory. A majority of the French are nominally Catholic, but few go to church, and fewer still, especially among the younger generations, understand the fundamentals of their faith. I recently surveyed my students on how many knew the significance of Ascension Day and Pentecost, both public holidays in France. Not one had a clue.

When I began teaching here, nearly twenty years ago, there was not a single veiled student on campus. Today I have at least one in every class; in some classes, a majority of students are Muslim, though that does not necessarily mean veiled women. Many of these students are from Algeria or Morocco, but many are French, and some are converts to Islam. To understand the appeal of their religion, I recently turned to the students themselves for their stories. There is Laetitia, who converted from Catholicism to Islam. She was born in Saint-Denis, into a nominally Catholic family that never set foot in church. Even as a young child she yearned to learn more about God. In Catholic primary school she turned to the nuns to learn more about the Catholic faith. All her decisions—to attend catechism, to be baptized at age eleven, and to take first Communion—were her own. Once she entered junior high school, many of her classmates were Muslim, and among them she met a girl who became her best friend. Though they did not practice the same religion, they shared the same love of God, which became the basis of a friendship that continues strong today. Within her family Laetitia had been alone with her faith in God, she told me; but with Islam she found a shared *discipline*, a fading word in French, and much of Western, society today: in Islam there were the fixed hours for prayer, the same prayers recited by millions all over the world, the same positions, standing or kneeling, in imitation of the Prophet, the same month-long fast, followed each evening by festive meals with family and friends. This sense of shared community is absent from Christianity, of course, but certainly it is absent from the practice of most French Catholics today. In many ways, Islam, now the second religion of France, presents itself as a welcoming faith with the power to bring the believer closer to God through the structure religion brings to daily life.

Laetitia converted to Islam five years ago. Like all Muslims, she accepts Jesus as a prophet, but she sees Christianity as incomplete. She would like to wear the veil as an outward sign of her religious convictions but refrains, for fear of hurting her mother, who has not easily accepted her daughter's religious choice.

There is Fatima, a Moroccan student from Agadir, born into a practicing Muslim family, who has been studying in France for seven years. She began wearing a veil at age sixteen, and her head is covered by a silk scarf the color of champagne. The entire oval of her face is visible, her forehead, her dark eyes, her lips. The veil covers her ears and neck and is expertly fastened beneath the chin. She is also wearing a long-sleeved tunic of light beige cotton and matching slacks. She seems very much at peace, confident that she is a force for good in the world; she is not as religiously rigid as another one of my students who informed me that it is a sin not to wear the veil, that unveiled women are in danger of hellfire, that miniskirts and low-cut tops are green lights, and that women who choose such clothes are declaring themselves for sale.

It is easy, perhaps, to be startled by such firm statements, and easy to object; but as I walk the streets of Paris, where naked women greet me from billboards all over the city, where buying a newspaper at a kiosk forces me to see how pornography takes precedence over the daily news, I understand her point of view. The French may consider me puritanical and prudish, but at times I am literally hurt—I feel a stab of pain to the heart—by the use of women's bodies in advertising in France, hurt as well by pornography on display to adults and children alike. Is this really freedom of expression, one of the pillars of democracy? Or is this incredibly superficial, incredibly demeaning to women?

The wonderful writer Fatima Mernissi, in her memoir *Dreams of Trespass*, describes the life of a girl born in 1940, in Morocco. Her father kept a harem, where his wives and daughters, though privileged and wealthy, lived among themselves, deprived of instruction and contact with the outside world. This was the traditional world of Islam, where the public sphere was reserved for men, and women spent their lives behind high walls and locked doors. Mernissi would have never learned to read or write had not the madrassas of Morocco been opened to women in 1943, as the country struggled for independence from France. To Mernissi, nothing in Islam over the past century has been as important as the entry of Muslim women into the public sphere; that they often do so veiled is far less important than that they do so, and perhaps the veil is even, oddly, a symbol of liberation, a symbol of the future of Islam, a symbol of what a mature Islam might become, a faith that does not imprison its women behind walls—and a faith that does not plaster their naked bodies on walls, either.

It was another of my students who articulated the most important aspect of the veil to Islamic women who wear it—it is a sign, a Muslim talisman, of St. Paul's exhortation to pray without ceasing. I think of this often now when I see veiled students, and conclude that while we have chosen different paths, we seek the same God.

ROBERT D. KAPLAN

Buddha's Savage Peace

FROM *The Atlantic*

I HAD ALWAYS WANTED TO GO TO KANDY, FOR NO OTHER REASON than that I was in love with the name: so airy, fanciful, and obviously suggestive of sweet things. I first found Kandy on a map of what was then called Ceylon, decades ago as a young man. Little did I know that it would one day have urgent revelations for me, more dark and poignant than sweet.

My journey began at Colombo's crumbling train station, with its white facade like a cake about to melt. The first-class ticket cost a little more than $3 for the three-hour journey from Sri Lanka's steamy Indian Ocean capital, through deep forest, to an altitude of 1,650 feet. The rusted railway car rattled and groaned its way uphill. Soon banana leaves were slapping against the train as we entered a relentless tangle of greenery.

The forest thickened with the crazy chaos of dark hardwood foliage. Vines choked every tree. The torrential rain of the southwest monsoon invigorated the pageant, shrieking and beating against the leaves as sheets of mist moved across the jungle. Then came swollen brown rivers, with water buffalo half sunk in mud near the pottery-red banks. Here and there the forest would break to reveal a shiny, rectilinear carpet of paddy fields, only to close in again, denser than before. I saw scrap-iron hutments and tiled rooftops the color of autumn leaves, and smoky blue hillsides creased by waterfalls and half-eaten by gray monsoon clouds. Other breaks in the forest revealed the occasional bell-shaped Buddhist *dagoba*, or stupa, with its soaring-to-heaven whiteness against the otherwise fungal-green tableau. As we drew near to Kandy, we passed through several narrow tunnels. In the pitch black, the creak of the train reverberated against the rock walls.

Kandy in early evening was a study in rust and mildew, with a crawling-uphill line of food stalls and other storefronts, so tattered and musty they seemed about to disintegrate. Yet that was only a first impression. Later ones would reveal how I had misjudged the scene. The storefronts—eateries, jewelers, mini-supermarkets, five-and-dime shop—were merely in need of new windows and paint jobs; they were in fact doing a brisk business. The streets were clean, the overhead fans worked in every shop I entered, and few beggars were visible. The middle class was evidently thriving, as demonstrated by the number of lavish, assembly-line weddings at my hotel during these auspicious days at the beginning of the monsoon.

A motorized rickshaw brought me to the Hotel Suisse, a seedy, dark-wooded British-colonial pile built in the mid-nineteenth century. It had a well-stocked bar with boxy sofas and a billiard room, and was half empty: a cliché, in other words. My room cost $50. It lay off a portico overlooking a garden and Kandy Lake, which at dusk was tinted a mystical gray and dotted with lizards that crawled out onto the rocks. A thing of rare beauty, the lake was created by the last king of Kandy, Sri Wickrama Rajasinha, at great cost. After a stretch in Colombo's punishing heat, I sat on the portico, yes, with a gin-and-tonic, and enjoyed the energizing coolness of a higher altitude, watching and listening to the rain on the lake.

Kandy defines quaintness, to such an extent that you begin to see the town in the black-and-white of a photo negative. But Kandy is also gaudy and magical. Within this forest town are Sri Lanka's principal Buddhist shrines, swimming in gold and Technicolor. Across the lake from the Hotel Suisse is the Temple of the Sacred Tooth Relic, or Sri Dalada Maligawa, a shrine complex that was built in the seventeenth and eighteenth centuries by Kandy's Sinhalese Buddhist kings and holds a tooth of the Buddha—Prince Siddhartha Gautama—said to have been taken from his funeral pyre in 543 B.C.

The Temple of the Tooth is a site of mass pilgrimage, where the tourist instinctively knows to dress modestly, remove shoes, stay quiet, and lurk in the background. Within the mottled stone walls of the complex is an immense layout of gardens lined with striped Buddhist flags: the blue stripe signifying loving-kindness, the yellow the middle path away from extremes, red the blessings of practice, orange the Buddha's teachings, and white the purity of the dharma, or universal truth, leading to liberation. Hundreds of Sinhalese sit in a two-story room in meditative positions, softly chanting and offering up mountains of pink lotuses, purple water lilies, and white jasmines in front of the gilded casket that holds the tooth. Babies are everywhere, remarkably silent, held tightly against the chests of women in long cotton wraparounds. Leaf monkeys watch the whole scene from the massive, fanlike roofs.

From this and the other temples and monasteries around Kandy radiates the overwhelming and studied richness of the two chief colors of Buddhism: a rich, maroonlike red and a dazzling gold, painted on stone statues and sumptuously draping the giant sitting Buddha in each temple. The murals in these temples are faded and blackened with age. Only in the Eastern Orthodox churches in the Balkans have I come across a clutter of magnificence to match what I have seen in the Buddhist sanctuaries of Sri Lanka. Even as you experience this whole sensual feast, your bare feet press against cold and wet stone, since the rains are constant during the southwest monsoon.

Here, you are alone with your thoughts. Sri Lanka is in general a less panicky, less frantic, less intrusive version of India. Only rarely are you hassled. And Kandy, up in the hills, away from the crowded coastal highway, is a concentrated version of the country's charms.

Alas, when you fall in love with a place, you encounter its history, which is often tragic. In fact, Kandy has remained seedily quaint, its monuments and ambience unravaged by mass tourism, only because Sri Lanka has experienced more than a quarter century of civil war between ethnic Sinhalese Buddhists and Hindu Tamils. And the origins and conduct of that savage conflict have drawn, in many ways, from the same emotional wellsprings as the tradition of worship at Kandy's tranquil Buddhist shrines.

Buddhism holds an exalted place in the half-informed Western mind. Whereas Christianity, Islam, Judaism, and Hinduism are each associated, in addition to their thought, with a rich material culture and a defended territory, Buddhism, despite its great monuments and architectural tradition throughout the Far East, is somehow considered purer, more abstract, and almost dematerialized: the most peaceful, austere, and uncorrupted of faiths, even as it appeals to the deeply aesthetic among us. Hollywood stars seeking to find themselves—famously Richard Gere—become Buddhists, not, say, orthodox Jews.

Yet Buddhism, as Kandy demonstrates, is deeply materialistic and demands worship of solid objects, in a secure and sacred landscape that has required the protection of a military. There have been Buddhist military kingdoms—notably Kandy's—just as there have been Christian and Islamic kingdoms of the sword. Buddhism can be, under the right circumstances, a blood-and-soil faith.

Kandy may be the Buddhist world's best example of this. From the late sixteenth to the early nineteenth centuries, the kingdom of Kandy sturdily held out against European invaders: the Portuguese, the Dutch, and the British in their turn. "Like many other armies in peasant and tribal societies," writes Channa Wickremesekera in *Kandy at*

War: Indigenous Military Resistance to European Expansion in Sri Lanka 1594–1818 (2004), "the Kandyan army fought in loosely organized and highly mobile units depending on a flimsy logistical base," making optimum use of its rugged, jungly terrain. It was very much like a twenty-first-century guerrilla insurgency, in other words—inspired, in this case, by the need to defend faith and homeland against heathen Europeans. The dense forest through which I had passed on my train ride constituted the graveyard of European attempts to reach Kandy, with many a Portuguese, Hollander, and Briton dying or giving up, exhausted and demoralized, afflicted by disease amid the cruel jungle so well described by Leonard Woolf in his 1913 novel, *The Village in the Jungle*:

> For the rule of the jungle is first fear, and then hunger and thirst. There is fear everywhere: in the silence and in the shrill calls and the wild cries, in the stir of the leaves and the grating of branches, in the gloom, in the startled, slinking, peering beasts.

Eventually, the improved muskets and light artillery developed in Europe proved too much for the Kandyans. The British, explains Wickremesekera, unlike the Portuguese and Dutch, had the added advantages of "mastery over the neighboring Indian subcontinent and an army of over 100,000 soldiers when they clashed with Kandy." They toppled King Wickrama of Kandy in 1815. He may have dug the lake, but he had been a tyrant and torturer. At least that was how the British rationalized their actions.

Thus the redoubtable kingdom of Kandy, for centuries such a rebuke to European attempts at conquest in Asia, became a trope in the warrior imagination of the Buddhist Sinhalese. To be sure, the quest to recover Kandy's lost honor and glory played a role in the bloody and morally unclean victory that the Buddhist Sinhalese won over an ethnic Tamil insurgency in May, after twenty-six years of fighting. More broadly, the history of Kandy—a cultural and artistic repository of 2,300 years of Buddhist worship that the Europeans rarely left in peace—has imbued Sinhalese with the sense of being repeatedly under siege.

Regional demography hasn't helped. Indeed, the majority-Buddhist Sinhalese, who constitute three-quarters of Sri Lanka's population of 20 million, have lived in fear of being overwhelmed by the Hindu Tamils, who, although they are only 18 percent of the population, can theoretically call upon their sixty million ethnic and religious compatriots living just across the Palk Strait in southeastern India. The history of Tamil invasions against the only homeland that the Buddhist Sinhalese possess is not just the stuff of ancient history, but a living reality underpinned by latter-day Tamil terrorism. Writes their Sri Lankan scholar K. M. de Silva:

> Sri Lanka's location off the coast of South India, and especially its close proximity to [the Indian state of] Tamilnadu, separated by a shallow and narrow stretch of sea serves to accentuate this sense of a minority status among the Sinhalese. Their own sense of ethnic distinctiveness is identified through religion—Therāvada Buddhism—and language—Sinhala. They take pride in the fact that Buddhism thrives in Sri Lanka while it has practically disappeared in its original home, India. Their language, Sinhala, has its roots in classical Indian languages, but it is now a distinctly Sri Lankan language, and one that is not spoken anywhere else.

The Sinhalese, argues de Silva, see their historical destiny in preserving Therāvada Buddhism from a Hindu revivalist assault, with southern India the source of these invasions. As they see it, they are a lonely people, with few ethnic compatriots anywhere, who have been pushed to their final sanctuary, the southern two-thirds of Sri Lanka, by the demographic immensity of majority-Hindu India. The history of the repeated European attacks on their sacred city, Kandy, the last independent bastion of the Sinhalese in that southern two-thirds of the island, has only accentuated the sense of loneliness.

The Sinhalese must, therefore, fight for every kilometer of their ethnic homeland, Bradman Weerakoon, an adviser to former Sri Lankan presidents and prime ministers, told me. As a result, like the Serbs in the former Yugoslavia, the Jews in Israel, and the Shiites in Iran, the Sinhalese are a demographic majority with a dangerous minority complex of persecution.

The Hindu Tamils, for their part, have been labeled a minority with a majority complex, owing to the triumph of Hinduism over Buddhism in southern India in the fifth and sixth centuries A.D., and the subsequent invasions from India's south against the rich and thriving Buddhist city-state of Anuradhapura in north-central Sri Lanka. These invasions resulted in the creation, by the fourteenth century, of a Tamil kingdom that, in turn, helped lay the groundwork for Tamil majorities in the north and east of the island.

Sri Lanka's post-independence experience, including its civil war between Sinhalese and Tamils, has borne out the worst fears of both communities. The Sinhalese have had to deal with a guerrilla insurgency every bit as vicious and suicidal as the better-known ones in Iraq and Afghanistan. The Tamils, for their part, have had to deal with coercion, discrimination, and the utter failure of Sinhalese government institutions to protect their communal rights. There is nothing crueler than a majority that feels itself a minority.

In 1976, a certain Velupillai Prabhakaran founded the Tamil New Tigers, who would later become known to journalists around the world as the Liberation Tigers of Tamil Eelam, or LTTE: "Tamil Tigers" for short. Prabhakaran would develop into one of the world's most hunted terrorists, as well as one of its most feared and capable guerrilla leaders. The young Prabhakaran had killed animals with a slingshot and air gun, and practiced building homemade bombs. He stuck pins under his nails to build up his tolerance for pain, and killed insects with needles to prepare himself to torture the enemy.

Prabhakaran turned the Tamil Tigers into a quasi-cult terrorist group that venerated him as a demigod. To comprehend the Tamil Tigers, wrote the late American scholar Michael Radu, "imagine Jim Jones' Temple cult of Guyana in possession of a 'navy' and 'air force,' as well as (at its height) some 20,000 fanatical and armed zombie followers." Indeed, Prabhakaran's Tamil Tigers constituted the world's first guerrilla insurgency with its own air force (Czech-made Zlín Z 143s) and navy (explosive-packed fishing trawlers and a small submarine force). He imposed a blood tax on the population under his control in the north and east, requiring each family to provide a son to the Tigers. One wing of the organization—the Black Tigers—was dedicated to murder and assassination. Until the early 1990s, the Tigers held a record for suicide bombings, a tactic that they had largely pioneered. The Tigers used many tens of thousands of civilians as human shields and children as porters during combat. The very history of the Hindu Tamil Tigers shows that perverse violence, the embedding of warriors amid large numbers of civilians, and the rampant use of suicide bombing are not crimes specific to Muslims.

To defeat such a group, the Buddhist Sinhalese relied on a powerful sense of communal religious identity. This identity has been embodied, in particular, by the current Sri Lankan government of Mahinda Rajapaksa and two of his brothers: the defense secretary, Gotabhaya Rajapaksa; and the president's most trusted adviser, Basil Rajapaksa. Together, the three brothers have marked a decisive break from previous Sri Lankan governments. Whereas the governments of the Senanayake and Bandaranaike family dynasties hailed from the relatively moderate Colombo-centric elite, the Rajapaksas are more representative of the somewhat xenophobic, semiliterate, and collectivist rural part of the Sinhalese Buddhist population. The Rajapaksas, with the full backing of the Buddhist clergy, have reconstituted something out of the Sinhalese past: an ethnically rooted dynasty, like the Buddhist kingdoms of Kandy of old, dedicated to ethnonational survival, unaccountable to the cabinet and parliament.

Mahinda Rajapaksa was elected in 2005 to win the war outright, and he succeeded in the most brutal fashion: by abducting or killing journalists and lawyers to silence the media, even as he conducted a counterinsurgency campaign that had no moral qualms about the deaths of the thousands of Tamil civilians that the Tamil Tigers were using as human shields. Of the seventy thousand people killed in the war since 1983, 10 percent, mainly civilians, were killed in the last few months of fighting in 2009.

I was in Sri Lanka on May 18, 2009, the day the war was declared over, and the body of Prabhakaran, killed in last-ditch fighting, was displayed on television, as government forces mopped up the final few hundred yards of Tamil Tiger territory. The next morning, May 19, I drove through the southern coastal heartland of the Buddhist Sinhalese. Everywhere there were parades and flag-bedecked, horn-honking rickshaw convoys, with young men, many of them unemployed, shouting and setting off masses of firecrackers. An effigy of Prabhakaran's body was dragged and burned. I sensed a scary and wanton boredom in these young men, as if the same crowds, under different circumstances, could be setting fire to Tamil homes, as had been done in earlier decades. I noticed that the closer I got to the ethnically mixed population center of Colombo, the fewer such demonstrations I saw.

President Rajapaksa came to Kandy a few days later, on May 23, to receive the blessings of the chief Buddhist monks at the Temple of the Tooth for winning the war. He expressed no apologies or remorse for the victims of the war, and he promised the monks, "Our motherland will never be divided [again]." He told them that there were only two types of Sri Lankans, those who love the motherland and those who don't. Because he conceives of the motherland as primarily Buddhist, his words carried too little magnanimity.

The monks had acquiesced in this descent into communal intolerance. They have long enjoyed the uses of political power and hark back to a past when they were the rousing nationalist force behind Ceylonese kings. Now they could close a long historical chapter that began at the Temple of the Tooth in March 1815, when the Kandyan Convention was signed, ceding all of Ceylon to the British after the defeat of the last Kandyan king, Wickrama. British rule in Ceylon, lasting until independence in 1948, was followed by decades of communal unrest culminating in the civil war. At last, these monks could look forward to a Buddhist-run state that would have full sovereignty over the island.

But even if the artistic grandeur of Kandy has helped form the emotional source of Buddhist nationalism, which has proved itself as bloody as other religious nationalisms, Kandy's religious monuments also offer a much deeper lesson: the affinity—rather than the hostility—between Buddhism and Hinduism. Buddhism arrived in Sri Lanka from India as part of the missionary activity of the great Mauryan emperor Ashoka in the third century B.C. And later eras of Indian history would witness an amalgamation of Buddhist teachings into Hinduism. A few miles from Kandy, deep in the forest amid glistening fields of tea, I saw statues of the Buddha and of Hindu gods under the same roofs, together in their dusky magnificence: in dark stone vestibules at the fourteenth-century temples of Gadaladeniya, Lankatilake, and Embekke. At the temple of Embekke, I lifted aside a veiling Hindu tapestry to behold the Buddha. At Lankatilake, I saw the Buddha surrounded on all four sides by *devales* (shrines) devoted to the deities Upulvan, Saman, Vibhisana, and Skanda—of mixed Hindu, Buddhist, and Persian origin. At the Buddhist shrine of Gadaladeniya, I saw stone carvings based on the style of the Hindu empire of Vijayanagar in Andhra Pradesh, in southern India. Each of these temples "reflects the fusion of Buddhism and Hinduism," writes SinhaRaja Tammita-Delgoda in *Eloquence in Stone: The Lithic Saga of Sri Lanka* (2008).

In fact, Wickrama, the Buddhist king who was deposed by the British, became the last in a dynasty, the Nayakkars, that was South Indian and Hindu in origin; even as its members patronized Theravada Buddhism, they sought Hindu brides for their male Buddhist heirs. The British, by ending this dynasty and thus breaking the link between Buddhism and Hinduism, helped set the stage for the polarization of politics in the postcolonial era. The truth was that Theravada Buddhism, so concentrated on ethics and the release from worldly existence, was too austere for the Kandyan peasantry, who were drawn to the color and magic of the Hindu pantheon. Kandy and its forests are a monument not only to Buddhism, but to Hinduism as well. The historical and aesthetic legacy of Sri Lanka that long predates modern statehood is, in the final analysis, deeply syncretic. Only when Sri Lanka's political leadership recognizes that legacy will communal peace be at hand—and with it the arrival of globalization and chain hotels, and the end of Kandy's quaintness.

JESSE KELLERMAN

Let My People Go to the Buffet

FROM *Commentary*

WHEN I WAS FOUR, WE WENT TO OAHU. IT WAS THE FIRST TIME WE celebrated Passover away from home. My only memory of the trip is of the ride to the Los Angeles airport. Our neighbor, Mr. Janis, drove a taxi. He loaded up our luggage and we all crammed in: my father up front and my mother in back with my sister Rachel and me. Rachel was then just shy of a year old, as yet incapable of communicating distress in any manner other than a wail. She was wailing as Mr. Janis started the car. We had not yet pulled away from the curb when she vomited explosively across the faux leather seats.

My father apologized. My mother ran back into the house for sponges and Lysol. Somehow we made our flight. I assume we had a good time, because we went back again the next year. What is clear in hindsight is that Rachel was trying to warn us.

For Jews who follow the laws governing Passover to the letter, the coming of the holiday is fraught. While people often think of Passover as eight days without bread, strictly speaking the ban applies to all foods containing *chametz*, or leaven; Ashkenazi Jews exclude all grains and legumes as well. Nowadays, when virtually every commercial food product contains some form of corn syrup, the ordinary supermarket is transformed into a religious House of Horrors. In preparation for the holiday, homes must be scrubbed and scoured until no trace of *chametz* remains, in a ritual that resembles spring cleaning for the obsessive-compulsive.

Before we began going away, my mother and grandmother would spend days sweeping out the cupboards, unpacking the special Passover dishes, layering the kitchen countertops with contact paper to prevent any conceivable contamination from even the tiniest speck of *chametz*. The task is so onerous that it is common for homemakers to spend the first Seder night falling asleep in their soup. Unsurprising, then, that a secondary market should have developed to address this problem, a market with an unassuming name: The Passover Program.

Such programs first took off at Borscht Belt hotels in the 1940s. Catering to well-to-do families, they offered eight days' worth of accommodation, entertainment, and kosher-for-Passover food. Though I am too young to have attended them, my understanding is that they were but a pale shadow of their successors. Today one can find a Passover program on virtually every continent. Wildly expensive hybrids of old-fashioned *heimish*ness and modern luxury, these second- and third-generation Passover programs speak volumes about the journey of contemporary Jewry. Yes, they murmur, you can have it all. And you can have seconds, too.

As a piece of real estate, the Palm Springs Desert Princess Resort was widely considered a dog. It wasn't actually in Palm Springs but one stop beyond, in Cathedral City, a working-class town stricken by poverty and gang violence. Out on the fringe of the desert, the area lacked Palm Springs's leftover 1950s swank. What Cathedral City did have was wind—hot, dry, sudden blasts of wind that could take your yarmulke off, send it turning across the desiccated plains like a tiny Hebraic tumbleweed. Wind that left you constantly thirsty; that interfered with tennis; that picked up grit and stung your eyes. Surrounded in all directions by exactly nothing, the Princess was unshielded from the fury of these winds, and consequently bore the brunt of them.

The hotel faced constant financial crisis, changing hands every few years as new ownership tried where others had failed to make a leaky business model sound. I later learned that the resort's most reliable source of revenue was the Passover program we began to attend yearly. Without the guarantee of eight days at 100 percent occupancy, the whole place would have gone under.

The people who ran the Passover program at the Princess were, like many of their customers, New Yorkers, and they had selected the hotel as the apotheosis of Southern California. It was big. It was pastel. It was stupefyingly hot. There was a pool. Sunsets washed the golf course in pinks and reds. To a Flatbush *balabusta*, it may have looked like the World to Come.

My father was not as moved. "I guess we're here," he said the first time we pulled up.

Upon arrival at a Passover hotel, you check in thrice. First you go to the normal front desk for your room key. Next you cross the lobby to a folding table staffed by an unsmiling woman in an ankle-length denim skirt. She checks your name against a list of program participants and grudgingly hands you a complimentary canvas tote bag printed with the program's logo and containing a schedule of events. She tells your mother what time to light the inaugural holiday candles, then directs you to the third check-in, which is for the children's day care, or more colloquially, "camp." This table is staffed by a girl no older than sixteen. She, too, is wearing a long denim skirt, although her hostility is latent, concealed by false cheer. Her name is Chavi or, less often, Adina.

"Are you excited for camp?" she asks. "It's going to be sooo much fun."

"She talks like Grandma," you tell your mother as you head toward the elevators.

"That's because she's from Brooklyn."

You are ten and from Los Angeles. "Where's Brooklyn?" you ask.

"Near Israel."

People say that the easiest way to understand a cruise is to think of it as a giant floating hotel. The easiest way to understand a Passover hotel program is to think of it as a land cruise.

Like a cruise, a good program is self-contained; you never need disembark in search of diversion. Nearly every hour of every day is planned. Simply consult the schedule you received in your complimentary canvas tote bag. Mealtimes are regular, as are prayer services. There are daily lectures by rabbinic "scholars-in-residence." There is always a "Wild West B-B-Q Nite." Often the schedule will call for a chess tournament to take place in the lobby. Upon showing up, you will discover that this so-called tournament consists of you, a creepy old man, and a seven-year-old Hasidic prodigy.

In Palm Springs, the big draw was bingo night. Run by a dour fellow with an enormous mustache, it was easily the best-attended event of the week, and very well may have drawn more people than the Seders. Some would corral as many cards as possible, one on the table and three hidden in the lap. A priggish child, I considered such cheating unconscionable, and I suppose I saw God's Hand in action when, in His infinite justice, on my very first Palm Springs bingo night, he caused me to win a brand-new microwave.

On paper, the day was packed. Really, though, attendance at most events was spotty at best. For many, the holiday ate up the bulk of their annual vacation time, and given the enormous expense involved in attending a Passover program (a family of four can easily spend $25,000, and many families in attendance are far larger), most people simply wanted to relax.

For the devout, this meant days spent praying, studying, eating, and lounging in the lobby in casual dress. Three thousand miles from home, free from the judgment of neighbors, they seized the chance to cut somewhat loose, to "go California." Shins (ankles, for women) saw the sun for the first time all year.

As my family fell toward the more modern (read: lax) end of the religious spectrum, we more typically avoided services, slept late, read. We played lots of board games, the cherished pastime of the Sabbath and holidays, when the use of electricity is forbidden.[1] Scrabble, Trivial Pursuit, Monopoly, cards—in Palm Springs we would hold marathon sessions of six hours or more, our loud laughter drawing glares from bewigged women and bearded men, who picked up their infants or their *Wall Street Journal*s or their Talmuds and moved across the lobby, where they once again tried to unwind in the Presence of the Divine.

Restless, we children wandered the hotel grounds. We swiped golf balls from the driving range. We tossed the Frisbee around. We stood outside the spa and imagined the Oriental tortures therein. We used the entire two-hundred-acre grounds for hide-and-go-seek. We traipsed up and down the employee-only stairwell; we went to the gift shop and stared sadly at the racks of interdictory candy bars. At night we played truth or dare by the empty, eerily lit pool, huddling under towels to shield ourselves from ferocious gusts of wind.

My partners in these adventures were, of course, other Passover program kids, friends I made at camp or roaming the halls. At some Passover hotels, Jewish guests share space with regular hotel guests, but in Palm Springs, the entire place belonged to us, ensuring that anybody I met was a Member of the Tribe. It astonished me that there were Jews I didn't know. These East Coast boys and girls—they opened their mouths and you could tell where they were from. My California accent sounded so flat by comparison; in fact, I didn't seem to have any accent at all. After a few days I would begin imitating them, the way they said *awnt* instead of *ant* and *awraange* instead of *ohringe*. I copied their slang. "That's *sick*," I said when they told me they went to school in a Manhattan high-rise. Other kids came from points west, cities with minor Jewish communities: Phoenix, Seattle, San Diego. One year a large family flew in from Mexico City on its patriarch's private jet. A friend told me they owned "all the banks down there."

Some of the people I met at the Princess lived in Los Angeles, and a few were even schoolmates to whom I never talked back home. Seeing them in Palm Springs was different from seeing them in LA, as though our journey into the desert had remade us. Displaced in space, displaced in time, we shed our regular identities for a few days and constructed ourselves anew. Girls who normally intimidated me became approachable. Boys I had nothing in common with would invite me to play four-man football. On the last night we would all trade addresses, writing once or twice before forgetting about one another until next year.

But where, you may ask, where was the festival itself? Where the *Mah Nishtana?* Where the parsley and the bitter herbs? Where the back-breaking preparation that so plainly evokes our former servitude? Where the ritual, the tradition, the Judaism? Where, in short, was the Passover?

Of course, there were Seders, which my family held in one of the hotel's conference rooms, waited on by polite men and women in bow ties and vests. These private rooms were highly sought-after and cost significantly more than the default option, which was to have one's Seder in the main dining room among dozens of *other* families leading *their* Seders, everyone singing and chanting at full volume, trying to drown out their obnoxiously loud neighbors.

Sometimes I took a break from our meal in Canyon Room C and went to visit my unfortunate friends stuck in the Oleander Ballroom, among the hoi polloi. The noise always gave me a shock: the clatter of eight hundred dishes, the shouts of busboys, the pernicious competition to see whose rendition of "Dayeinu" would reign supreme. In the distance, I saw my friends, looking bored, waiting to deliver their prepared "words of Torah" before sinking back into the clangorous silence. I felt guilty going back to our quiet little piece of property; guilty, and relieved that we could read the Haggadah aloud without having to shout ourselves hoarse.

But even with the added privacy, and even as I began to forget what it was like to have Passover at home, I could never manage to convince myself that Seder in a conference room was anything but a simulacrum. Sometimes I complained to my parents: Without that backbreaking preparation, how were we to appreciate the freedom that comes with the fourth and final cup? It all seemed too easy.

Of course, I'd never been the one to vacuum the house, polish the flatwear, grind the horseradish. Resenting my parents for taking me on a lavish vacation—especially when the alternative placed such a heavy burden on my mother—was the height of ingratitude. Yet my sense of unease persisted as I slipped back into Canyon Room C, persisted and grew as I got older. Every year we went back to Palm Springs. Every year I had a good time. And every year I could not escape the feeling that something was not right.

I wanted Passover to be harder. Then, as now, what I felt was more than just nostalgia for some imaginary Old Days, more than just Jewish Puritanism, the belief that pleasure without corresponding suffering yields decadence. What I felt was a symptom of something much more unsettling: an awareness that the raison d'être of Passover hotels is to make it seem as though you are not celebrating Passover at all.

A good Passover program is, from start to finish, an act of forgetting, and that's what makes it so seductive, so sybaritic, so American. Such willful amnesia presents a deep irony, insofar as Passover, more than any other Jewish holiday, celebrates collective memory. On

Passover, the past is supposed to barge in on the present, disrupting routine in every conceivable way. Some Sephardic Jews, for example, physically reenact the enslavement and the Exodus, whipping one another with leeks and tramping around their Seder table with packages on their backs. We Ashkenazim, less theatrical by nature, nevertheless spend the night steeped in over-the-top symbolism. The *charoset* we eat stands for the mortar used by our forefathers to build Pharaoh's cities; the salt water in which we dip our vegetables stands for the tears of the oppressed.

It is no accident that this night is different from all other nights. Those differences are designed to awaken us to what is rich and novel and compelling in our own history, because without such insight we would doubtless seek novelty elsewhere. Without Passover, our national identity would shortly disappear. It is a holiday that calls attention to itself: profoundly disorienting, profoundly unmodern. "Look," it says. "Look at yourself. At your people. At your strange, retrograde ways. Look—and wonder."

To spend Passover pretending that everything is business as usual— to ask *Why is this vacation different from any other vacation*, and then to answer *It isn't*—is to flout the purpose of Passover. Which is precisely what successful programs do. The successful Passover program works very, very, very hard to obscure the holiday and its intrusions, and it achieves this in two ways: by overwhelming the senses and by engaging in sleight of hand.

Which brings us to the buffet.

The internet tells me that while the buffet was first developed in eighteenth-century France, it was not taken to its logical conclusion until the 1940s, when a Las Vegas hotel manager named Herb Mc-Donald introduced the concept of "all-you-can-eat." The Passover hotel constitutes, by itself, a third stage in the world-historical development of the buffet. If the French originators were Aristotle to

McDonald's Nietzsche, then the architects of the Passover programs are the Foucaults and Derridas of the buffet world, for whom satiety is not a physical state but a psychological construct. Feeling full is only the first step. The real goal of the Passover buffet is to clog the mind, and so merely setting out a huge spread will not suffice.

In general, keeping kosher demands lots of time spent scrutinizing labels and monitoring kitchen standards, and on Passover an already onerous task becomes Herculean. Rules upon rules upon rules! But for good reason: Eating on Passover is not just eating. It is eating in a specific religious and historical context. Every time we feel a craving for real bread, every time we submit to lousy fake condiments, we're supposed to remember that we were once enslaved and are no longer.

At a Passover hotel, though, these exertions are not your responsibility. You pay for the right to avoid checking labels or watching pots. You pay for the right to avoid adjusting your recipes; pay for the right to avoid cooking at all. You pay, in short, for the right to avoid thinking about Passover, and by extension, to avoid thinking about your history as a slave.

To the contrary: On a Passover program, you eat like a king, assuming that that king is Caligula. Even the meals served tableside include some form of buffet component, be it a stir-fry station or ice cream sundae bar. More important, that a meal is brought by waitstaff does *not*, in any way, imply a limit on the number of items one may order. It's quite common to see people ordering two and three and nine entrées, either because they didn't approve of their first choices or because they've finished and are still hungry. Some people simply order all the available entrées right at the outset, thus guaranteeing that they get to taste every single dish on offer. In effect, the served meal is simply another form of buffet, except that you don't have to get up and walk across the ballroom.

I always reach a point, usually halfway through the holiday, when

I make a grumbling remark about the last days of the Roman Empire. Then I ask to try the lamb.

If you've ever seen an institutional kitchen, you've probably been startled by the scale of the equipment, the cauldron-sized mixing bowls and walk-in freezers most New Yorkers would be happy to live in. There's something nauseating about seeing a lot of food in one place at one time. In Palm Springs I discovered that there's also something dangerous about it. One year a waiter in a hurry slipped while dashing past a huge pot of *cholent*, the traditional Sabbath stew. Usually *cholent* consists of meat, potatoes, and barley, but on Passover grains are off-limits, leading to a slightly thinner consistency than usual, one that provides little resistance to a full-sized man plunging headfirst into its depths. It sounds funny until you learn that he got third-degree burns. Then it's funny in a different and awful way.

As I mentioned earlier, every program worth its salt features a barbecue. Weather permitting, the event is held outdoors, on the patio overlooking the putting green, or adjacent to the pool. The theme is always "cowboy." Tiki torches frequently make an appearance; these cowboys, it seems, are Polynesian.

And what do they eat, these hula-hula buckaroos? Well, it seems that they eat hamburgers and hot dogs and schnitzel breaded in a non-*chametz* crust. Sweet-n-sour chicken and lamb and various kinds of sausage. Beef tips. Peking duck. Carving stations, so many carving stations: pastrami in schnauzer-sized chunks; smoked turkey breasts; artillery shells of roast beef. Given the limited number of kosher animals—Jews seldom eat anything other than beef, lamb, turkey, chicken, and duck—it's frankly staggering how many permutations show up in the chafing dishes. And it never ceases to amaze me that, having gorged themselves for days, people will get into a line forty minutes long for steak.

The watchword "quantity"; but what truly commands awe is the presentation. Because the list of acceptable ingredients shrinks so dramatically on Passover, Jews have, from time immemorial, striven to make certain foods look and taste like other foods, foods to which the original ingredients bear no resemblance whatsoever. This never, ever works. As long as Jewish mothers have sought to make cake out of potato starch and matzah meal, their children have been there to inform them that it tastes like Astroturf. Cooking well on Passover thus requires a Bach-like capacity to push a restrictive form to its limits. It requires, in a word, magic. And it is here, in creating the illusion of normalcy, that Passover programs shine brightest.

Every magician knows that the best way to cover an awkward movement is to create a distraction. Look at my left hand, holding my top hat, and you fail to notice my right hand moving to my pocket. Watch the cloud of smoke and you miss the trapdoor.

Passover programs have got this routine down, from the ornate decoration that accompanies theme meals (sombreros and tricolors on the Mexican station, Asian chefs preparing mock sushi with quinoa "rice"), to the plating (a five-pound mass of whitefish molded in the shape of a five-pound fish), to the raucous carnival atmosphere that pervades (mariachi music).

The attempt to subjugate the senses through sheer quantity finds its purest expression in a place called the Tea Room. The name conjures up an English seaside inn, with scones and cucumber sandwiches and Earl Grey in a strainer. But at the Passover hotel, there is no tea in the Tea Room; or, if there is, you can't find it, obscured as it is by soaring heaps of nuts, dried fruits, and kosher-for-Passover chocolate. Open at all times save during official meals, the Tea Room makes it possible to spend every waking moment of a Passover program eating.

In recent years some programs have begun setting up more than one Tea Room, putting, for example, a satellite Tea Room out by the pool. And the menu has grown. Where they once offered only junk food, many Tea Rooms now feature meat grilled to order, Viennese tables, full bars stocked with nongrain alcohol, and more mixers than a high-end stereo emporium.

For those who "want to get their money's worth," the Tea Room becomes a kind of challenge. You can pick and pick and pick at the piles of stuff—and they'll keep on bringing out more. You may never reach the top of the mountain, but that's never stopped anyone from trying. If all else fails, you can take a plate back to your room.

My family eventually departed the sunny climes of the Palm Springs Desert Princess, entering a period of wandering that continues to this day. I have since celebrated Passover in Kona, San Diego, Los Angeles, Scottsdale, New York City, Fort Lauderdale, Lake Las Vegas, and Palm Beach Gardens.

Some of my nomadism is attributable to my wife. I knew soon after we met that we had to get married, because she was the first person I had met who had spent more time at Passover hotels than I had. She has never celebrated Passover at home, not once. To me she is the veteran who has done four tours of duty in the swamps of Vietnam before returning home to work in inner-city Baltimore, teaching English as a second language to the disabled. I worship her. She told me that her family had gone to the same program in Florida for sixteen years running, with one exception, when they tried out the West Coast.

"Where did you go?" I asked.

"The Palm Springs Desert Princess," she said. "Nineteen eighty-nine."

My first year there. I was ten. She was eight.

We never met.

These days we trade off, one year at a hotel with my family and the next at a different hotel with hers. Though the location may change, there is an essential sameness to these holidays. The Jews in shorts.

The all-you-can-eat midnight dessert extravaganza. The meat hang-
overs. The jogging in penance, the hours spent in hot tubs, boiling
like flanken, futile attempts to sweat out toxins. The vows to go light
at lunch, just some fish and egg salad and perhaps a tiny tiny tiny
slice of cheesecake. And fruit.

When I am honest with myself, I will admit that there is some-
thing I love about these programs. I love them in the same way that
I love Las Vegas, the same way that I love the movies: as a hyperreal
expression of the American Dream. Often I swear I'll never return,
declaring that next year, we will stay home. A few times we have even
made good on this promise, and though these Passovers are delight-
ful and private, they never happen two years in a row. They exhaust
my mother or mother-in-law. We can't handle them anymore, any-
way. Our systems have been reconditioned, weakened; our tolerance
for endless matzah with jam, all but atrophied. *Where's the buffet?* we
ask. We may sing about next year in Jerusalem, but by the following
April we have reverted to form, boarding a plane ten hours before
Seder night, bound for another grand hotel, our bags crammed with
sunscreen and neckties, our hearts full of longing and dread.

---

[1] Of Passover's eight days, only the first two and the last two are considered holidays.
One is still required during the four intervening days to eat no leaven, but otherwise
these are regular working days.

BRUCE LAWRIE

Who Am I, Lord, That You Should Know My Name?

FROM *Portland*

MY SIX-YEAR-OLD SON AND I SHARE A NIGHTLY RITUAL, JUST THE TWO of us alone in the fading light of his bedroom. Matty, who is severely mentally retarded, loves routine because life comes at him as if blasted from a water cannon, the millions of sights and sounds we all unconsciously assimilate every second of every day an undecipherable roar. Even more than most children, Matthew craves the safety that comes from learning the rhythms of his life, thrives on repetition. And of all his daily routines, winding down to bedtime might be the best. For a few minutes every night, I can turn down the white noise for him and help him ease into the peaceful joy of drifting off to sleep. We start out sitting on the floor with his favorite board book about monkeys drumming on drums, dumditty, dumditty, dum, dum, dum . . . The book is worn with love, all four corners gnawed off—Matthew chews up books the way other kids do grilled-cheese sandwiches, starting at the corners and working his way to the center. As we reach the last dumditty on the last page, he lets out a sigh that tells me everything's right in his world and he's looking forward to climbing into bed.

I rise to my feet and begin singing, *Lord, I lift your name on high* . . . as I reach down to help him into bed. He's unable to walk on his own but he can aim himself in the general direction of the bed. He knows where this is heading and he's ready for it. He pauses at the bedside to feel the blankets and pillow for a moment as if to make sure the bed is still stationary. Legally blind in one eye, he's learned that things have a disturbing way of disappearing right when you're ready to lean on them. But, as always, he finds the cool sheets safe, slings a skinny leg over the bed, and hauls himself up on top, moving rapidly before the bed can escape. He lies on his back rocking back and forth in bed, body rigid, a crease-eyed smile lighting his face, letting out an ecstatic *aaahh*.

I turn out the light and kneel beside his bed in the dark room, still singing, *you came from heaven to earth . . .*

Matty holds his arm out in my direction, a tentative groping for me in the sudden blackness. I wrap his hand in mine and press it to my face. I start singing the next song in our nightly rotation as I brush his hand against my whiskers, first his palm and then the back of his hand. He explores my face with his fingertips and then he covers my mouth gently. I sing into his palm, imagining the reverberations vibrating down into his little soul. How does he experience me? What am I in his world? I don't know. I may never know.

I keep singing. *Only you can look inside me . . .*

Who will care for Matty when I am gone? Who will keep him safe? Or maybe I'll outlive him. Many children like Matthew don't live out a normal life span. Would it be better if he went first? As is often the case with Matty, I don't have the answers. What I *do* have, though, is this moment in the dark with him, his soft hand gently brushing my lips, the source of the soothing song, the same song he's heard nearly every night of his six years on the planet. Those hazel eyes of his that so seldom look into mine are easing shut.

Who am I, Lord, that you should know my name?

I finish the song and stand up and wonder what heaven will be for my son. Maybe it'll be a place a lot like here, a place where his own son will run from him across a wide open field of green, every nerve-end in his little body singing, where afterward, Matty and I can tip back a beer together at a pub. Where he has a healthy body and a lovely wife and our family can linger long over pasta and home-made bread and salad and red wine. Where his son, my grandson, will fall asleep in my lap, a sweaty load of spent boy pinning me to my chair on the deck, the night sounds stirring around us, the stars rioting in the dark sky.

I look down on Matty's peaceful sleeping face. So often peace has eluded him: the operations, the IVs, the straps tying his hands to the hospital bed rails so he wouldn't pull the needles out, the countless blood draws when they couldn't find the vein, all the insults descending out of the blue onto my little boy who couldn't understand why the people around him had suddenly begun torturing him. But he is at peace right now. And a time is coming when he will have peace and have it to the full. And all the other things he's been robbed of. Meeting a girl. Playing catch with his father and his son. Making love. Calling his mother's name aloud. Talking with his twin sister. Eating a pizza. Drinking a beer. Running. And I'll get to be there with him. God will carve out a little slice of eternity for us; our own private, do-over where the breeze carries the smell of fresh-cut grass, where the sky is bluer than you ever thought it could be, where the air feels newborn.

Soon, Matty. Soon.

PHILIP LEVINE

1934

FROM *The New Yorker*

You might hear that after dark in towns
like Detroit packs of wild dogs took over
the streets. I was there. It never happened.
In the old country before the Great War,
my people were merchants and butchers,
and then the killings drove the family
first to England, then Canada, then here.
My father's brother had a shoe repair shop
for a time on Brush Street; he'd learned
the trade from his father back in Kiev.
My mother's family was in junk. The men
were huge, thick chested, with long arms
and great scarred hands. My uncle Leo
could embrace a barrel of scrap metal,
laugh out his huge laugh, and lift it up
just for the joy. His wife, Rebecca,
let her hair grow out in great wiry tangles
and carried her little fists like hammers.
Late summer Sundays we'd drive out
to the country and pick armloads
of sweet corn, boil them in sugar,

and eat and eat until we couldn't.
Can you believe those people would let
dogs take what was theirs, would cross
an ocean and a continent to let
anyone or anything dictate?
After dark these same men would drink
out on the front steps. The neighbors claimed
they howled at the moon. Another lie.
Sometimes they told stories of life
back in Russia, stories I half-believed,
of magic escapes and revenge killings,
of the gorgeous Ukrainian girls they had.
One night they tore up the lawn wrestling, until
Leo triumphed, Leo in his vested suit,
gray and sweat-stained. My uncle Josef
was different; tall and slender, he'd
come into the family through marriage
here in Michigan. A pensive, gentle man,
when stray dogs came to the back door
of the shoe shop he'd let them in, even
feed them. Their owners, he told me,
barely had enough to feed themselves.
Uncle Josef would take a battered pair
of work shoes and cut the soles off
with a hooked cobbler's knife and then,
drawing one nail at a time from his mouth,
pound on a new sole. He'd pry off
the heel and do the same. I was just a kid,
seven at most, and never tired of watching
how at the polishing wheel the leather
took on its color and began to glow.
Once he made a knife for me, complete

with a little scabbard that looped
around my belt. The black handle, too,
was leather, taken from a boot no one
reclaimed. He pounded and shaped it
until it felt like stone. Whenever you're
scared, he told me, just rub the handle
three times and nothing bad can happen.

BARRY LOPEZ

An Intimate Geography

FROM *The American Scholar*

IT WAS NIGHT, BUT NOT THE COLOR OF SKY YOU MIGHT EXPECT. THE sun was up in the north, a few fingers above the horizon, and the air itself was bluer than it had been that afternoon, when the light was more golden. A friend and I, on a June "evening," were sitting atop a knoll in the Brooks Range in northern Alaska. We had our spotting scopes trained on a herd of several hundred barren-ground caribou, browsing three miles away in the treeless, U-shaped valley of the Anaktuvuk River. The herd drifted in silence across an immensity of space.

Sitting there, some hundreds of feet above the valley floor, we joked that the air was so transparent you could see all the way to the Anaktuvuk's confluence with the Colville River, 90 miles down the valley. The dustless atmosphere scattered so little light, we facetiously agreed, it was only the curvature of the Earth that kept us from being able to see clear to Franz Josef Land, in the Russian Arctic. I braced the fingers of my left hand against a cobble embedded in the tundra by my hip, to shift my weight and steady my gaze. The orange lichen on the rock blazed in my eye like a cutting torch before I turned back to the spotting scope, and the distant caribou.

Years later, at the opposite end of the planet, I was aboard a German ecotourist ship, the 403-foot *Hanseatic*, crossing the Drake Passage from the Falkland Islands to South Georgia. The vessel was yawing through 40-foot seas, pitching and rolling in a Beaufort Force 11 storm, one category shy of a hurricane. Dressed in storm gear and gripping a leeward rail outside on one of the upper decks, I stood shoulder to shoulder with a colleague. The surface of the gray sea before us had no point of stillness, no transparency. Veils of storm-ripped water ballooned in the air, and the voices of a flock of albatrosses, teetering in incomprehensible flight, cut the roar of the wind rising and collapsing in the ship's superstructure. In the shadowless morning light, beyond the grip of my gloves on the rail, beyond the snap of our parka hoods crumpling in the wind, the surface of the ocean was another Earthly immensity, this one more contained, and a little louder, than the one in the Brooks Range.

In April 1988 I was traveling across China in the company of several other writers. In Chongqing, in Sichuan Province, we made arrangements to descend the stretch of the Yangtze River that cuts through the Wushan Mountains, the site of the famed Three Gorges, upriver from Yichang. At that time, years before the completion of the Three Gorges Dam, the Yangtze still moved swiftly through the bottom of this steep-walled canyon, falling, as it did, 519 feet between Chongqing and Yichang. Despite the occasional set of rapids, the water in the gorges teemed with commerce—shirtless men paddled slender, pirogue-like boats down, up, and across the Yangtze; larger passenger vessels, such as ours, plowed through; and we passed heavily-loaded lighters and packets laboring against the current. The air was ripe with the smells of spoiling fish, fresh vegetables, and human waste. The scene, a kind of Third World cliché, didn't fully engage me—until I caught sight, unexpectedly, of great runs of vertical space on the right bank, variegated fields rising straight up, perhaps 900 feet, into a blue sky. The terraced slopes were as steep as playground slides, a skein of garden plots and traversing rice paddies, dotted with sheds and houses. These images might be visible between sections of bare cliff for no more than 30 seconds as the ship passed them, but the convergence of cultural and physical geography was spectacular. The boldness of the farming ventures made my heart race. And in that mute, imposing gorge I discovered a different type of seductive Earthly immensity. I wanted time to ferret out all the revealing detail in those densely patterned clefts. But our riverboat bore on. I inhaled sharply the damp perfume of human life around me, and gazed instead at the bolus of light shattering endlessly on the turbid water of the bow wave.

Like other persistent travelers, I have often viewed the surface of the Earth from high-flying aircraft, but those intangible expanses have rarely had the emotional impact of the stillness I experienced that night in the Anaktuvuk River Valley or the more circumscribed view I had later of the chaotic Southern Ocean, let alone the detail and animation of the Yangtze River scenes. What's missing in views from high-flying aircraft is the sensual immediacy of a place. The sound and the smell of it, the press of tempered air on the skin that accompanies what one sees. It's the full reach of the landscape that's not apparent, what you could call the authority of the land. The impression of distance in the valley of the Anaktuvuk that night was intensified by seeing the brilliance of a few lichen-covered rocks close to my hand, by being able to make a connection, in that same instant, between the near and the far. Also, a ground-level view, unlike the view from a plane, has both a foreground and a middle ground— my yellow gloves grasping the rail of the *Hanseatic*, and the albatrosses flying between the ship and the horizon. Or the variegated gardens rising from riverbank to canyon crest.

I don't mean to imply that someone can never establish an intimate connection with the Earth from an airplane, though this seems to happen only at low altitudes and slow speeds. Many years ago, when I was doing research for a book about the Arctic, I flew regularly with a bush pilot named Duncan Grant. He traveled routinely and widely in a twelve-passenger Twin Otter across Canada's Queen Elizabeth Archipelago, north of the North American mainland, ferrying scientists and their gear to and from remote summer campsites. Most bush pilots in that country tended to fly in a straight line from point A to point B, cruising at an unvarying altitude of 3,000 feet. Duncan flew zigzag courses, like an Arctic fox searching for something to eat, always at an altitude of about 300 feet. As his passenger, you never quite lost touch with the Earth. He would habitually follow leads in the summer pack ice, hoping for a glimpse of narwhals. He'd throttle the aircraft back nearly to a stalling point so he could pass a flock of snow geese more slowly.

I learned from Duncan, who maintained close visual contact with the varied and active surface of the planet whenever he flew, what Saint-Exupéry, Anne Morrow Lindbergh, and other writer-pilots meant by the phrase "the romance of flight." It was not freedom from the Earth they sought as much as a release from the tyranny of distance. And what they discovered, what was genuinely new in their explorations, was a different kind of intimacy with Earthly places, both the ones they were already familiar with and those they were seeing for the first time.

Books like Saint-Exupéry's *Wind, Sand and Stars* and Beryl Markham's *West with the Night* held my attention because of the pilots' allegiance to the physical Earth, including their own trackless paths through the atmosphere. Their descriptions revealed more deeply the complex relationships to place that are the hallmark of strong human feelings about geography. They particularized the dull abstractions—the purple plain, the shining river, the amber waves of grain. They enlivened and humanized them.

. . .

When I think of my own attempts to maintain intimacy with the Earth, what first comes to mind is not any arduous encounter with the Earth's terrain or a deliberating hour on my hands and knees somewhere, but the Paleolithic cave complex at Altamira. In the spring of 1991, the director of the Museum of Prehistory at Altamira offered me a private tour of this underground gallery of early human art, in Cantabrian Spain. Accompanied by a guide and with no limit on my time, I was able to move through its various sections at my own speed, grateful for the guide's patience with my slowness. I observed each tableau of animal life, studiously altering my perspective before each one, feeling all the while the damp closeness of the walls and the darkness crowding in. I speculated, like any visitor, about the meaning of what was before me, but these intellectual efforts were the least important thing going on. Surrounded by this vivid, riveting evidence of human imaginations at work, and with the humid silence exaggerating the paintings' starkness, I felt a tenuous identity with its creators. In some sense, these people were my Cro-Magnon ancestors. Holocene history—the domestication of wheat, the codification of law under Hammurabi, the emergence of the Chinese dynasties—none of that entered my mind. All I could see was this glistening testament that Magdalenian hunters had left behind, and myself standing before it, the staring, slow-breathing, distant relative.

When I exited the caves on a promontory and looked out across a Mondrian patchwork of kitchen gardens, corralled stock, and simple, two-story houses at the edge of the town of Santillana del Mar, I felt a surge of empathy for all humanity, as if the paintings and the cultivated soil before me had been created by human beings separated by no more than a few generations.

Intimacy with the physical Earth apparently awakens in us, at some wordless level, a primal knowledge of the nature of our emotional as well as our biological attachments to physical landscapes. Based on my own inquiries, my impression is that we experience this primal connection regularly as a diffuse, ineffable pleasure, experience it as the easing of a particular kind of longing.

I recall diving once on a nameless seamount in Dixon Entrance, near the southern tip of Prince of Wales Island in British Columbia's coastal waters, a kind of flooded landscape. I was working with a team of ecologists surveying benthic communities in the area. Diving is a highly-charged form of human inquiry and many divers become aware of a renewed sense of intense, amorous contact with the Earth almost immediately upon entering the water. A limit on the supply of air you can take along lets you know that your time here will be relatively short. The resistance of the water tells you you won't be going very far. And the projecting frame of your mask suggests, like a monk's cowl, that much will likely go by you unnoticed. Gravity, however, will clearly not be a restraint on your desire to examine things here, where you are "out of your element." You can swim up and down the face of 100-foot cliff walls, and if you have good neutral buoyancy skills, you can suspend yourself a few inches from that wall and scrutinize every movement a tiny creature makes, minute after minute, while it feeds.

That day, diving at Dixon Entrance, I felt like an astronaut, untethered, on an extravehicular excursion. The seamount, which rose to within 60 feet of the surface and was only about 200 yards in diameter, fell away into abyssal darkness on every side. While our mother ship, the NOAA vessel *Alpha Helix*, floated overhead in station-keeping mode, the six of us split up to inspect the complicated contours of this isolated formation. Predictably, in these cold, nutrient-rich waters, the mount was thickly covered with sponges, hydrocorals, anemones, tubeworms, basket stars, and brilliantly colored nudibranchs. Crustaceans appeared in nearly every crevice, and one of us saw an octopus. Small fish darted about, larger fish lumbered past. The scene was generally familiar from other cold-water dives I'd made in the Pacific North-west, until I passed within a few feet of a hole about the size of my fist. The blunt head of an eel protruded from it—an ancient, bald, almost terrifying face. A wolf eel, I realized, and I pulled back sharply. Later, I encountered another wolf eel, this one about three feet long, undulating across the expanse of the seamount in its eerie, limbless way. It triggered the same sudden alarm in my mammalian cerebellum, but the rocky field of bright color over which it moved, pale greens and dark browns, dappled with the shadows of surface waves and accentuated by luminous spots of chartreuse, apricot, carmine, and lavender, gave the eel a kind of innocence and vulnerability with which I identified, suspended there in the open ocean.

I feel fortunate to have been able to experience so much of the physical world directly, to have had time to linger and observe, to ask questions, and to listen while someone explained some subtle characteristic of his local landscape. I have felt pulled since early childhood toward the raw materials of geography and toward its local interpreters, though the pull has not always been toward unpopulated places like those I've been describing here. On a visit to Kabul, in the fall of 2007, my host offered me the services of a Pashtun driver and a battered car, which gave us a lower profile. Over two days the driver and I made our way through virtually every quarter of that blasted, crowded, dust-choked, and heroic landscape. I had told my host that I wanted to see what was actually going on in the streets of his city. What were people really doing in this place?

I watched men in open-air foundries taking infinite care as they hand-peened pieces of scrap metal into parts for cars. I watched a man sell a single pomegranate from a tiny tray of pomegranates, the entirety of his wares. I watched herdsmen moving their goats through reeking heaps of street-corner rubbish—and recalled a dinner conversation I'd had a few days earlier with one of Afghanistan's ministers, a man anxious about plans for his country's economic survival and development. It is from observing the interplay of minute details like these within the larger, overall picture, sensing the tension between the revelatory particular and the general condition, that the written stories we most trust about life begin to take shape. For me, those stories have very often been about human drama in actual places—Melville's Pacific, Faulkner's Yoknapatawpha County, Saigyo's Honshu, Gordimer's Johannesburg.

Geography, some scholars believe, has subtly but directly influenced the development of our cultures, our languages, our diets, our social organization, and to some degree even our politics. Whenever I travel in remote or in still largely tribal places, I'm often conscious of watching for something modern man might have misplaced on his way from Altamira to Rome and Tenochtitlán—specifically, the understanding that geography was central to any idea of his destiny. Once, I can easily imagine, we each had a fundamental sense of well-being that grew directly out of our intimacy, our back-and-forth, with the profundity embedded in the places we occupied.

From time to time I've been asked, as a traveler, which landscape I favor most. Would it be, the interviewer inquires, the Tanami Desert in Australia's Northern Territory? The terraced hills of Bali, or perhaps the intracoastal waterway of southern Chile? I always respond in the same way, saying no, it would be my home in western Oregon, where I have lived since the summer of 1970. It's with this place that I have had the longest conversation.

The house is situated on a bench above the north bank of the McKenzie River, in mixed old-growth forest. The valley here is too steep for farming, so human settlement has been light. Industrial logging has taken a toll, sweeping the mountain slopes clear of trees in many places. But Chinook salmon still spawn in front of the house and, just glancing out the windows, I've seen bobcat, mink, and black bear. Elk and mountain lion are nearby in the woods, as are coyote, beaver, river otter, and black-tailed deer. I often come upon their tracks. From the river, I regularly hear ospreys and belted kingfishers call; and from the trees, ravens, pileated woodpeckers, and a host of other birds—warblers, tanagers, and thrushes among them.

Douglas-firs, cedars, hemlocks, and big-leaf maples surround the house so tightly they take away the horizon. Sometimes, when their crowns sway in the wind, I have the sense that I'm living at the bottom of a kelp forest. The expanse of this montane forest, like the expanse of the Pacific Ocean, is something I feel, and against this volume of space I array the details of life here: the late-night caterwaul of a gray fox, so like the wail of a terrified child; claw marks on the broken boards of an outbuilding, dismantled by a black bear; a rubber boa, pale as the stem of a mushroom, curled up by the kitchen steps one morning; the glint from an obsidian spear point, a broken section of which I unearthed one evening with a trowel while laying a brick walk in the forest.

Over the years I have seen, heard, tasted, palpated, and smelled many remarkable things around the place. I do not recall a single day of attentiveness outdoors, in fact, when something unknown, something new, hasn't flared up before me. I'm kept from the conceit that there is anything remarkable in this, however, by steady streams of weekend tourist traffic that speed past the house, en route to recreation areas in the mountains or to launch points on the river. To most, my landscape, I have to think, must appear innocuous, ordinary.

Still, I'm happy in this undemonstrative, rural place. In my conversations with it I know, once more, who I am. It inundates me continually with mystery, because its nature is too complex to be fully known. If I want the comfort of intimacy with it, of integration and acceptance, my only choice is participation—to learn from it by participating. I imagine my choice here is very like that of Magdalenian cave painters in their time, one of stepping into the physical world as fully as circumstances permit. Of not opting for the expediency of detachment.

Accelerated global climate change, an abstraction around elements of physical geography, has become an inexorable force in the alteration of the Earth's biological fabric. As climatic change begins to affect long-range strategic planning for human survival, as the Earth's stocks of pelagic food fish plummet, as dry-land aquifers are drained, we can easily believe we've been shortsighted in a loss of intimacy with place, in largely ignoring the impact geography has on our daily lives. As humans in Africa and Asia migrate today from their derelict lands in search of ground more habitable—or simply in search of gainful employment—we can even wonder whether, in not providing a central role for geographical awareness in the shaping of our country's domestic and international policy, we've erred fatefully.

The Jack Hills in Western Australia lie about 400 miles north-northeast of Perth. There, in the 1980s, scientists found a lode of zircon crystals that at the time represented the oldest known bits of the Earth's crust. One of these extremely hard and durable crystals was dated at 4.27 billion years, about 250 million years after the formation of the planet. After reading in *Nature* about the discovery, I felt compelled to see the region. I didn't want to spirit away any specimens. I just wanted, if I could, to become for a moment a part of the flow of time there.

From the regional airport at Meekatharra I drove overland in a rented four-wheel-drive about 200 kilometers to a sheep station near the site of the find. The next morning, the manager of the station offered to fly me slowly over the section of the Jack Hills I was trying to reach, to help get me oriented in a roadless area. Employing that overview, and using a hand-drawn map given to me by one of the geologists involved in the research, I located by mid-morning the dry wash in which the crystals had first been discovered. I parked in a copse of eucalyptus trees and walked slowly uphill, studying the ground closely. Distant, almost mythic events in the Archean Eon came to mind while flocks of small, bright, green-and-yellow budgerigars zoomed close overhead. Galahs and crested cockatiels called from trees in the distance. I sat for a while at the edge of a dry watercourse and, from time to time, studied open sections of the broken, hilly country with a pair of binoculars. Nothing moved. I saw no sheep, no feral cats or goats, only the arid contours of a brittle land with little soil, one that carried few footprints distinct enough for me to read.

By early afternoon I was satisfied that I'd located the precise spot where the crystals had first been noticed. The geological exposure was unequivocal. I lingered there for an hour, viewing all I saw in light of the tiny crystals glittering in the rock formation at my feet.

On my way back to the truck I stopped to focus my binoculars ahead on a small flock of gray-and-pink cockatoos with white crowns—galahs. The late afternoon light inflamed their pink chests and I could now easily distinguish female galahs, with their red eyes, from brown-eyed males. The heated air buzzed with their raucous calls, erupting from the upper limbs of the eucalypts under which I'd parked. From the upper end of the wash, my line of sight carried out over the crowns of those trees into a plain beyond, a sun-drenched expanse of savannah under a massive, pale blue sky. It was too far off, on the plain, to catch and identify the voice of any bird there, but perhaps, just then, birds unknown to me were announcing themselves in that welter of space.

ROBERT MIOLA

Sisters & Daughters

FROM *First Things*

IT STARTED BACK IN MAY 2001, AT A GRADUATION PARTY IN MY daughter's tiny New York apartment, just off Broadway, five flights up. Christine has won prizes in classics and Italian, a set of other honors, and she has no use for any of them. She has dropped two decades of aspiration and academic achievement, two decades of building a self in society, two decades of dreams about the future, without so much as a whistle.

"I'm not interested in that anymore," she says. I am proud of her. She has achieved the success we both hoped and worked for—through private schools, travel abroad, summer programs, enrichment opportunities, and family activities. We step out on the roof for some air. One distinguished female scholar, who was on the committee that awarded her a prize for her senior thesis, sidles up: "So what are you going to do with all that Greek and Latin now?" "That's really up to God, isn't it," she replies coolly, meeting her eyes. I keep reminding myself of Thomas Aquinas's dictum: The end of all learning is love of God. "She is just skipping the middle steps," I tell myself and others again and again. Who wouldn't be proud of that?

But I am disappointed, too. She won't be going through the long-anticipated rituals of academic accreditation, and I won't be offering all the cheers, consolations, and advice I have stored up. And

I am worried. Is this a free choice or an unhealthy compulsion, born of some deep-seated neurosis or fear or wound? Will she be safe and healthy and happy? Can we see her, and how often, and on whose say-so? She will never have a husband. She will never have children. What about all that nurturing love and motherly good sense she showed her brother Dan and younger sisters, Rachel and Rosie, babysitting, helping her parents, organizing chores, providing entertainment? And, of course, she will always be a beggar, despite her talents and the tens of thousands of dollars spent in tuition. (The IRS and the alumni surveys have yet to provide a category marked "No income now or ever.")

So, a second-generation Italian American Catholic, I have mixed feelings. No easy, comfortable path for my eldest daughter, no grandchildren, and no success in the New World, at least as people conventionally construe both success and that world.

But it is some consolation to think that there may be larger rhythms at play here. My mother reminds me that her mother, Francesca Cappadona, spent her youth in a convent in Italy.

Christine found her vocation during her year abroad in Rome, which had coincided with the 2000 jubilee. "In Rome I tried to be normal, to stay away from daily Mass," she says, "but I was miserable. I needed to go to church. And all around the city I kept running into those blue habits. Those women were so joyful and peaceful and free."

I tried to reason with her: "You are going into a Servants of the Lord novitiate, and that is by definition a time to try things out, to discern. Take it easy and see if it is right for you." "No," she told me firmly. "I love passionately and want to give everything now—no holding back."

"You should use the talents God gave you and the education I paid for," I respond, all but oblivious to the folly of that coordination. "You can work in a soup kitchen and feed twenty or you can write food-stamp legislation and feed twenty thousand." She shakes her head and looks at me with amusement and, perhaps, a touch of pity.

In January 2004, Sr. Maria del Fiat (formerly Christine Miola) is walking in step with three other sisters, carrying a heavy backpack of books up the hill to the Centro di Alti Studi. Elderly Italian ladies, wrapped in shawls, call out to chat and hug and scold Sr. Fiat in mock anger for not visiting often enough. She laughs with them and asks about their aches and pains. They give full reports and talk about their husbands, children, and grandchildren. They invite us for coffee.

When we arrive at the Centro she introduces me to her students, seminarians as well as sisters from South America, Europe, and Africa. "Who knows more Latin, you or La Maestra?" Fr. Mario asks me, with a mischievous grin. She begins class with a prayer and then gets right to the Latin drills, conducted in Italian. That afternoon I give a lecture on early-modern Jesuit martyrs. I tell them of St. Philip Neri, who used to greet seminarians at the English College in Rome with the phrase, *Salvete flores martyrum*, "Hail, flowers of martyrs." I tell them of Edmund Campion, ministering in disguise and secret to Catholics, evading detection but challenging all of Protestant England to debate: "We shall never despair your recovery while we have a man left to enjoy your Tyburn, or to be racked with your torments, or to be consumed with your prisons. The expense is reckoned. The enterprise is begun; it is of God, it cannot be withstood."

I have given the lecture a hundred times but this one is different. The air crackles with an electric attention and energy. A half hour later I see four seminarians from the back of the room standing together in the piazza. "*Salvete flores martyrum*," I say in jest. Andres, a handsome Argentinian priest with a beautiful tenor voice, closes his eyes and responds immediately, "*Utinam*"—Would it were so.

That night I meet my daughter in the small convent chapel, cut out of a mountain side, for vespers. It is cold and windy but the stone chapel is warm with candlelight; the nuns kneel in silent adoration. Sr. Fiat plays a small organ and leads the hymns, "Tantum Ergo," "Salve Regina," her voice high and clear. The psalms and antiphons echo in the Italian night. The sisters kiss their breviaries before closing them.

But then, in 2005, I find myself saying with dismay, "You can't be serious." Another daughter, Rachel this time, looks at me with deep blue eyes. Her lip quivers. Robert Kaske's book of medieval sources, my gift to her before she heads to graduate school at Notre Dame, sits on the table, already a relic from another dispensation.

"You are wholly different from Chrissy and wholly unfit for that life," I insist. "She loves rules and you can't stand them. You were a feminist at the University of Chicago, and this is a life of submission and obedience."

She struggles to remain calm. "It's not a matter of rules or my sister. It's not even a matter of who I am, and, I'm not sure you know me anymore anyway. Don't you trust that I have thought about this at length?" Her temperature rises. "Do you really want to argue with joy now and the hope of eternal life later?" she says sharply.

"There are no guarantees for eternal life," I retort, my temperature rising. "Are you sure you are not just following your big sister?" I charge, half-conscious of the absurdity of the question, posed as it is to my most flamboyant and theatrical daughter, always fiercely independent, "Or perhaps it's just a coincidence that no one we know enters religious life and you follow your sister in the same choice, in the same order?"

"There are a lot of ways to serve God," I lecture. "Human love is good. Are you afraid of human love, afraid of marriage, afraid of sex?"

"Daaad." She rolls her eyes in exasperation.

"Listen, Ray." I plead, "Ten years from now you will wake up and discover that this life is not or ever was right for you; then you will be too strapped with guilt and an ethic of self-abnegation to do anything about it. Why don't you proceed along with your graduate school plans or go for a year and enter later if you still want to?"

"I already told them I am not coming. I told them to give the fellowship to someone else." I feel a fiery swirl of panic, fear, and anger rise up. Scenes from her life flash before me—reading books together on the porch in blankets, her performances in high school cross-country and theater; her study of medieval Latin paleography in college; her gaining entrance to the Vatican library, officially closed to undergraduates; her pluck; her swing dancing.

I close with brutal sarcasm, feeling cut off, confused, dizzy from worry and anger. I rise from the table, saying, "I'm sorry, Ray. I love you, but I can't support a course of action I think is wrong for you. I don't think I can see you anymore. Maybe that is part of your cross."

"That would make me very sad," she says, as her blue eyes fill slowly with tears.

In Washington, October 2008, I watch Sr. Panagia (formerly Rachel Miola) in action, poised and purposeful. Of course I have seen her many times after that painful day in 2005—in fact, the very next day, filled with love, contrition, and anxiety—but I have rarely seen her in *in propria persona* before.

The children seek her out, and she kneels to see them eye to eye, producing holy cards and medals for them from the mysterious folds of the habit. They are mesmerized. Some adults lead her to the side for confidential and intense conversation, sharing their stories and (I assume from their expressions) their griefs. She moves naturally and easily through the crowd of strangers, young and old; everyone wants to talk to her.

I watch Sr. Fiat, my older daughter, prepare for the ceremony, the declaration of her final vows, and I see her pray and tremble in anticipation, watched by her father and her younger sister, in habit. The priests and sisters process in. The cardinal formally and finally accepts Sr. Fiat and five others, after more than seven years of intense prayer and preparation, as spouses of Christ. At the climactic moment at the altar in the crypt, she stands up and says, "Lord, you have called me; here I am." She makes "an oblation to God of all my being . . . in order to be a concrete imprint which the Trinity leaves in history that all men may discover the attraction and longing for the divine beauty." She vows to remain "forever chaste, for the sake of the kingdom of heaven, forever poor, manifesting that God is the only true wealth for man, forever obedient, even to death on the cross."

My little girl, now twenty-nine, lies prostrate while a priest intones the litany of the saints, calling each to witness and help her fulfill her vow—the Virgin Mary, St. Peter, St. Paul, St. Thomas Aquinas, Padre Pio, Elizabeth Ann Seton, the angels, one by one, St. Teresa, St. Joseph, St. Francis, a divine roll call. Crowned with a wreath of flowers, she completes the mystical marriage by taking a ring on her right hand—my father's wedding ring. My mother, kneeling behind me, weeps for joy to see their marital love thus renewed. At times it seems the thousand others in the grand cathedral fade away and there is no one else there but my daughters.

Many people congratulate me after, as if I had something to do with all that. "You must be very proud," they say, but the opposite is true. I am embarrassed at how poor a part I have played in their lives. I am humbled into silence to see the girls I helped bring into the world, diapered, assisted with homework, watched on playing fields, paid tuition for—now turned into holy persons of God, missionaries, radiant with presence and power.

What does it all mean? I've been thinking about those lines I inscribed to Sr. Panagia the day she took the habit, those famous lines about apprehending the intersection of the timeless with time being the occupation of a saint. Most of us live our lives experiencing normal pleasures and normal pains. Occasionally we experience something beyond all that, something of grace, another reality.

But they live every day in that reality, in the gentle, constant presence of Christ. It is our world of power, pleasure, pain, and pride that is secondary, shadowy, and unreal. Unimaginable, one might say, but there they are, laughing and praying, singing and working, emptied of disordered passions and filled with peace. There they are, big as life, robed in gray and blue.

At the reception they talk with excitement of missions they have just visited—Sr. Fiat in Ireland, Sr. Panagia in Guyana. Everything seems new and possible. I breathe prayers for their health and safety and happiness, and for that of all my children. I have no idea what's next for any of them. But then again, *Deo gratias ago*, I never did.

SEYYED HOSSEIN NASR

We and You—Let Us Meet in God's Love

FROM *Sophia*

> In the Name of God, the All-Good, the Infinitely
> Merciful and blessings and peace be upon the Prophet
> Muhammad and upon all the messengers.

Your Holiness, Eminences, Excellencies,
Distinguished Scholars:

It is asserted by the Word of God, which for us Muslims is the Noble
Quran, "And God summons to the Abode of Peace," and by Christ
(may peace be upon him), who is the Word of God in Christianity
and also a prophet of the highest order in Islam, "Blessed are the
peacemakers." The goal of attaining peace is thus common between
our two religions and we are here precisely with the hope of attain-
ing peace between Christianity and Islam. Furthermore, what can be
more important and foundational in the quest for peace than creat-
ing peace between our religions—for only from this peace will it be
possible to establish peace between peoples and nations, more spe-
cifically the Islamic world and the West. Whether we are Christians
or Muslims, we are beckoned by our religions to seek peace. As peo-
ple of religion meeting here at the center of Catholicism, let us then

dedicate ourselves to mutual understanding, not as diplomats, but as sincere religious scholars and authorities standing before God and responsible to Him beyond all worldly authority.

When one ponders the remarkable similarities between Islam and Christianity, one wonders why there has been so much contention between the two religions over the centuries. As Muslims we share with Christians faith in the One God, the God of Abraham, and see in the beginning of the Catholic declaration of belief, *credo in unum deum*, the deepest confirmation of the first *shahādah* or testimony of our religion, namely *lā ilāha illa 'Llāh* (there is no divinity but God), which we consider to be foundational not only to our religion, but to every authentic religion. Our religion and yours share, therefore, the same foundation and basis despite differences among us in the interpretation of the doctrine of *tawhīd*, or unity, that is so central not only to Islam but also to Christianity since the doctrine of the Trinity certainly does not negate Divine Unity in mainstream Christian theology.

Moreover, for us God is the Creator and Sustainer of the universe, at once Transcendent and Immanent, as He is for you. Over the many centuries of our history men and women of our two communities have stood in awe before the majesty of God as Transcendent and felt His closeness as the Immanent, for as the Noble Quran asserts God is closer to us than our jugular vein. And there have been those in our two communities who have smelled the perfume of Divine Proximity, have become immersed in the Ocean of Oneness and been blessed by the beatific vision of God.

For both of us God has a personal dimension and we can address Him as the "Thou" to whom we both pray. For Muslims as well as Christians God is both Merciful and Just and the harmonization of these two apparently contradictory Qualities has been the subject of countless studies by both your theologians and ours. And of course we both associate God with love, with different interpretations of this central Divine Quality in our two religions. Christians speak of the love of God and some view Islam as lacking in emphasizing this Quality. Muslims would respond that God being infinite, surely His love for His creation could not have become exhausted by the advent of Christianity. Some of that love must in fact have remained to be manifested in Islam and we, no less than Christians, live the life of faith in the glow of Divine Love. That is why one of the greatest spiritual masters of Islam, Jalal al-Din Rumi, identified God with the Beloved, as did so many other Sufis, and could utter in a poem:

> *Hail to Thee O our Love with goodly passion,*
> *O physician of all our ailments,*
> *O remedy of our pride and honor,*
> *O Thou our Plato and Galen besides.*

Both you and we believe that God has created the human soul which is immortal and reject all those views that consider man as a clever machine brought about through accidental and haphazard biological events. We both associate human dignity with men's and women's eternal soul. Consequently we both emphasize the ethical character of human life and believe that having been given free will to act, we are responsible to God for our earthly actions. Our theologians may have debated about free will and determinism for many centuries but both religions have always insisted upon morality and the ethical nature of human actions with consequences beyond the grave. We all affirm the reality of good and evil and their basic distinction, without which belief in ethical action and its effect upon our immortal soul would be meaningless. And our ethical norms are in fact similar in so many ways. That is why we both seek to avoid what classical Catholic theology calls the seven deadly sins. That is why on the social plane we both emphasize the importance of the family and on the individual level the crucial significance of sexual ethics, which, although dealing primarily with the individual, has such a major impact upon society at large.

For both you and us it is our common eschatological beliefs, in their general principles and not details, that provide the framework for the religious understanding of human actions and their consequences upon our souls. We all believe in the reality of posthumous states, in various paradises, infernos, and at least in the case of Catholic Christianity the purgatories. All of us expect to meet God and rely on His mercy and forgiveness. We even have fairly similar historical eschatologies with of course some differences, but in any case we both expect the second coming of Christ, who is at once the center of Christianity and such a major figure in the Islamic religious universe.

We Muslims and Christians, like followers of other religions, pray, and although the external forms are different, there are remarkable similarities in our prayers. Some of us say "O God forgive us our sins" and others *astaghfiru 'Llāh,* that is, "I ask forgiveness of God." The life of the pious person, whether Christian or Muslim, is intertwined with prayer and both religions are witness to a vast spectrum of prayers from the simple petition to God for some need or want to the prayer of the heart, of the saints who only want "Thy will be done" or "I want not to want."

Also over the centuries both Christians and Muslims have made pilgrimage and many continue to do so, Christians to such places as St. James of Compostela, Lourdes, and in earlier Christian history Canterbury, and Muslims primarily to Makkah and Madinah but also many other sites including Jerusalem which has been shared by both Muslims and Christians as a site of pilgrimage. Indeed, the external forms are different but how similar was and is the inner experience of pilgrimage in our two religions!

"How precious is the gift of faith!" Such an assertion can be made equally by a Christian and a Muslim. Whether one speaks of *fides* or *īmān* one is dealing with a most profound reality shared by Muslims and Christians alike. Moreover, both religious communities have encountered the relative significance of faith and works in their religious life. Remarkably enough every theological position taken in Christianity as a whole on the question of the relation and relative significance of faith and works has its equivalence *mutatis mutandis* in Islam.

Such is also true of the question of free will and determinism. Islamic thought is not confined to Ash'arism nor Christianity to Calvinism. It is false to assert that Islam is fatalistic and deterministic while Christianity is based on free will. In reality the rich theological and philosophical schools of both religions present a full spectrum of views on this crucial subject. Nor could this have been otherwise, for the followers of both religions experience in an immediate way, as do all human beings, their freedom to act. Yet along with Jews, they stand before the God of Abraham whose Will reigns supreme.

How strange that Muslims have been accused of being opposed to reason while it was a Muslim philosopher and jurist, Ibn Rushd or Averroes, who is considered to have been the single most important figure in the introduction of rationalist arguments into medieval Christian theology. The reality of the matter is that both Christians and Muslims have presented and held many diverse views concerning the relation between reason and faith or reason and revolution and practically every view in one religion finds its counterpart in the other, except that of course Islam did not encounter Enlightenment rationalism in the eighteenth century and did not surrender to its tenets as did certain strands of Christianity. In any case, persons of faith in both religions stand before the Majesty of God and His all-powerful Will as well as all-encompassing knowledge. And among them those who have had philosophical and theological tendencies have had to ponder over the relation between reason and revelation and have come often to similar conclusions. It is true that in Christianity God is a mystery hidden from man and in Islam it is not He who is hidden and a mystery but man who is hidden from God. And yet, the question of the relation between reason and faith, far from being a source of contention between the two religions, is a source of common accord if one considers the full spectrum of the traditional theologies and philosophies of Christianity and Islam.

Both religions having been sent by God to lead human beings back to Him, Christianity and Islam are channels of grace and make possible not only salvation but also the experience of sanctity as well as the attainment of inner illumination. The pious life of both religions has, through the centuries, been involved with the reality of sanctity in one way or another despite the eclipse of this dimension of religious life in recent times in both religions, in Western Christianity due to the advent of secularism and in Islam as a result of the rise of what has now come to be known as "fundamentalism." One can only ask what the relation between Christianity and Islam would be if saints, men and women whose being is rooted in God, represented each religion in dialogue. In any case, the reality of sanctity as well as spiritual leadership, whether associated with an *imām* or a superior of a Catholic order are shared between us. In Shi'ism and certain schools of Sunnism, we speak of *walāyah* which means spiritual power, sanctity, and inner guidance. Surely Christians would find in this concept and reality deep similarities to their own doctrines.

It is also important to recall that both Islam and Christianity have created major civilizations with their own social structures, sciences, philosophies, arts, etc. Both have created sacred architecture of the highest order whether it be Chartres or the Mezquita in Cordova. Both have produced most outstanding examples of literature imbued with the values of the religions in question. Outward forms differ but the inner meanings of traditional Islamic and Christian arts and sciences—and not the humanistic and modernistic distortions of the traditional norms—are very close and should be a means of bringing the two religions closer together.

Speaking of Christian and Islamic civilizations, it must be noted that the name of both religions has been associated with violence in certain periods of their history. To associate only Islam with violence is to overlook the fact that over the centuries many more Muslims have been killed by Christians than Christians by Muslims. If there is more violence today carried out in the name of Islam than of Christianity, that is not due to the support of violence by one religion and opposition to violence by the other, but rather the result of the relative strength of each religion today. If Christianity in the West is no longer associated with violence, it is because of the weakening of Christianity before the onslaught of secularism. One could hardly imagine calling French or British soldiers to war these days in the name of Christianity, in contrast to older days from the Crusades to the destruction of natives in the Americas when Christianity being strong, was used oftentimes by political forces to legitimize wars and violence. To associate Islam simply with violence and Christianity with non-violence is to make virtue out of necessity. The task to confront and oppose violence in all its forms is in fact a task in whose realization both Muslims and Christians must work hand in hand.

When we ponder over what unites us, we are confronted with the issue of human dignity. The views of the two religions are indeed close in this crucial matter. Traditional and classical Christianity and Islam both believe in human dignity because as both religions have asserted "God has created man in His image" whatever different meanings we attach to the word "image." Furthermore, God has breathed into us His Spirit and that is the origin of human dignity we both accept and the source of human rights. To base human rights and freedoms on humanistic, evolutionary and secularist conceptions of man is merely to espouse a position that is based on sheer sentimentality bereft of any theological foundation and opposed by serious theological thought, both Islamic and Christian.

These are but a few of the realities shared by us and you. Why then has there been such confrontation and opposition between Christianity and Islam? One must consider first of all the fact that Islam appeared after Christianity and from the dawn of Islam Muslims have had respect for Christianity as a revealed religion, and have protected the Christians living among them and as they continue to in sizeable numbers in several Islamic countries. In contrast Christianity preceded Islam and its mainstream religious thought did not accept and for the most part does not accept even now Islam as an authentic religion revealed by God and given the power to bring about salvation to its followers. There are also formal differences many of which were divinely ordained in order to keep the two religions distinct. Had not those providential distinctions existed, we would not be speaking to each other as followers of two religions today, both of which have not only survived but possess a global presence to this day, a situation surely willed by God for those of us who accept God as the Almighty whose Will rules supreme. Let us then turn to some of those differences.

Islam emphasizes Divine Unity which being Absolute cannot enter into any relation, for that would imply relativity; hence the Islamic rejection of the Trinitarian doctrine and the possibility of Divine Sonship. Christianity on the contrary emphasizes the Triune nature of God while like Islam accepting His Oneness. Likewise, the two religions differ in their account of the end of the life of Christ who plays such an important spiritual role in the Islamic religious universe as well as being the heart and center of Christianity. The question between the two religions that remains is the following: was Christ crucified or not? And the answer to this crucial question is not the same as far as Islam and Christianity are concerned.

On the social plane, Islam emphasizes the centrality of the Divine Law (*al-Sharī'ah*) whose main sources are the Noble Quran and the *Sunnah* or wonts of the Prophet of Islam while for Christianity the law of Christ is a spiritual law and in everyday affairs Christianity incorporated much of Roman Law and later Germanic common law. The result is different views concerning the significance of laws that govern human society. Likewise, on the social plane Christianity preached giving unto God what is God's and unto Caesar what is Caesar's. This meant the complete separation of spiritual and temporal authority, although in practice after Constantine the two became intertwined resulting practically in a situation not very different from that of Islam which has never accepted the separation of the domains of God and Caesar. Today both religions struggle with this question but for different reasons.

When we come to the organization of religion we again detect important differences. In Catholic Christianity there is the ordained priesthood and only priests can perform certain ritual actions, especially the consecration of the Eucharist. In Islam every man is a priest and there is no religious hierarchy as we find in Christianity in general and Catholicism in particular. Even the hierarchy found in Shi'ism is not the same as that found in Catholicism and a Shi'ite, like his Sunni brothers, is a priest in being able to conduct all the rites of the religion from performing or leading the daily canonical prayers to leading the prayer for the dead.

What or who is the Divine Word? To this question a Christian would answer Christ and a Muslim the Noble Quran, although in certain schools of Islamic thought each prophet including Jesus has been identified with an aspect of the Divine Word. In any case, for Christians the body of Christ is the "container" of the Word, while for Islam it is the Quranic Arabic language which, as the result of the Islamic revelation, became by God's Will the sacred language of Islam and the "container" of God's Word. Christianity has had many liturgical languages, including, besides Latin, Aramaic, Greek, Russian, Slavonic and even Arabic which is thus the sacred language of Islam as well as the liturgical language of Arab Christians. This different understanding of the role of language in religious rites has had many significant consequences. Not only Arabs, but all Muslims, whether Malay, Indo-Pakistani, Persian, Turk or African, all having mother tongues other than Arabic, pray five times a day in Arabic, whereas in the West after nearly two millennia of the use of the beautiful Latin liturgy, it was put aside in favor of vernacular languages after Vatican II.

Many have said that for Christianity, Islamic teachings have been too close for comfort and there is what one might call family enmity towards Islam that Christianity has not had towards other religions, the case of Judaism being an exceptional one. Yes, Christians read in the Holy Bible about Noah, Abraham and Moses, all of whom along with many other prophets are also mentioned in the Noble Quran. Christians, especially Catholic and Orthodox, venerate the Virgin Mary and so do Muslims. For Christians, Jesus is the Son of God, who was born miraculously from a virgin mother and who performed of many miracles. For Muslims he is not the son of God but one of the foremost prophets dedicated to spiritual guidance, the prophet of inwardness, born miraculously of a virgin mother. Yes, Muslims also venerate Mary, the only woman after whom a chapter of the Quran is named. Moreover, they not only accept the virginal birth of Jesus as do Christians, but also affirm his performance of miracles. Despite differences, the similarities are great enough to have aroused suspicion and special enmity among many Christians against Islam even after the political threat of Islam to Europe had disappeared.

There are also significant differences between Islam and Christianity due to their very different encounters with modernism and secularism. Obviously in dealing with Christianity today, we Muslims are not confronted with St. Thomas Aquinas, Dante, and the builders of the Cologne Cathedral, however real these dimensions of traditional Western Christianity might still be. Rather, we face a Christianity that bears the deep wounds of five centuries of battle with forces opposed to religion, from the secular humanism and skepticism of the Renaissance to the materialism associated with the seventeenth century Scientific Revolution and the subsequent secularization of the cosmos to the rationalism of the Age of Enlightenment, to the historicism and evolutionism of the nineteenth century to the current post-modern critique of religious texts and the virulent atheistic attacks being made recently in the West against religion as such. Western Christianity has had to face such figures as Montaigne, Bayle, Feuerbach, Marx, and Freud, all of whom were products of the West and not from a land far away as has been the case of Islam in its confrontation with such figures. Islam, moreover, did not experience various phases of modernism in a gradual manner as did Western Christianity, but experienced it rapidly and in quick order. Of course there are those in the West who claim that the problem is precisely that Islam did not experience in depth modernism and especially the Enlightenment to which Muslims would respond, thank God that this did not happen to us. Otherwise the number of Muslim worshippers performing the Friday prayers at the Sultan Hassan Mosque in Cairo would be the same as the number of Christians participating in the Mass on a Sunday at the Saint Sulpice Church in Paris.

In seeking to come together we must be fully aware of the differences created by the advent of modernism. Western Christianity has fought against but also in many cases surrendered to the foe as we see in the abandonment of the cosmos to a secularist science or the adoption of certain Marxist themes in some of the currents of liberation theology. As for Islam, its encounter with modernism has been confined to a short period. Within the span of a century Muslims

have had to face the challenges of five centuries of European antire-
ligious thought. Their reaction has, therefore, been different from
that of Western Christianity. Islam's encounter with modernism has
not produced an army of influential secularist thinkers, nor a strong
wave against religion as we see in modern European history. But
there have been severe reactions, sometimes unfortunately violent, to
modernism throughout the Islamic world recently, resulting in what
is called problematically in the West fundamentalism which, how-
ever, also has its equivalents in both Judaism and Christianity not to
speak of Hinduism.

Let us understand the roots of our differences not only as based in
scripture and tradition, but also as resulting from our very different
experiences of modernism and secularism. Simple criticism of the
other without understanding and empathy cannot bring accord de-
spite all the elements common between Islam and Christianity to
which some reference has already been made. We are situated in the
same boat floating over very dangerous waters. The vilification of the
other through accentuation of differences without deeper understand-
ing of causes of these differences and disregard for all that unites us,
especially the love of God and the neighbor, cannot but lead to our
own perdition.

Forgetting and casting aside the remarkable accord on so many basic
doctrines and values and exaggerating differences used often to bring
about purposefully discord and opposition have characterized much
of the history of relations between our two religions. As we now all
stand at the edge of a precipice it is time to turn a new page and seek
to come together in the bosom of Divine Love. Of course our coming
together does not and should not mean the destruction of divinely
ordained formal structures of each religion. You and us: We must in
fact be able to continue our distinct religious lives without constant
threat of the destruction of our faith from the other side before even

embarking upon dialogue. That is why we Muslims oppose aggressive proselytizing which seeks to reward conversion with worldly advantages. We wish to preserve our religion, as do the Jews, who in 1988 passed a law in Israel banning religious proselytizing, as would Christians if they were placed in our situation. To be friends requires that we first exist as ourselves. The other must be respected as the other, not as potential material for conversion from the category of otherness. Yes, both Christianity and Islam envisage for themselves a universal message, but if we are to live together in peace, we cannot try to destroy the religious identity of the other at all costs, imposing what we consider to be our right on the other, and disregarding his right for self-preservation.

Our attitudes in this matter as in so many others will change if we realize not only theoretically, but also concretely, that we belong to the same family of religions, worshipping the same God. The great tragedies of the twentieth century have helped to expand the usage of the term "Judeo-Christian." It is now time to realize that we have to speak of "Judeo-Christian-Islamic" if we are to be honest, and also reverential towards Abraham, who is the father of monotheism. It was God's Will that the Abrahamic tradition should be comprised of the three religions of Judaism, Christianity and Islam. You cannot sever bonds that have been forged by God. If we are to accept in our hearts, and not only diplomatically, that we are members of the same religious family (seen in the positive sense of family based on accord and not discord), then we must discourse with each other as family members and respect each other in every way without hatred and above the fray of family feuds. Our dialogues must not be based on suspicion, hidden agendas, and duplicity, but on sincerity and honesty, which are so much needed in our world. We are not each other's enemies, but members of the same divinely ordained family. Therefore, we should not try to destroy each other, but seek to vie with each other in goodness, as the Noble Quran asserts.

One might understand that a thousand years ago, when we both lived in a world impregnated by faith, some Christians might have called Muslims their enemies, and vice versa, although even then many Christians and Muslims lived as friends as can be seen in the long history of Christian communities in the Islamic world. In any case, we no longer live in a traditional world of faith and are confronting other enemies. We live in a secularist world in which religions are each other's best friends. In any case, today our enemy, which in fact is common between us, is the materialistic, hedonistic, nihilistic and God-negating world-view that is so wide-spread, the world-view that negates the spiritual nature of humanity, denies the sacred and the transcendent, and seeks to shatter our hopes for a blessed life everlasting. We have much to offer to each other in the central battle between truth and falsehood. But the offer can only be accepted if we first recognize each other as friends and not as enemies.

In this effort to reorient ourselves toward each other, all of us, Christian and Muslim alike, can play a role. But there is no doubt that the main responsibility lies on the shoulders of religious leaders, thinkers, and scholars, those whom we call *ulamā* in Islam. Those who are guides and trailblazers in religious matters must come forward and seek to bring about understanding to those in their own communities who hearken to their call. They should bring about further knowledge about the other whom they should present as friend, not enemy, to be loved and not vilified. And surely the carrying out of such a task on our part is one that is not always easy. It requires—besides the necessary knowledge—selflessness, honesty and truthfulness in conjunction with love and compassion.

We as Muslims from different schools of Islamic thought and countries have come together to extend to you our hand of friendship, seeking to meet you in God's love, beyond all our theological differences and memories of historical confrontations. Surely we, who respect and love Christ as you do, can meet and come together under the banner of what he has stated to be the two supreme commandments: to love God and to love the neighbor. We can also seek to extend, often in harmony with each other, the border of the definition of neighbor to include not only you and us but the whole of humanity, and even beyond that the rest of God's creation. As the Holy Bible asserts, "With God, all things are possible." We submit to Him, and ask for His help and affirmation in carrying out this momentous task of meeting with you in friendship and peace under the banner of that common word that unites us. There can be no more blessed act in our times than the creation of deep accord between God's religions, especially the two religions that have the largest numbers of followers in the world, namely Christianity and Islam. Indeed, God summons us to the Abode of Peace, and blessed are the peace-makers.

This is the full text of a paper prepared for the Catholic-Muslim Forum held at the Vatican November 4–6, 2008. An abridged version was delivered to His Holiness and participants on November 6.

MARILYN NELSON

The Contemplative Life

FROM *Image*

Abba Jacob said:
Contemplation is both the highest act
of being human, and humanity's highest language.
If the language of things reaches beyond things
to designate the Absolute,
the silent interior mantra
bespeaks a profound communion
with that Someone further than ourselves—
and communion within
ourselves, for the two go together.
When we meditate, we enter
paschal mystery, the frontier between death and life.
Egyptian mythology has a wonderful image
of the pass from life to death: a great ship
which bears us to eternity. Charon
is the great passer of Greek mythology,
helping souls cross the River Styx from life to death.
Christianity turns it around: Christ
is the greatest passer, helping us pass
from death to life.
Contemplative life is always making the passage

from death to life, from humanity to divinity.
It is always taking the risk of being human.

There is an extraordinary message from the grave
as to what it takes to be human: a letter
from a Cistercian monk, one of seven
who had their throats cut
by Muslim fundamentalist terrorists
in their monastery in the mountains of Algeria
about ten years ago. Their prior
left a letter, just in case:
they knew it was probably coming,
they knew they were at great risk.
The letter was found and published.
Here is how it ends:

To the one who will have killed me:

and also you, Friend of my final moment,
who would not be aware
of what you are doing,
yet, this: Thank you.
And adieu to you.
For in you, too,
I see the face of God.

Abba Jacob wiped his eyes.
Interval of birdsong from the veranda.

He's seeing not an abstract God,
but a God who has assumed a face,
a God who shows him this face

in every one of those Muslim brothers and sisters,
including the one who kills him.

Contemplative life has no frontiers.
And it is the heritage of all humanity.
Through contemplation we enter
into communion with everybody.
And this leads to service.
But that's a subject
for another day.

Based on a talk given by Père Jacques de Foiard Brown.

MELISSA RANGE

Pigs (see Swine)

FROM *The Hudson Review*

> According to official Library of Congress rules, one must
> classify children's books about pigs under "pigs" and
> adult books about pigs under "swine"; the terms are not
> interchangeable.

On the books, the rules for subjects long assigned:
For children's tales, use *pigs;* for grown-ups', prefer *swine.*
How now, white sow, on which one will you dine?
Wilbur is "some pig"; Napoleon, some swine.

But there's a book whose pigskin bindings shine
For youth and aged alike, in which the terms align,
Pigs and swine; and in its stories, sow supine,
Your litter's better bacon in a poke done up with twine.

The Evangels spin a story from the silken ears of swine:
The swineherds eat their lunches by the mountain's steep
       decline,
By the tombs, where wind's perfumed with marjoram and
       thyme,
With the sweet smell of the cedars, the sweet reek of the swine;

And by the tombs, a bruised man roots for acorns, as benign
In his iron fetters as the Son of Man, the Vine,
Who withers branches, makes blood out of wine.
The shackled shouting man's a temple with no shrine,

Or two thousand shrines, and every one maligned
By other gods, other incarnations, so this text opines:
Gods unclean as hordes of hogs, scores of swine,
Hooves divided, eyes savage, tails serpentine.

O lardlings, your Lord cometh, and you know not his design.
He sails across still waters and his lips are caked with brine.
Piglets, he will not give this generation a sign,
Unless that sign be read in demons, in the bristling flesh
    of swine.

For swine, see pneuma, see daimon, see the soul unconfined.
See incarnation thistle-pink with hock and flank and rind.
See madman counsel madman, chapter, verse, and line.
See spirits seek for bodies, and see the spirits find.

See the book consign the flock, loin and heart and mind,
To a tumble through the salty sky, their transport undefined.
Over the cliff, swine see pigs, and pigs see swine—
Legion, yet one: porcine, insane, divine.

PHILIP SCHULTZ

Bleecker Street

FROM *The New Yorker*

It's a lovely June afternoon
and I'm heading up Bleecker Street
for a hazelnut espresso latte,
the kind made out of real hazelnuts,
not syrup, hoping it will empty me
of all my bickering ideas about love
and fate and immortality
so I can hear the fertile songs of spring.
Miguel de Unamuno—whose name
is impossible to say without smiling—
believed "self-love widens into love of all that lives."
Thank God for Unamuno! For hazelnut lattes!
But the infinite archeology of my stupidity
prefers the charms of self-pity
to the equilibrium of self-love.
Perhaps these three Chinese girls
giggling into cell phones, lavishly spending
each moment of their youth, truly believe
the mountain of self has no top
and each breath is a reckoning with fate?
Perhaps these shiny boutiques, each

so resolute, so eager to please, are weary
of decorating the illusions of another century,
prefer the runaway slaves they hid in their root cellars,
their dreams of slaughter and deliverance?

Perhaps this beautiful blond woman,
screeching to a stop in a lilac Mercedes,
pursued by wailing police cars, finally
understands that it is not only for the soul
but for the mind that happiness is a necessity?
"Is the rich bimbo stoned or just stupid?"
an old man, radiant with rage, screams.
Perhaps everyone secretly admires
something momentous about himself,
with the mass and "inner life" of a cathedral,
in the tradition of the Spanish saints and mystics
who cherished the bliss of infinite sacrifice?
Perhaps this street remembers the loneliness
of war widows, the roll calls of absent names,
its first kisses on the corner of West Tenth Street,
the swooning confetti heat of victory,
the scalding springs of defeat? Indeed,
this street is a wave of advocacy
and streaming window peonies and tulips,
a fierce glimpse of history, an echoing
of nightly gunshots, a flag of black pigeons
flowing east toward the end of a continent,
a hunger for immortality, a tiny brusque city,
a bickering idea, a useless boutique,
a fertile song widening into a love for all that lives.

ANITA SULLIVAN

Scordatura: Upon Listening to Biber's Rosary Sonatas

FROM *Image*

> *Scordatura: Abnormal tuning of a stringed instrument in order to obtain unusual chords, facilitate difficult passages, or change the tone color.*
>
> —*Harvard Dictionary of Music*, second edition

ALTHOUGH I AM A PIANO TUNER WHO USED TO PLAY A VIOLIN, I would not dream of referring to the violin as a simple instrument, at the risk of calling down the ire of contemporary violin builders and their hefty spiritual ancestors, who might rant loudly to me in Italian in the middle of the night. Yet, from an instrument maker's point of view, a piano is much more difficult to build than a violin, a cello, even a harpsichord. But what means "simple"?

I have worked as a professional piano tuner for almost three decades. Because of the many tuning pins, and how deeply they are embedded into the pinblock, the job is lengthy, complicated, and physically demanding. For this reason, pianists have not tuned their own instruments since—well, possibly since the very beginning, in 1700 in Florence, when the piano was conceived and presented to the world as an instrument totally different from a harpsichord by the Medici family's chief musical instrument curator, Bartolomeo Cristofori. But what means "complicated"? Violins have only four strings that can be adjusted fairly quickly by the performers without the aid of tools. The pitches are easy to hear, and the traditional tuning places them a fifth apart. What could be simpler and more elegant? The music that comes out of these four strings is nonetheless phenomenal.

Most pianists have no idea that their pianos can be tuned in a variety of ways—hundreds, actually—because pianos have been tuned only one way for almost a hundred years. Similarly, many violinists have never heard of "scordatura" tuning for their instruments unless they play traditional fiddle music. As a pre-teen I played classical and popular pieces on the violin, and my teachers never told me that GDAE was only one of many possible tuning patterns. I first learned of the renegade Italian tuning term at roughly the same age I became fully aware of the concept of sin. Why would an instrument I considered to be almost holy, ever be tuned *abnormally on purpose?* Why would anyone want to do that? My head would not wrap itself around the concept, so I put it aside: as it turns out, for something like fifty years.

In the fifteen *Rosary* Sonatas by Heinrich Ignaz Franz Biber (1644–1704) for violin and unspecified accompanying instruments, the violin is tuned differently for each sonata, and fourteen of these tunings are scordatura. This is a good word to roll around in your mouth, in your bad imitation of an Italian accent, and recognize as mildly wicked. Or, more to the point, *be reminded* of something wicked. What? You can find the word in musical dictionaries alongside more familiar terms such as *adagio, allegro, piano,* and there you discover why the "scord" part gives you a little shiver: it began life as the Italian word *discordare,* which even today still means "out of tune." In English we say "discord," meaning anything from a family argument to "an inharmonious combination of musical tones sounded together." But somewhere in the early seventeenth century the Italian word *discordare* labored and brought forth—perhaps we should say discarded—a fledgling that flourished for roughly a hundred years as a name for a particular kind of beauty, rather than just a general term for its opposite.

Furthermore, in the seventeenth century when this deliberate abnormal—meaning atypical, but not bad or ugly—tuning of non-keyboard stringed instruments (lutes, guitars, viols, and the members of the violin family) was in common use among composers and performers, the normal, or "accordare" way of tuning was not so widely agreed upon and rigidly followed as it is today. In fact, some stringed instruments (viola d'amore, for example) had no single "accordare" tuning standard to deviate from. Not only was the music improvised on these small instruments, but so was the very scale structure upon which the music found its rest. This means that for a hundred years or so, a large body of stringed instruments in Europe were regularly permitted, cajoled, and urged over an extra threshold in order to make their music. It was that kind of threshold that angels are especially loathe to cross.

Keyboard instruments, in order to make music, also must be tuned by some physically dictated guidelines. But harpsichords, clavichords, and pianos have many more strings than violins, lutes, viols, or guitars. As a result, a tuning pattern (also called a temperament) for keyboards is quite a difficult thing to settle upon. There is no orthodoxy here; any temperament will be based on a somewhat whimsical core idea, rather than one firmly sanctioned by the physical harmony of musical acoustics. Thus, all keyboard tunings are, in a sense, scordatura. But this, of course, is a total paradox—how can you diverge from "normal" if there is nothing normal to diverge *from?*

Scordatura has now revealed an odd symmetry. A violinist has the option of tuning her instrument either the normal way, or not. The orthodox tuning has the pattern GDAE, which is based on the natural harmonics of musical strings, and has been sanctioned over and over again by the demanding ears of musicians throughout many centuries. Hence, any deliberate deviations from this pattern would require moving away from an easy and traditional purity. On keyboard instruments (organs, harpsichords, clavichords, pianos), such easy purity is not physically possible; nonetheless, a series of twelve perfect fifths remains the mathematical and musical template that all keyboard temperaments aspire to, in theory.

So, the odd symmetry goes like this: the violins don't stick with perfection even though they know they can have it any time; the keyboards keep trying to counterfeit such perfection even though they know they can't ever have it. The (abnormal) tuning of a violin in scordatura and the (abnormal) tuning of a keyboard in one of many possible temperaments represent two distinct aesthetic impulses. Like two different reasons for misbehaving. Not only that, but two different *beautiful* reasons.

When Biber composed the *Rosary* Sonatas in honor of the sufferings and ecstasies of the Blessed Virgin Mary, he specified fourteen scordatura tunings and one usual one. A scordatura tuning involves tightening or loosening one or more of the strings to change the pitch from the normal pattern, in increments of a half or whole tone. This can be done to expand the range of the instrument, or to make certain passages easier (or even possible) when the performer is playing double stops, for example.

In this composition Biber was using scordatura also, or perhaps only, for a third reason: by deliberately and radically pushing the physical limits of the instrument so that it would seem to be speaking from a variety of highly emotion-charged responses, he would bring about a mystical union between the performer, the listener, and the larger, holy story being thus musically sanctified. Tightening strings makes the violin sound harder, closer to what we would call nasal or keening; loosening strings brings about a weaker, more husky or throaty sound. By varying these effects, Biber jerks the listener around through a turmoil of conflicting aesthetic responses based merely on the tuning, never mind what the music itself is doing. This adds an entire dimension to the music that we have lost the ability to understand or require, and which can set a first-time listener almost staggering.

For example, in the "Ascension" he set out the pattern CEGC, which means the bottom G is raised three whole tones and the top E is lowered two. These alterations mess with the violin's physics in intriguing and disturbing and marvelous ways that go beyond beautiful or ugly. Biber is drawing the instrument, by a variety of paths, close to the brink of noise. The notes themselves are normal enough, but each alternation of string tension changes the violin's voice. You hear the instrument speaking regular words in an irregular tone of voice— like a mother right on the edge of a breakdown. You begin to receive a very ancient message directly through your sinews as they engage harmonically with those of the stressed-out instrument. Your sense of music, and of suffering, is enlarged.

Because only two instruments are playing, and because both are mistuned according to their symmetrically opposite physical responses to the rules of musical physics, something pristine can take place. The listener is forced to hear that the violin *by nature* operates in a different space than the harpsichord does; they render different realities. As if the fact that they are musical instruments is not precisely the essential element of their ensuing actions. As if, unknown to us, music were actually born twice. Our attention is drawn to music as a raw material rather than as an art; and even though we can continue to rest on the assumption that this familiar and beloved phenomenon we have always taken for granted has to do with sound, we begin to acknowledge that more than one member of the Grendel family of music is out there stalking the world, and we have hitherto never run into its mother. Apparently at least two different gods had the music idea at the same time and released it through two different doors: the up and the down doors, perhaps? The division door and the multiplication door, magnitude and multitude? Like Homer's two gates for dreams.

One recent night I dreamed that my son Timothy (now thirty-three), at age two, wandered away from the glassed-in spaceship we were occupying, out into the alien, tropical landscape of an earth-like planet. I was half asleep on a divan (not a sofa), and when he went out I lulled myself into complacency by noticing that he was accompanied by a young man employed inside our vehicle. Gradually, reason nudged me into full wakefulness by reminding me that this employee was not a babysitter, and very probably assumed I was watching out for my child. By this time it was dusk, no sign of my little son or the young man. I cried "Tim!" in increasing panic, and eventually he showed up whitely in the dim light.

I woke up stifling from guilt and nostalgia. The dream had called up a similar scene from years ago. I was looking out the window into the backyard where Tim and his older brother were just coming up through the trees towards the house. Patrick, my older son, was not yet visible, but for some reason Tim glowed just a little as he rustled over the grass in his paper diapers; his little fat knees caught at my heart like candles. I was overwhelmed with love and with the simple beauty of the scene; but also, I remember, by that irrational dark that afflicts all mothers, the fear of losing the child. More than that, I felt—as I did in the dream—guilt for not paying enough attention to the possibilities of wandering. But how silly!

My sons are alive despite all the mistakes, the accidents, the near-misses that actually took place during the time their father and I were bringing them up. I never seriously neglected my children. Why should a simple dream, a simple glance out the window remind me of things that never actually happened? At some base level of human existence all possible actions and outcomes do become equally likely, no longer beautiful or ugly, good or bad, but deeply, whimsically, terrifyingly available. The dream reminded me of that, as did the *Rosary* Sonatas when I listened to them for the first time, also on a recent night.

How powerful is a rendition of scordatura tunings when presented in such a piece of music! The simple result in this case is two different versions of beauty, trading places in the listener's ear throughout the performance like figure and ground. But here, in the violin part, the voice of the *instrument* is being permitted to insert a primal response to the fundamental circumstances in which it is designed to make music: like a dialect of wood and gut. Thus—in this unpublished piece of music, of which only one copy is known to exist— there is the intimation of much more: of *at least* two entire worlds; *at least* two opportunities for exquisite secrecy and nuanced pain, for reasons for things. This happens so casually by the mere tightening or loosening of four strings. Or rather, so gratuitously. Through our ears—which are a direct pathway to the self—we are helpless and even terrified before such a simple manifestation of infinity.

But then, with so much infinity expressly, if fleetingly, available, might this not suggest more than one *essential* way through the world? Perhaps if beauty arises out of the Is-ness of things, spontaneously, irrevocably, and if this Is-ness exists hugely, obliviously but all around at all times, we need only a tiny shift in the magnification of our seeing or hearing, a miniscule twitch of angle, and it will explode into us: a series of caverns inside the veins of each leaf, the lavish turquoise bleedings from the under-surface of the sea. If this is so, then how can suffering be merely what it seems?

The recording that inspired this essay features Andrew Manze on baroque violin and Richard Egarr on organ and harpsichord: Harmonia Mundi 907321 (2004).

TERRY TEACHOUT

Believing in Flannery O'Connor

FROM *Commentary*

IN 1952, THE LANDSCAPE OF AMERICAN FICTION WAS DOMINATED BY a group of literary celebrities who had published their first novels after or near the end of World War II. James Baldwin, Saul Bellow, Truman Capote, Ralph Ellison, Norman Mailer, J. D. Salinger, Gore Vidal: these were the up-and-comers about whom everyone was talking in the days when serious fiction still mattered to the educated public, the ones who were expected to do great things.

But while all of them are remembered today, none save Bellow came anywhere near living up to his promise. And though the most consequential American book of 1952 was undoubtedly Ellison's *Invisible Man,* the year's most significant literary debut turns out in retrospect to have been a slender, poorly reviewed novel about a half-crazed itinerant evangelist who preached the gospel of the Church Without Christ, a book whose all-but-unknown author was a young woman whose home was not New York but a small town in rural Georgia.

It took a number of years for Flannery O'Connor's *Wise Blood* to be recognized as a modern classic, but once recognition came, it was decisive. Today O'Connor, who died in 1964 at the age of thirty-nine, is generally acknowledged as one of the foremost American fiction writers of the twentieth century. Not only has she emerged as

a key figure in postwar American letters; she is by far the most criti-
cally acclaimed of the many Catholic writers who came to promi-
nence in this country after World War II, as well as one of the most
widely read novelists, short-story writers, or poets to have been born
in the American South. As Brad Gooch points out in *Flannery: A Life
of Flannery O'Connor* the first full-length biography of O'Connor,
the Library of America's 1988 volume of her collected works "outsold
[William] Faulkner's, published three years earlier."

That an author who published only two short novels and twenty
stories (not counting student work) in her lifetime should now be
the subject of such posthumous acclaim is the stuff reevaluations are
made of. Might some of the attention now being paid to O'Connor
and her modest oeuvre arise from the fact that she died so young? Or
could it be that certain of her admirers are going out of their way to
praise a writer who—unlike the once-big literary guns of the fifties—
was a woman?

Tempting though such mean-spirited speculation may be, it is mis-
guided. O'Connor's laconic, formidably tough-minded novels and
stories are fully as good as their reputation, and vastly better than any-
thing published by Baldwin, Capote, Mailer, Salinger, or Vidal. After
she died, Thomas Merton wrote that "when I read Flannery O'Connor,
I do not think of Hemingway, or Katherine Anne Porter, or Sartre, but
rather of someone like Sophocles." Though O'Connor herself would
surely have scoffed at such praise, she is among a bare handful of
American writers, modern or otherwise, of whom such a thing might
plausibly be said.

But her reputation rests in part on a persistent misunderstanding.
Unlike most of the other major American novelists of the twentieth
century, O'Connor wrote not as a more or less secular humanist but
as a believer, a rigorously orthodox Roman Catholic. Her fiction was
permeated with religious language and symbolism, and its under-
lying intent was in many cases specifically spiritual. Yet most of

O'Connor's early critics failed to grasp her intentions, and even now many younger readers are ignorant of the true meaning of her work.

Brad Gooch's excellent book is likely to clear up this misunderstanding once and for all. *Flannery: A Life* is attractively written, thorough but not obtrusively detailed and—most important—wholly to the point. Unlike much of what has been published about O'Connor in recent years, it is the work of a biographer whose goal is not to advocate or justify but simply to tell the story of O'Connor's too-short life and (insofar as possible) show how it was mirrored in her fiction.

As Gooch makes clear, O'Connor's religious beliefs were central to her art. She was a "cradle Catholic," one of the very few novelists of her generation to have been born into the church rather than converting to Catholicism as an adult, and she appears never to have weathered any crisis of faith. What inspired her to write fiction, however, was not her own reasonably straightforward relationship to the Catholic Church so much as the church's more complex relationship to the world around her.

Roman Catholicism has long been viewed with suspicion in the South, where evangelical Protestantism in all its myriad varieties is woven into the fabric of a culture that is, in O'Connor's oft-quoted phrase, "Christ-haunted." O'Connor, on the other hand, was both a Catholic and an intellectual, a pair of traits that set her as far apart from the common life of rural Georgia as did the chronic illness that forced her to lead the reclusive existence of a semi-invalid.[1]

Yet O'Connor, to her credit, took the homespun beliefs of her fellow Southerners with the utmost seriousness. Even more surprisingly, she regarded them with exceptional imaginative sympathy, seeking to portray in her fiction the sometimes bizarre ways in which spiritual enthusiasm manifested itself in the lives of people who, lacking an orthodoxy to guide them, were forced to re-create the forms of religion from scratch. As she explained in a 1959 letter:

The religion of the South is a do-it-yourself religion, something which I as a Catholic find painful and touching and grimly comic. It's full of unconscious pride that lands them in all sorts of ridiculous religious predicaments. They have nothing to correct their practical heresies and so they work them out dramatically.

Her sympathy, she added, arose from the fact that "I accept the same fundamental doctrines of sin and redemption and judgment that they do."

Hence the ambiguity of *Wise Blood*, a concisely picaresque novel about Hazel Motes, an uneducated Southerner who longs to free himself from the Christianity in which he was raised but "cannot get rid of his sense of debt and his inner vision of Christ" (as O'Connor put it) and ends by blinding himself in order to better "see" his inner vision of divine grace. What gives *Wise Blood* its characteristic tone is that O'Connor plays Motes's desperate struggle for laughs—but without ever making the mistake of viewing it, or him, with contempt.

O'Connor, as *Wise Blood* proves, was no run-of-the-mill religious novelist. In addition to having a deeply philosophical turn of mind, she was a thoroughgoing modernist who adhered no less devoutly to the Jamesian precept to "dramatize, dramatize!" Moreover, her youthful reading of Jacques Maritain, the Catholic philosopher who argued in *Art and Scholasticism* (1930) that "the pure artist considered in the abstract as such . . . is something completely unmoral," had persuaded her that the serious Catholic fiction writer had no moral obligation to be preachy.

Between them, these two inclinations led O'Connor to write stories in which religious faith (or its absence) and its effects on her characters were portrayed with little or no explanatory authorial comment. Because these stories are in the broadest sense comic—and because they portray a culture of which most educated Americans of the fifties knew little or nothing—it was inevitable that they would be misunderstood by many of their first readers, who wrongly pigeonholed their author as a purveyor of the same Southern gothicism and grotesquery that they had previously encountered in such novels as Erskine Caldwell's *Tobacco Road* (1932) and Truman Capote's *Other Voices Other Rooms* (1948).

To be sure, the undeniable brilliance of O'Connor's writing won her near-immediate acclaim from the American intelligentsia. Her cause was promptly taken up by such noted editors and writers as Robert Giroux, Robert Lowell, Katherine Anne Porter, and Philip Rahv, who published two excerpts from *Wise Blood* in *Partisan Review*. But it soon became evident that some of those who most admired her writing failed to grasp its point, and the middlebrow publications of the day reviewed her with a blend of puzzlement and disdain.

Typical of the critical response to O'Connor's early work was *Time*'s unsigned review of *A Good Man Is Hard to Find* (1955), her first short-story collection, in which sympathetic detachment was mistaken for cutting satire:

> Georgia's Flannery O'Connor has already learned to strip the acres of clay-country individuality with the merciless efficiency of a cotton-picking machine. . . . The South that simpers, storms, and snivels in these pages moves along a sort of up-to-date *Tobacco Road,* paved right into town.

O'Connor was unsurprised by such obtuseness. "I have found," she wrote with dry amusement, "that anything that comes out of the South is going to be called grotesque by the Northern reader, unless it is grotesque, in which case it is going to be called realistic." Yet it vexed her all the same, and when *Wise Blood* was reissued in 1962, it was accompanied by a newly written author's note in which she called the book "a comic novel about a Christian *malgré lui*."[2]

Some of O'Connor's friends were dismayed by her decision to speak so frankly about the book's religious implications, no doubt because many of them, as Brad Gooch makes clear in *Flannery,* preferred not to believe that orthodox belief was so salient an aspect of her work. Even the usually sympathetic Gooch describes the note to *Wise Blood* as "rather heavy and blunt." By then, however, it had become apparent to most of O'Connor's critics that she was writing from a specifically religious perspective, though only a few saw that she identified herself with her Christ-haunted preachers and prophets.

Consider, for instance, the critical reception of *The Violent Bear it Away* (1960), a dark and shocking short novel whose protagonist, Francis Tarwater, is a fourteen-year-old boy torn between the crude but passionate Protestantism of his great-uncle, an angry old man who believes himself to be a prophet, and the bloodless secularism of his uncle, a school teacher who longs to bring the boy "out of the darkness into the light." Francis is ignorant, willful, and violent, and there is nothing obviously sympathetic about the way O'Connor describes him—but he has still been touched by grace, and so she sides with him in his quest. "The modern reader will identify himself with the school teacher," she told a friend, "but it is the old man who speaks for me." Yet *Time,* though its reviewer sensed something of O'Connor's larger purpose, failed to perceive her sympathy, claiming that the book showed "the secure believer poking bitter fun at the confused and bedeviled."

It was not until 1979, fifteen years after her death, that the full extent of O'Connor's orthodoxy became widely known. In that year a collection of her letters, *The Habit of Being,* was published, revealing her to have been a witty, engaging correspondent.[3] Paradoxically, it was *The Habit of Being* that cemented O'Connor's reputation, displaying her as a person in a way that her fiction never does (though *Flannery* reveals that a considerable amount of her private life made it onto the page, albeit in cryptic form). But O'Connor also tore the veil of symbolism away from *Wise Blood*, *The Violent Bear It Away*, and such widely anthologized stories as "A Good Man Is Hard to Find," writing with straightforward specificity about their religious aspect.

After the publication of *The Habit of Being*, there was no longer any excuse for readers to ignore or misinterpret the religious underpinnings of O'Connor's fiction, or to fail to take at face value her categorical statement that "I write the way I do because (not though) I am a Catholic. . . . The stories are hard but they are hard because there is nothing harder or less sentimental than Christian realism." By then, though, O'Connor's work had taken on a life of its own, and to this day it remains common for readers to assume that her comic portraits of Southern Protestantism are hostile rather than sympathetic.

Therein lies the O'Connor "problem," if problem it is. To what extent is her fiction accessible to those who do not take its religious wellsprings seriously? This is far more of a problem today than it was in the fifties and sixties, for American intellectual culture has lately become almost entirely secularized, and it begs a hard question: Will O'Connor's work survive only by being misunderstood?

It is true that she has much to offer beyond her spirituality. O'Connor was also a consummate craftsman whose stories are both beautifully wrought and closely observed. A case in point is "Parker's Back," a story from *Everything That Rises Must Converge* (1965), her second and last collection, on which she was working at the time of her death. She describes a small-town boy who sees a man covered with tattoos at a fair and immediately undergoes something like a conversion experience:

> Parker had never before felt the least motion of wonder in himself. Until he saw the man at the fair, it did not enter his head that there was anything out of the ordinary about the fact that he existed. Even then it did not enter his head, but a peculiar unease settled in him. It was as if a blind boy had been turned so gently in a different direction that he did not know his destination had been changed.

In many of O'Connor's best stories, "Parker's Back" prominent among them, the religious theme is so subtly dramatized that it can be overlooked by casual readers unaware of the author's larger purpose. Whatever else her fiction is, it is not Catholic propaganda.[4] In the end, though, a critical approach that denies or downplays O'Connor's faith will necessarily result in only a partial appreciation of her work. It is no more possible to understand a book like *Wise Blood* without taking Catholicism seriously—if only to reject it—than it is possible to understand the fiction of Isaac Bashevis Singer without taking Judaism seriously.

The difference, of course, is that Singer viewed religion with reluctant skepticism, O'Connor with unswerving certitude. As I once wrote in these pages:

> O'Connor's Christ-haunted characters differ profoundly from Singer's demon-infested Jews. In O'Connor, unbelievers living in a fallen world tainted by modernity suddenly find themselves irradiated by grace, but, like Hazel Motes . . . they struggle in vain against its revelatory power. In Singer's world, by contrast, there are no sudden revelations, only the

unquenchable desire to believe, against all evidence to the contrary, that life has meaning.[5]

Might O'Connor's faith cause the brilliance of her art to fade in an age of increasingly militant secularism whose cultural tastemakers do not share her beliefs? The fact that her reputation has continued to grow when so many of her contemporaries have become critical also-rans says something about her staying power. Yet there have always been doubters. In 1972, O'Connor was posthumously given the National Book Award for an omnibus volume of her complete stories. Robert Giroux, her longtime editor, was accosted at the ceremony by a dubious colleague who asked, "Do you really think Flannery O'Connor was a great writer? She's such a Roman Catholic."

It will be interesting—and revealing—to see whether that question is asked with increasing frequency in the years to come.

[1] Throughout her adult life O'Connor suffered from lupus, a physically debilitating autoimmune disease that ultimately led to her death.

[2] That is, a believer in spite of himself. The reference is to Molière, the greatest of comic playwrights, and his play *The Physician In Spite of Himself* (*Le médecin malgré lui*).

[3] Most of the letters originally published in *The Habit of Being* are included in *Flannery O'Connor: Collected Works,* along with twenty-one additional unpublished letters.

[4] Nor is it conservative in any meaningful sense of the word, though critics on the Right have long warmed to the savagely funny parodies of liberal humanism that are found in *The Violent Bear It Away* and such stories as "Good Country People" (from *A Good Man Is Hard to Find*) and "The Lame Shall Enter First" (from *Everything That Rises Must Converge*). O'Connor's "conservatism," such as it was, was exclusively religious in its orientation. She had no political interests of any kind beyond a Southerner's understandable interest in racial segregation (which she opposed).

[5] "I. B. Singer and Me," *Commentary*, September 2004.

RICHARD WILBUR

Trismegistus

FROM *The New Yorker*

O Egypt, Egypt—so the great lament
Of thrice-great Hermes went—
Nothing of thy religion shall remain
Save fables, which thy children shall disdain.
His grieving eye foresaw
The world's bright fabric overthrown
Which married star to stone
And charged all things with awe.

And what, in that dismantled world, could be
More fabulous than he?
Had he existed? Was he but a name
Tacked on to forgeries which pressed the claim
Of every ancient quack—
That one could from a smoky cell
By talisman or spell
Coerce the Zodiac?

Still, still we summon him *at midnight hour*
To Milton's pensive tower,
And hear him tell again how, then and now,

Creation is a house of mirrors, how
Each herb that sips the dew
Dazzles the eye with many small
Reflections of the All—
Which, after all, is true.

ROBERT LOUIS WILKEN

Christianity Face to Face with Islam

FROM *First Things*

No event during the first millennium was more unexpected, more calamitous, and more consequential for Christianity than the rise of Islam. Few irruptions in history have transformed societies so completely and irrevocably as did the conquest and expansion of the Arabs in the seventh century. And none came with greater swiftness. Within a decade three major cities in the Byzantine Christian Empire—Damascus in 635, Jerusalem in 638, and Alexandria in 641—fell to the invaders.

When reports began to circulate that something unusual was happening in the Arabian Peninsula, the Byzantines were preoccupied with the Sassanians in Persia who had sacked Jerusalem in 614 and made off with the relic of the True Cross. And in the West they were menaced by the Avars, a Mongolian people who had moved into the Balkans and were threatening Constantinople. Rumors about the emergence of a powerful leader among the Arabs in the distant Hijaz seemed no cause for alarm.

Even on the eve of the conquest of Jerusalem, when Arab armies had encircled the holy city and blocked the road to Bethlehem, the patriarch of Jerusalem, Sophronius, assured the faithful: "We will laugh at the demise of our enemies the Saracens [as Christians first called the Muslims] and in a short time see their destruction and complete ruin." Fourteen hundred years later the Muslims are still in Jerusalem, and with each passing decade Islam figures larger in the minds of Christians, penetrates more deeply into Christian societies, and, by its fixed and impermeable tenancy of a large part of the globe, circumscribes the practice of Christianity.

From the day Caliph Umar was met by the patriarch Sophronius in Jerusalem in the mid-seventh century, Christianity has found itself face to face with Islam. Though the circumstances have varied from place to place and century to century, Islam has always presented a challenge. Yet, in the course of a long history, during which Islam expanded all over the world, Christians, with the exception of those who lived in the Middle East in the early centuries of Muslim rule, have seldom taken Islam with the seriousness it deserves or recognized it for what it is—a religion in the biblical tradition in which piety is wedded to statecraft. A "complacent ignorance" (in the phrase of the modern scholar Lamin Sanneh) has prevailed, especially in the West.

Before the Muslim conquest, Christians could look back confidently on six hundred years of steady growth and expansion. By the year 300, churches were found in all the cities of the Roman Empire, from Spain and North Africa in the west to Egypt and Syria in the east, as well as in Asia Minor and the Balkans. In the fourth century the Armenians embraced the new religion, and on the eastern shore of the Black Sea the preaching of St. Nino led to the conversion of the Iberian royal house and the adoption of the Christian faith by the Georgians. To the south, Christianity reached Ethiopia in the fourth century and Nubia a century later. And there were Christian communities in Roman Gaul already in the second century and in Britain by the third century.

No less impressive was the spread of Christianity eastward. Accustomed to the colorful maps of Paul's missionary journeys printed in study Bibles, we are inclined to think that the initial expansion took place in the Mediterranean world. But in the vast region east of

Jerusalem—Syria, Jordan, and Iraq, where Aramaic was the *lingua franca*—the majority of people had become Christian by the seventh century. The Christian gospel was carried even farther east to ancient Persia, and from there it traveled along the Silk Road into Central Asia: Uzbekistan, Tajikistan, Afghanistan. At some point during the first six centuries it reached the western shore of India and even China. In the seventh century, the global center of Christianity lay not in Europe but to the east of Jerusalem.

Though the people of this vast area spoke many languages and had different customs, through Christianity they were linked together in the confession of the creed of Nicaea. They baptized their infants in the name of the Father and of the Son and of the Holy Spirit, offered the sacrifice of the Eucharist in their churches, were governed by bishops, revered the lives of ascetic men and women living in monastic communities, and had in common a holy book.

Archaeologists have uncovered fragments of ancient Christian texts that make the point powerfully. At both Antrim in Northern Ireland and in Panjikent, near Samarkand, in present-day Uzbekistan, copybooks were found from about the year 700 (wax on wood in Ireland and potsherds in Asia), each containing verses from the Psalms. In Ireland, the schoolboy whose language was Irish had written the psalm verses in Latin, and in Panjikent, the boy whose language was Soghdian had written his lesson in Syriac.

When one considers the extent of Christianity in the year 600, the deep roots Christians had set down all over the world as they knew it, and the interconnectedness of the churches, it is no wonder that Christians had difficulty grasping that the Arab armies occupying their cities were not simply conquerors seeking booty but heralds of a spiritually potent religion and architects of a new civilization.

The first recorded comment of a Christian reaction to Muhammad dates from only a couple of years after his death. When tales of a prophet among the Arabs reached Christian Syria, someone asked an old man, "What can you tell me about the prophet who has appeared with the Saracens?" The old man groaned deeply and said, "He is false, for the prophets do not come armed with a sword." He had in mind of course the Hebrew prophets, Elijah or Isaiah or Amos. A prophet is one called to *speak* for God.

But his memory of the Bible was imperfect, for he had overlooked the greatest of the prophets before Jesus: Moses. Like the later prophets, Moses was certainly called to speak for God, but, unlike Isaiah or Ezekiel, Moses was also a political and military leader and, let it not be forgotten, a lawgiver. And he carried a sword: In the Book of Numbers, we learn that he armed a thousand men from each tribe of Israel to take vengeance on the Midianites.

It is this biblical prophet, Moses, who was the model for Muhammad. Though Muslims see Abraham as the first to believe in the one God—and thus the first *muslim* and the ancestor of the Arabs through Ishmael—the prophet mentioned most often in the Qur'an is Moses. Muhammad was, like Moses in the words of St. Stephen in the Acts of the Apostles, "powerful in words and deeds."

And the early spread of Islam was an affair of deeds: vigorous, venturesome, irresistible deeds. In the span of less than a hundred years, Arab commanders made their way from the edge of Egypt along the North African littoral until they reached the Atlantic Ocean. From the Arabian Peninsula they also advanced northeast through Persia and across the Asian steppes to India. The Arabs reached Sind, today a province in Pakistan, in 711. And within the same decade, after crossing the Strait of Gibraltar into Christian Spain, they crossed the Pyrenees and penetrated southern France, to be halted finally at the battle of Poitiers in 732.

By the beginning of the eighth century, Muslims had created in these disparate and distant regions a new community formed by common beliefs and practices and held together in a loose unity by the caliphate established in the ancient Christian city of Damascus. As new territories were conquered, garrison towns arose. The Arabs brought their wives and children, built mosques, and over time founded such new cities as Basra and Kufah in Iraq, Fustat (old Cairo) in Egypt, and Kairouan in Tunisia. By keeping themselves apart initially from the local societies, they were able to maintain their identity in a sea of strange people and gradually displace the culture that had dominated the region for a thousand years.

Soon Islam began to take hold among the conquered peoples— and one reason was that they were already familiar with the biblical tradition on which the Qur'an drew. For example, an entire surah is devoted to the biblical Joseph, the son of the patriarch Jacob, viceroy of Egypt.

At first Arabic was spoken only by the Arabs, but by the end of the seventh century, during the caliphates of Abd al-Malik and his son Hisham, Arabic became the language of administration, commerce, and learning as well as of religion. To replace the Byzantine currency, gold coins were minted with Arabic legends carrying a reproach to Christians: "There is no god but God alone. He has no companion." A public cult supported by political authority was established, calling for an annual month of fasting, prayer five times a day, recitation of the Qur'an on Fridays, and the *khutba,* an address before prayers.

In other ways Abd al-Malik claimed the public space for Islam. In a dramatic political gesture, he built the Dome of the Rock on the Temple Mount in Jerusalem, altering forever the skyline and character of the holy city. On interior as well as exterior walls, inscriptions emphatically proclaim the central tenets of Islam. "There is no God but God and Muhammad is his prophet." The phrase "God has no companion," an explicit critique of the Christian doctrine of the Trinity, occurs no less than five times. Abd al-Malik also appointed judges to administer the emerging body of law on matters of ritual, marriage, inheritance, and property. Over time, the law of Shari'a, more an evolving body of social practices than a fixed code, became a defining mark of Muslim identity. Its significance for the Muslim is as much psychological as legal, which helps explain why it packs such emotional force in Muslim countries to this day.

Within the space of a century, the movement inaugurated by the prophet Muhammad had planted a permanent political and religious rival to Christianity in historic Christian lands. Its advance both to the West and to the East meant that a large part of the globe was claimed for Islam, fulfilling the words of the Qur'an: "We appointed you successors on the earth after them." For Christians these territories proved irrecoverable. Four hundred years later, when the Crusaders arrived in the East, the Arab historian Ibn Athīr said that they had entered "the lands of Islam."

Little of this was apparent to Christian observers in the early years, or at least few were willing to acknowledge what was happening before their eyes. John of Damascus, who lived during the reign of Abd al-Malik at the beginning of the eighth century, wrote a polemical account of Muhammad based on his reading of the Qur'an. But in his book he places Muhammad in the section on "heresies" and depicts him as a descendant of the arch-heretic Arius: a teacher of a truncated version of Christian truth. At some abstract level that may be true, and it does show that he thought Islam and Christianity share a common spiritual lineage, but it is noteworthy that he treats Muhammad solely in theological or religious terms, ignoring the cultural and political changes that he wrought.

About the same time, a monk writing in Syriac in the region of Basra had a keener sense of what Islam meant for Christians. In a dialogue between a Christian monk and a Muslim official, he has the Muslim official say: If your religion is true, "why has God handed you over into our hands?"

By the year 750, a hundred years after the conquest of Jerusalem, at least 50 percent of the world's Christians found themselves under

Muslim hegemony. In some regions, most notably North Africa, Christianity went into precipitous decline. At the time of the Arab conquest there were more than three hundred bishops in the area, but by the tenth century Pope Benedict VII could not find three bishops to consecrate a new bishop. Today there is no indigenous Christianity in the region, no communities of Christians whose history can be traced to antiquity. Though originally conquered by the sword, most of the subject peoples eventually embraced the religion of their conquerors. By a gradual process of soft coercion, Islam was able to gain the loyalty and kindle the affections of those who were subjugated and make them part of the Muslim *umma*—no small accomplishment.

In greater Syria—including the Holy Land, Egypt, and Iraq—the rights and privileges of Christians were limited by their legal status as *dhimmis*: members of a restricted and inferior minority subject to an onerous tax. Still, Christian intellectual life flourished. In the early centuries under Islam, Christians participated in the vigorous and enterprising culture being created by the Muslims. They gradually made the transition to Arabic—a delicate undertaking, because much of the religious vocabulary in Arabic came from the Qur'an. They wrote apologetic works in defense of Christianity and engaged in debate with Muslim thinkers on points of practice, doctrine, and philosophy. Even a partial listing of Christian thinkers writing in Arabic during this period is impressive: theologians such as Theodore Abu-Qurrah (a bishop in Harran, in southeastern Turkey) and Timothy I (catholicos of the Church of the East in Baghdad), such translators as Anthony David of Baghdad and Stephen of Ramlah in Palestine, and such philosophers as Hunayn ibn Ishāq and Yahya ibn 'Adi in Baghdad. Though their names have been mostly forgotten, their writings have endured, offering a precious resource for Christians as they address Islam today.

By the eleventh century, however, Christianity had begun a long demographic decline in its eastern homeland, and, carried by the militancy of the Turks, Islam resumed its relentless drive westward. The end of the eleventh century also marked the beginning of the First Crusade.

In recent years, there has been much moralistic posturing over the brutality of the Crusaders and thoughtless pontificating about their historical import. Out of ignorance, many conveniently ignore that the Crusades were part of a Christian counteroffensive against the occupation of lands that had been Christian for centuries before the arrival of Islam. In the Iberian Peninsula, Christians had begun to reconquer lost territories in the center of the country (including Toledo), the Byzantines had launched new offensives in Syria and Anatolia, and, further east, the Georgians and Armenians had rebelled against Muslim overlords. The Crusades do not stand alone; they were an understandable attempt on the part of the Christian world to halt the advance of Islam and reclaim Christian territory, including the holy city of Jerusalem.

But the Crusades ended in failure. For a brief period Christian kingdoms were established in the Holy Land and in parts of Syria, but in less than two centuries the territories were reclaimed for Islam. No doubt that is why Muslim memory (until recently) viewed the Crusades as a transient epoch, a regretful intervention by outsiders but less significant than the devastation brought by the Mongols. The Franks were simply another enemy. Only as the Crusades have been put at the service of contemporary agendas, both in the West and in the Muslim world, have they become viewed as a cause célèbre.

In the long view of history, and especially from a Christian perspective, the Turkish conquest of Asia Minor was of far greater significance. The arrival of the Turks prepared the way for the displacement of the Greek-speaking Christians in Byzantine Anatolia, the planting of Islam in the Balkans, and the fall of Constantinople in 1453. Though many books have been written about Constantinople, most notably Steven

Runciman's gripping narrative, little has been said about the gradual dissolution of Christianity in Asia Minor in the centuries leading up to the fall of Constantinople. There is no more heart-rending chapter in Christian history than this and, in the telling of the Christian past, none more completely forgotten—a reminder, as W. H. Auden once wrote, that "dreadful martyrdom must run its course in a corner." In poignant contrast to the Crusades, what happened in Asia Minor had far greater consequences, not merely as an event for historians and pundits to debate but in the hard intractable facts of demography.

Consider some statistics. In the eleventh century, the population of Asia Minor was almost wholly Christian. By the sixteenth century, Muslims constituted 92 percent of the population. During those centuries, the Church lost most of its property, its ecclesiastical structures were dismantled, and its bishops prohibited from caring for their dioceses. At the beginning of the period, there were four hundred bishops; by the end, 97 percent had been eliminated. Because there was no centralized state, only petty rulers, a *dhimmi* system was never put fully into place. As Muslim institutions flourished, the Christian population fled, and the disoriented and dispirited who remained gradually adopted the religion of their masters. Today there are only tiny remnants of ancient Christian communities in Turkey.

As a result of Turkish victories, by the beginning of the sixteenth century Islam had a new powerful political center in Constantinople and was putting down roots in southeastern Europe, where it remains to this day. The establishment of Turkish kingdoms in Asia Minor and the Balkans accomplished for the lands northeast of the Mediterranean what the Arabs had done in the countries on its southern shore, in greater Syria, and in the Fertile Crescent.

When Edward Gibbon introduced the prophet Muhammad in his *Decline and Fall of the Roman Empire*, he observed that the rise of Islam was "one of the most memorable revolutions, which have

impressed a new and lasting character on the nations of the globe."
Gibbon saw that Islam did not just inaugurate a religious revolution.
Its unparalleled expansion changed the course of history by altering
the map of the world and creating a new geography.

It is that singular and adamantine fact that we must ponder in
thinking about Christianity as it faces Islam. A few years ago *National Geographic* published a handsome volume with the title *The Geography of Religion*. As one would expect, besides its beautiful pictures of religious buildings and of rituals from all parts of the globe,
it also includes a map of the world. On it the continents are colored
to identify the dominant religions in the various regions. India, for
example, where 75 percent of the population is Hindu, is colored
orange. Orthodox Russia and Eastern Europe are colored purple, and
Catholic Latin America is colored lilac. But the largest contiguous
area, colored green, is occupied by Islam, which occupies a huge land
mass extending from the Atlantic Ocean in the West to Pakistan and
Bangladesh in the East.

We are all familiar with textbook accounts of Christianity as a
tale of growth and expansion as it spread from the countries on the
shores of the Mediterranean into northern Europe, flowered in the
High Middle Ages, was rent by the Reformation, crossed the Atlantic
Ocean, was chastened by the Enlightenment, and then, in the wake
of the great missionary movements of the nineteenth and twentieth
centuries, underwent a period of phenomenal growth in the Southern Hemisphere and in Asia. In this rendering of the last two millennia, Christianity and the West sit atop the summit of civilization.

If, however, one injects into this sanguine narrative the story
of Islam, things take on a different coloring. Set against the history of
Islam, the career of Christianity is marked as much by decline and
extinction as it is by growth and triumph. By a selective choice of
periods, events, and geographical regions, the conventional account

(the one imagined from the perspective of Europe and North America) gives the impression of continuous progress.

But seen in global perspective, that may be illusory. To state the obvious: Most of the territories that were Christian in the year 700 are now Muslim. Nothing similar has happened to Islam. Christianity seems like a rain shower that soaks the earth and then moves on, whereas Islam appears more like a great lake that constantly overflows its banks to inundate new territory. When Islam arrives, it comes to stay—unless displaced by force, as it was in Spain. But the shameful expulsion of Muslims from Spain is hardly an event Christians would wish to celebrate today.

There are exceptions, of course: Ancient Christian lands such as Greece, Armenia, and Ethiopia remain Christian. Yet when the matter is viewed geographically, these countries seem perched on the edge of a much larger and expanding Islamic world. There is good reason to be troubled over the supine acquiescence of Europeans today at the collapse of Christianity as a social and cultural force and over the mounting number of Muslims living in France, Germany, and Britain. Though Christianity was able to create a great civilization, it seems incapable of preventing its dissolution.

Europe's place in Christian history is singular and without parallel. Rome, the most hallowed city in Western Christianity, was the home of a Christian community at the beginning, as St. Paul's letter to the Church in Rome attests. Centuries later, in alliance with Rome, Christians north of the Alps created Europe and, in modern times, European Christians and their descendants carried the faith to all parts of the world. And in the younger churches, at least in the early years, it was European forms of Christianity that were set in place.

Christianity has had an abiding physical presence in Europe. The bonds of affection are attached to place: Its churches, shrines, tombs, and pilgrimage sites were imprinted deeply on the Christian soul.

The demise of Christianity in Europe and the ascendancy of Islam would be a crippling blow to the continuity of Christian memory and the sense that the Church is the carrier of an ancient, unbroken, living tradition that reaches back through time to the apostles and to Jesus. Memory is an integral part of Christian faith, but unattached to things it is infinitely malleable, even evanescent, like a story whose veracity is diluted as its particulars are forgotten. Without tangible links to the past mediated through communities tethered to the earth, something precious is lost. "Walk about Zion," sang the psalmist, "go round about her, number her towers, consider well her ramparts, go through her citadels, that you may tell the next generation that this is God, our God for ever and ever."

If Christianity continues to decline in Europe and becomes a minority religion, its history will appear fragmentary and episodic and its claim to universality further diminished by the shifting patterns of geography. And without the bridge of Western Europe, the Slavic Christians in Eastern Europe and Russia, bearers of the ancient Byzantine tradition, would be isolated from the Christian world. At the end of *After Virtue,* Alasdair MacIntyre wrote that we are waiting for another St. Benedict. In my wanton and admittedly darker ruminations, I sometimes wonder whether what Christianity needs is not so much a new Benedict as a new Charlemagne.

But, of course, that is an idle thought. No matter how great the accomplishments of Christian kings and emperors, that chapter in Christian history is closed. True, one can point to the astonishing growth of Christianity in the Southern Hemisphere, especially in Africa and Asia, and to the unbounded enthusiasm evangelicals and Pentecostals have brought to the Christian mission. But energy and enthusiasm are no substitute for deep roots, vital and durable institutions, and a thick and vibrant culture. Will the younger churches have the staying power to pass on the faith in its fullness generation after generation and give rise to distinctly Christian societies? And how will they fare in the face of aggressive Muslim communities alongside which some live?

Which brings me back to the geography of religion. The Islamic revolution is more far-reaching than could be sensed when Gibbon was writing in eighteenth-century Europe. Take Africa, for example: Though Christianity came to Mediterranean Africa in the second century, with the exception of Ethiopia and Nubia it did not spread south into the continent. Islam, however, penetrated early into sub-Saharan Africa from Libya and Morocco and crossed the Red Sea from the Arabian Peninsula to Zanzibar to reach trading centers along the eastern coast of Africa. With its deeper roots, Islam has had far greater cultural influence on that continent than has Christianity. Here, too, looking at a map is instructive. Islam is dominant not only in North Africa but also across a band of contiguous states in sub-Saharan Africa: from Senegal in the west to the Sudan in the east and down the coast. When we hear statistics of the growth of Christianity in Africa, it must be remembered that they apply only to the southern third of the continent.

In Nigeria, for example, there are many Christians and the number is growing, but Christianity is a relative newcomer to the region. Where Islam traces its history in western Africa to the eleventh century, and a Muslim kingdom was established in what is now Nigeria in the fifteenth century, the Christian mission in Nigeria began in earnest only in the nineteenth century. The northern regions of the country are largely Muslim and share a common culture with the belt of Islamic states stretching across Central Africa. In recent decades, the Muslim population in the north of the country has grown increasingly assertive, calling for a wider application of Islamic law within society. This effort has been resisted by Christians, but in 1999 and 2000 various forms of Islamic law were implemented in twelve of Nigeria's thirty-six states. Muslims have also pressed Nigeria to join the OIC, the Organization of the Islamic Conference, an association of fifty-six Islamic states promoting Muslim solidarity in economic, social, and political affairs.

Of even greater significance is the growth and establishment of Islam in Southeast Asia, in the archipelago between the Bay of Bengal and the China Sea. From India, Islam spread along trade routes into the region and, by the sixteenth century, Muslims had become the dominant religion in what is today Malaysia and Indonesia. Here Islam made its way not by military conquest but peaceably, through the gradual conversion of people who had contact with Muslim traders and through the quiet labors of itinerant Sufi preachers. With Muslim growth came Muslim culture and law and, eventually, Muslim rule.

In a way that is not true of Christianity, Islam is territorial. One of Islam's most enduring innovations was that religious law became also the law of the body politic. Shari'a is more encompassing than the Church's canon law, and historically its authority depended on a community with territorial boundaries and political jurisdiction. This understanding is of course being tested today and has been debated by Muslim thinkers since the nineteenth century. But most Muslims in the world live in countries in which Islam occupies a conspicuous public space in society. Even in countries such as India, where Muslims do not make up the majority, the feeling of solidarity and belonging runs deep.

There is a moment in E. M. Forster's *Passage to India* in which the British headmaster Cyril Fielding and his young Muslim friend Dr. Aziz are having a conversation about their different approaches to life. Fielding says, "I travel light." Aziz thinks: "So this is why Mr. Fielding and others were so fearless! They had nothing to lose. But he [Aziz] himself was rooted in society and Islam. He belonged to a tradition which bound him, and he had brought children into the world, the society of the future. Though he lived so vaguely in this flimsy bungalow, nevertheless he was placed, placed."

This sense of placement, of being defined by one's social world, is still very much alive among many Muslims. For centuries Islam has been the bearer of a spiritual and prophetic vision of the ordering of human society on the basis of worship of the one God. This vision continues to discipline the lives and marshal the energies of millions of people in different social, political, ethnic, and linguistic settings.

There is no sign that it is faltering today. As a religion, Islam has had remarkable tenacity. Although in science, in the humanities, in technology, and in statecraft the West has far outdistanced the Muslim world, the practice of Islam has not been dislodged by the political and cultural hegemony of the West. As Muslims have struggled to come to terms with modernity as we know it in the West, Islam as a religion has not gone into remission. The remarkable truth is that the peoples and societies that were part of the Muslim world five centuries ago have remained resolutely and unreservedly Islamic.

Turkey is a good example of the resilience of Islam in modern times. Here is a historically Muslim country whose constitution, law, institutions, schools, and mores were forcibly stripped of religion early in the twentieth century—reshaped to conform to a coercive secularism based on ideas of *laïcité* derived from the French. Religious teachers were divested of authority and religious schools closed. Men were required to give up the traditional head covering and adopt Western brimmed hats that made it impossible to prostrate in prayer. Women were forbidden to wear the veil. The traditional day of prayer and rest, Friday, was abandoned and Sunday put in its place.

In the last several decades, however, the practice of Islam has undergone a revival, and religious Turks have gained political power through democratic means. Though the roots of the Justice and Development Party, the present government, are Islamist, its leaders have behaved as centrists, and some have compared them to the center-right Christian democratic parties in Western Europe. Even the *New York Times* and the *Washington Post* portray their opponents, the secularists, as old-fashioned, ideological, and undemocratic. Almost a century after Kemalism, an authoritarian secularism, was imposed on the Turkish people, the overwhelming majority of the population remains Muslim, and Islam has reasserted itself in the public square. It is hard to imagine something similar happening to Christianity in Britain or France.

By focusing on what went wrong, on Islamic terrorism, on Wahhabism, or on radical Islamists, we miss ways in which Islam is adapting constructively to a changing world. The Columbia University historian Richard Bulliet argues that, until there is a fundamental reconsideration of Islam, the word will continue to sound to Western ears "like a rattlesnake's rattle." If we see Islam as a historical relic, incapable of change and betterment, inimical to reason and science, a form of religion that is disadvantaged in the modern world, we will never grasp the formidable challenge it presents to Christianity. Bulliet calls attention to what he calls "edge" situations, areas of Muslim life where significant developments are taking place: in Muslim diaspora communities in Europe and North America; in democratically oriented political parties in Muslim majority countries, such as Turkey; and in education, either traditional religious schools or universities, as in Indonesia.

I am no apologist for Islam. Over its long history, Islam has been very bad for Christianity. In North Africa and Asia Minor, the arrival of Muslim armies led in a short period of time to the destruction of Christian communities. In the Middle East, *dhimmitude* was a suffocating institution that eventually sucked the oxygen out of communities, turning them in on themselves as they bent their energies to the sole end of survival. Although during the early centuries of Muslim rule there was fruitful intellectual and cultural intercourse, it did not last and has largely been forgotten. To this day a great part of the world remains effectively closed off to Christians.

Violence has been a persistent strain in Muslim history. Even as sympathetic an interpreter as Marshall Hodgson, in his magisterial *The Venture of Islam,* acknowledged that the vision of the prophet Muhammad "led inevitably to the sword." It is a "peculiar test of Islam," he says, as to "how Muslims can meet the question of war." So there is much to ponder and, for Christians living in the Muslim world, much to fear.

Given the experience of centuries, it is tempting for Christians to see Islam as the enemy: Often it has been the enemy. But if that remains our dominant paradigm for looking at the religion, we deny something of ourselves. Christianity's historic mission was to bring the worship of the one God, the God of Abraham and Isaac and Jacob, to the nations. Let us not forget that the first and greatest sin is idolatry, to worship something other than the one God as god. "You shall have no other gods before me," reads the first commandment. Christians confess, "We believe in one God, the Father, the Almighty, Maker of heaven and earth," and Muslims recite, "There is no god but God and Muhammad is his messenger."

The kinship between Christianity and Islam is deeper than the centuries of conflict would lead one to think. To mention only one example: the collaboration of Christians and Muslims in the ninth and tenth centuries in the translation and interpretation of philosophical works from Greek antiquity into Arabic and their transmission to the West in translations from Arabic into Latin in the eleventh and twelfth centuries.

The significance here is twofold. First, long before the major writings of Aristotle were known in the West, Muslim thinkers had appropriated the Greek philosophical tradition. The continuity of Western philosophical thought depends in part on the contribution of Muslim thinkers. Second, because Islam, like Christianity, is grounded in the revelation of a transcendent God, a free creator, Muslim thinkers addressed a series of philosophical and theological topics—God and the world, creation out of nothing, the freedom of God, faith and reason—

that Christian thinkers would also take up. The resulting dialogue raised the level of sophistication of Western thought and helped Christian thinkers clarify and deepen their own approach to similar issues.

Although the divide between Christianity and Islam is great and the search for a usable past looks unpromising, Christians must learn, as the bishops at Vatican II put it, to look on Muslims "with respect." For "they worship the one God living and subsistent, merciful and almighty, creator of heaven and earth, who has spoken to humanity and to whose decrees, even the hidden ones, they seek to submit themselves whole-heartedly, just as Abraham, to whom the Islamic faith readily relates itself, submitted to God."

Within the last two years, there have been two serious efforts by Muslim leaders to reach out to the Christian world. The first was an open letter to Benedict XVI a month after his lecture at the University of Regensburg. The violence that erupted in the Muslim world after the speech made the headlines, but the letter, largely ignored in the American press, was more significant. In it Muslim leaders from all over the world prepared an irenic, thoughtful, and critical response to the pope's comments on the use of reasons—the heart of the pope's speech—and criticized Muslim extremists.

A year later, in fall 2007, a longer statement of Muslim leaders was addressed to Christian leaders East and West, Roman Catholic, Orthodox, Protestant, and Evangelical, entitled "A Common Word Between Us and You." In the long history of Muslim-Christian relations, it is unprecedented that a group of Muslim thinkers from different parts of the world and differing views should collaborate on a positive overture to Christians. From the beginning Islam has been a harsh critic of the central teachings of Christianity. "A Common Word Between Us and You," however, draws extensively on the New Testament to argue that Christians, like Muslims, teach that love of the one God is the first and greatest religious truth.

The authors link the words of the Prophet's message directly to the biblical tradition. In proclaiming "there is no god but God," these Muslim leaders write, the Prophet Muhammad was echoing the first and greatest commandment to love God with all one's heart and soul, as found in the Bible. "That is to say . . . the prophet Muhammad was perhaps, through inspiration, restating and alluding to the Bible's first commandment."

Still, Islam is more than a faith, and Christianity cannot relate to it simply as one religion to another without reference to social, cultural, and political factors. As useful as theological dialogue may be, one cannot ignore the facts on the ground. And the most significant fact is this: The vast geographical extent of the Muslim world offers an exceptionally sturdy base of piety, learning, and culture for expansion. It is often said that the great story of the twenty-first century will be the conflict between Christianity and Islam. From the partial view of these first few years in the century, that certainly seems true. But if the Islam we imagine is the one that makes the morning headlines or the evening news, our sight will be as constricted as that of the Christian inhabitants of Byzantine Syria when the Muslims began to construct a new civilization in their midst. Only if we move to a higher elevation to view Islam on a large historical and geographical panorama will we have the vision to take the measure of the determination, strength, and resources Muslims are likely to display in the decades to come.

Christianity cannot escape Islam's political geography. A part of the world will remain off limits for Christian witness, and the future is bleak for Christians living in Muslim countries. In the Middle East (with the exception of such countries as Egypt and Lebanon, where Christians are still numerous), Christians will have difficulty existing even as minorities. And in countries on the edge of the Muslim world, such as Nigeria, where Christians make up a large and growing part of the population, they will find themselves on the defensive as Muslims seek to implement Muslim law in society. And, of course, as their numbers mount in Europe, Muslims will be increasingly assertive in claiming public space for the practice of Islam.

The question to be asked, then, is whether, face to face with Islam, Christians will be able to sustain, rebuild, and create strong and resilient communities that provide institutional anchorage for the faith to endure and flourish. Will they have the imagination to form the spiritual architecture of the societies of which they are a part? This is a task for which Christianity is particularly well suited. It has a much longer lineage than Islam, it has taken many different cultural forms in the course of its history, and it has passed through the fires of modernity. It has a deeper and more coherent relation to its own tradition, including the cultural patrimony of classical antiquity. And it commands the intellectual resources to understand and engage other religious traditions as well as to provide moral inspiration for secular societies.

Unlike Islam, Christianity began as a community distinct from the body politic, and for three hundred years it existed independently of political authority. This early history has never been forgotten. Even in the time of Christian hegemony in the West, during the age of Charlemagne, Abbot Wala of Corbie insisted that the Church constituted a parallel sovereignty. The king, he said, should have public properties for the maintenance of his army, and the Church should have "church properties, almost like a second public domain."

Augustine's metaphor for the new life in Christ was not that of an individual's being born again but that of becoming part of a city with its own form of governance. "Happy the people whose God is the Lord," wrote the psalmist. Though some may eschew the term, in the decades to come the great challenge for Christians will be to fashion, within the cultural and political conditions of the twenty-first century, a new kind of Christendom.

NANCY WILLARD

Ian's Angels

FROM *Image*

The first angel Ian drew
was silent as the sun
on empty fields of snow.
Nothing was fast or slow,
the world not yet begun.

The second angel Ian drew
sang green out of the ground.
Birds of the air, rejoice.
Let fire find its voice,
each river its own sound.

The third angel Ian drew
wore vestments pale as sand.
A message printed there
would let earth speak to air.
But from whose hand?

The fourth angel Ian drew
packed darkness in its wings
for planets, bright or dim,

for moons riding the rim
of day. For unborn things.

The fifth angel Ian drew
turned into a door.
It opened into space.
I never saw its face,
only the light it wore.

C. K. WILLIAMS

The Foundation

FROM *The New Yorker*

1.
Watch me, I'm running, watch me, I'm dancing, I'm air;
the building I used to live in has been razed and I'm skipping,
hopping, two-footedly leaping across the blocks, bricks,
slabs of concrete, plaster, and other unnameable junk . . .

Or nameable, really, if you look at the wreckage closely . . .
Here, for instance, this shattered I-beam is the Bible,
and this chunk of mortar? Plato, the mortar of mind,
also in pieces, in pieces in me, anyway, in my mind . . .

Aristotle and Nietzsche, Freud and Camus and Buber,
and Christ, even, that year of reading "Paradise Lost,"
when I thought, Hell, why not? but that fractured, too . . .
Kierkegaard, Hegel, and Kant, and Goffman and Marx,

all heaped in the foundation, and I've sped through so often
that now I have it by heart, can run, dance, be air,
not think of the spew of intellectual dust I scuffed up
when in my barely broken-in boots I first clumped through

the sanctums of Buddhism, Taoism. Zen, and the Areopagite,
even, whose entire text I typed out—my god, why?—
I didn't care, I just kept bumping my head on the lintels,
Einstein, the Gnostics, Kabbalah, Saint This and Saint That . . .

2.
Watch me again now, because I'm not alone in my dancing,
my being air, I'm with my poets, my Rilke, my Yeats,
we're leaping together through the debris, a jumble of wrack,
but my Keats floats across it, my Herbert and Donne,

my Kinnell, my Bishop and Blake are soaring across it,
my Frost, Baudelaire, my Dickinson, Lowell and Larkin,
and my giants, my Whitman, my Shakespeare, my Dante
and Homer; they were the steel, though scouring as I was

the savants and sages half the time I hardly knew it . . .
But Vallejo was there all along, and my Sidney and Shelley,
my Coleridge and Hopkins, there all along with their music,
which is why I can whirl through the rubble of everything else,

the philosophizing and theories, the thesis and anti- and syn-,
all I believed must be what meanings were made of,
when really it was the singing, the choiring, the cadence,
the lull of the vowels, the chromatical consonant clatter . . .

Watch me again, I haven't landed, I'm hovering here
over the fragments, the remnants, the splinters and shards;
my poets are with me, my soarers, my skimmers, my skaters,
aloft on their song in the ruins, their jubilant song of the ruins.

CHRISTIAN WIMAN

My Bright Abyss

FROM *The American Scholar*

> *My God my bright abyss*
> *Into which all my longing will not go*
> *Once more I come to the edge of all I know*
> *And believing nothing believe in this:*

AND THERE THE POEM ENDS. OR FAILS, RATHER, FOR IN THE THREE
years since I first wrote that stanza I have been trying to feel my
way—to will my way—into its ending. Poems in general are not
especially susceptible to the will, but this one, for obvious reasons,
has proved particularly intractable. As if it weren't hard enough to
articulate one's belief, I seem to have wanted to distill it into a stanza.
Still, that is the way I have usually known my own mind, feeling
through the sounds of words to the forms they make, and through
the forms they make to the forms of life that are beyond them. I have
always believed in that "beyond," even during the long years when I
would not acknowledge God. I have expected something similar
here. I have wanted some image to open for me, to both solidify my
wavering faith and ramify beyond it, to say more than I can say.

In truth, though, what I crave at this point in my life is to speak more
clearly what it is I believe. It is not that I am tired of poetic truth, or

that I feel it to be somehow weaker or less true than reason. The opposite is the case. Inspiration is to thought what grace is to faith: intrusive, transcendent, transformative, but also evanescent and, all too often, anomalous. A poem can leave its maker at once more deeply seized by existence and, in a profound way, alienated from it, for as the act of making ends, as the world that seemed to overbrim its boundaries becomes, once more, merely the world, it can be very difficult to retain any faith at all in that original moment of inspiration. The memory of that momentary blaze, in fact, and the art that issued from it, can become a kind of reproach to the fireless life in which you find yourself most of the time. Grace is no different. (Artistic inspiration *is* sometimes an act of grace, though by no means always.) To experience grace is one thing; to integrate it into your life quite another. What I crave now is that integration, some speech that is true to the transcendent nature of grace, yet adequate to the hard reality in which daily faith operates. I crave, I suppose, the poetry *and* the prose of knowing.

If you return to the faith of your childhood after long wandering, people whose orientation is entirely secular will tend to dismiss or at least deprecate the action as having psychological motivations—motivations, it goes without saying, of which you are unconscious. As it happens, you have this suspicion yourself. It eats away at the intensity of the experience that made you proclaim, however quietly, your recovered faith, and soon you find yourself getting stalled in arguments between religion and science, theology and history, trying to nail down doctrine like some huge and much-torn tent in the wind.

In fact, there is no way to "return to the faith of your childhood," not really, not unless you've just woken from a decades-long and absolutely literal coma. Faith is not some remote, remembered country into which you come like a long-exiled king, dispensing the old wisdom, casting out the radical, insurrectionist aspects of yourself by which you'd been betrayed. No. Life is not an error, even when it is. That is to say, whatever faith you emerge with at the end of your life is going to be not simply affected by that life but intimately dependent upon it, for faith in God is, in the deepest sense, faith in life—which means, of course, that even the staunchest life of faith is a life of great change. It follows that if you believe at fifty what you believed at fifteen, then you have not lived—or have denied the reality of your life.

To admit that there may be some psychological need informing your return to religion does not preclude or diminish the spiritual imperative any more than acknowledging the chemical reactions of romantic attraction lessens the mystery of enduring human love. Faith cannot save you from the claims of reason, except insofar as it preserves and protects that wonderful, terrible time when reason, if only for a moment, lost its claim on you.

On the radio I hear a famous novelist praising his father for enduring a long, difficult dying without ever "seeking relief in religion." It is clear from the son's description that the father was in absolute despair, and that as those cold waters closed over him he could find nothing to hold on to but his pride, and drowned clutching that nothing. This is to be admired? That we carry our despair stoically into death, that even the utmost anguish of our lives not change us? How astonishing it is, the fierceness with which we cling to beliefs that have made us miserable, or beliefs that prove to be so obviously inadequate when extreme suffering—or extreme joy—come. But the tension here is not simply between belief and disbelief. A Christian who has lived with a steady but essentially shallow form of faith may find himself called to suffer the full human truth of God—which is the absence of God—may find himself finally confronted with the absolute emptiness of the cross. God calls to us at every moment, and God is life, *this* life. Radical change remains a possibility within us right up until our last breath. The greatest tragedy of human existence is not to live in time, in both senses of that phrase.

I don't mean to suggest that the attitude of stoic acceptance is not at times a worthy one. I don't know what was going on in the mind of the novelist's father, but what was going on in the mind of the novelist himself is quite clear: it's the old fear of religion as crutch, Freudian wish fulfillment, a final refusal of life—which in order to *be* life must include a full awareness of death—rather than a final flowering of it. Christians love to point to anecdotes like that of Nietzsche, idolater of pure power, going insane at the end of his life because he saw a horse being unmercifully beaten; or Wallace Stevens, the great modern poet of unbelief, converting to Catholicism on his deathbed. But there are plenty of anecdotes to contrast with these: Freud's courage when suffering his final illness, Camus' staunch, independent humanism in the face of the utter chaos and depravity he both witnessed and imagined ("What we learn in time of pestilence: that there are more things to admire in men than to despise"). There is not a trace of resignation or defeat in Camus. Indeed, there is something in the stalwart, stubbornly humane nature of his metaphysical nihilism that constitutes a metaphysical belief. If it is true—and I think it is—that there is something lacking in this belief, that it seems more like one man's moral courage than a prescription for living, more a personal code than a universal creed, it is also true that all subsequent Christianity must pass through the crucible of unbelief that thinkers like Camus underwent.

If God is a salve applied to unbearable psychic wounds, or a dream figure conjured out of memory and mortal terror, or an escape from a life that has become either too appalling or too banal to bear, then I have to admit: *it is not working for me.* Just when I think I've finally found some balance between active devotion and honest modern consciousness, all of my old anxieties come pressuring up through the seams of me, and I am as volatile and paralyzed as ever. I can't tell which is worse, standing numb and apart from the world wanting Being to burn me awake, or feeling that fire too acutely to crave anything other than escape. What I do know is that the turn toward God has not lessened my anxieties, and I find myself continually falling back into wounds, wishes, terrors I thought I had risen beyond.

Be careful. Be certain that your expressions of regret about your inability to rest in God do not have a tinge of self-satisfaction, even self-exaltation to them, that your complaints about your anxieties are not merely a manifestation of your dependence on them. There is nothing more difficult to outgrow than anxieties that have become useful to us, whether as explanations for a life that never quite finds its true force or direction, or as fuel for ambition, or as a kind of reflexive secular religion that, paradoxically, unites us with others in a shared sense of complete isolation: you feel at home in the world only by never feeling at home in the world.

It is this last complacency to which artists of our time are especially susceptible, precisely because it comes disguised as a lonely, heroic strength. Sometimes it truly is a strength: Giacometti, Beckett, Camus, Kafka. Yet it is a deep truth of being human—and, I would argue, an earnest of the immortal Spirit who is forever tugging us toward him—that even our most imaginative discoveries are doomed to become mere stances and attitudes. In this sense, art does advance over time, though usually this advance involves a recovery of elements and ideas we thought we had left behind for good. This is true not only for those who follow in the wake of great accomplishments, but also for those who themselves made those accomplishments. What belief could be more self-annihilating, could more effectively articulate its own insufficiency and thereby prophesy its own demise, than twentieth-century existentialism? To say that there is nothing beyond this world that we see, to make death the final authority of our lives, is to sow a seed of meaninglessness into that very insight. These artists knew that, and made of that fatal knowledge a fierce, new, and necessary faith: the austere, "absurd" persistence of spirit in both Camus and Beckett, the terrible disfiguring contingency that, in Giacometti's sculptures, takes on the look of fate. There is genuine heroism here, but there is also—faintly at first, but then more persistently, more damagingly—an awareness of heroism. (Only Kafka seems to fully feel his defeat: he is perhaps the most "spiritual" artist in this group, though he treasures his misery too much ever to be released from it.) This flaw—the artist's adamantine pride—is what made the achievement possible, but it is also the crack that slowly widens over time, not lessening the achievement but humanizing it, relativizing it, causing what had once seemed an immutable, universal insight to begin to look a little more like a temporal, individual vision—a vision from which, inevitably, there comes a time to move forward.

Christianity itself is this, to some extent. To every age Christ dies anew and is resurrected within the imagination of man. This is why he could be a paragon of rationality for eighteenth-century England, a heroic figure of the imagination for the Romantics, an exemplar of existential courage for writers like Paul Tillich and Rudolf Bultmann. One truth, then, is that Christ is always being remade in the image of man, which is to say, his reality is always being deformed to fit human needs, or what humans perceive to be their needs. A deeper truth, though, one that scripture suggests when it speaks of the eternal Word being made specific flesh, is that there is no permutation of humanity in which Christ is not present. If every Bible is lost, if every church crumbles to dust, if the last believer in the last prayer opens her eyes and lets it all finally go—Christ will appear on this earth as calmly and casually as he appeared to the disciples walking to Emmaus after his death, who did not recognize this man to whom they had pledged their very lives; this man whom they had seen beaten, crucified, abandoned by God; this man who, after walking the dusty road with them, after sharing an ordinary meal and discussing the scriptures, had to vanish to make them see.

When I think of the years when I had no faith, what I am struck by, first of all, is how little this lack disrupted my conscious life. I lived not with God, nor with his absence, but in a mild abeyance of belief, drifting through the days on a tide of tiny vanities—a publication, a flirtation, a strong case made for some weak nihilism—nights all adagios and alcohol as my mind tore luxuriously into itself. I can see now how deeply God's absence affected my unconscious life, how under me always there was this long fall that pride and fear and self-love at once protected me from and subjected me to. Was the fall into belief or into unbelief? Both. For if grace woke me to God's presence in the world and in my heart, it also woke me to his absence. I never truly felt the pain of unbelief until I began to believe.

When I assented to the faith that was latent within me—and I phrase it carefully, deliberately, for no white light appeared, no ministering or avenging angel tore my life in two; rather it seemed as if the tiniest seed of belief had finally flowered in me, or, more accurately, as if I had happened upon some rare flower deep in the desert and knew, though I was just then discovering it, that it had been blooming impossibly year after parched year in me, surviving all the seasons of my unbelief—*when I assented to the faith that was latent within me*, what struck me were the ways in which my evasions and confusions, which I had mistaken for a strong sense of purpose, had expressed themselves in my life: poem after poem about unnamed and unnamable absences, relationships so transparently perishable they practically came with expiration dates on them, city after city sacked of impressions and peremptorily abandoned as if I were some army of insight seeing, I now see, nothing. Perhaps it is never disbelief, which at least is active and conscious, that destroys a man but unacknowledged belief, or a need for belief so strong that it is continually and silently crucified on the crosses of science, humanism, art, or (to name the thing that poisons all these gifts of God) the overweening self.

They do not happen now, the sandstorms of my childhood, when the western distance ochred, and the square emptied, and long before the big wind hit, you could taste the dust on your tongue, could feel the earth under you—and even something in you—seem to loosen slightly. Soon tumbleweeds began to skip and nimble by, a dust devil flickered tirelessly in the vacant lot across the street from our house, and birds began rocketing past with their wings shut as if they'd been flung. Worse than snow, worse than ice, a bad sandstorm shrinks the world to the slit of your eyes, lifting from the fields an inchoate creaturely mass that claws at any exposed skin as if the dust remembered what it was, which is what you are—alive, alive—and sought return. They do not happen now, whether because of what we've learned or because the earth itself has changed. Yet I can close my eyes and see all the trees tugging at their roots as if to unfasten themselves from the earth. I can hear the long-gone howl, more awful for its being mute.

Lord, I can approach you only by means of my consciousness, but consciousness can only approach you as an object, which you are not. I have no hope of experiencing you as I experience the world—directly, immediately—yet I have no hunger greater. Indeed, so great

is my hunger for you—or is this evidence of your hunger for me?—
that I seem to see you in the black flower mourners make beside a
grave I do not know, in the ember's innards like a shining hive, in the
bare abundance of a winter tree whose every limb is lit and fraught
with snow. Lord, Lord, how bright the abyss inside that "seem."

RUTH R. WISSE

The Shul at Loon Lake

FROM *Commentary*

THE LOON LAKE JEWISH CENTER, ABOUT TWO-THIRDS OF THE WAY between Plattsburgh and Saranac Lake, New York, is a log cabin, a former hunting lodge, consisting of one large square room that serves as the sanctuary; an adjoining back room with a refrigerator, sink, and table; and a small corner bathroom with toilet and sink. Until about ten years ago, a moose head hung above the blocked-up fireplace in the main room, but a humorless caretaker had it removed as an offense to the spirit of the place.

At one end of the main room is a wooden ark holding a Torah scroll that is taken out during the service and unfurled for reading. The velvet Torah mantle, the breastplate that covers it, the curtain before the ark, and the cloth covering the large lectern on the bimah— the raised platform with the reading table on which the Torah is spread out—were all carved or embroidered by members of the congregation in honor of deceased relatives.

The Jewish Center is a summer congregation, its parishioners hot-weather vacationers, many of whom make a six-hour drive from New York or Toronto or a two-hour drive from Montreal. For the five decades of its existence, it has never failed to hold services at the prescribed times on Friday night, Saturday morning, and at the conclusion of Sabbath, following the Orthodox ritual and prayer book. There have been years when the president has canvassed the members to see whether there can be a minyan on the Sabbath before July 4, and occasionally enough members have stayed beyond Labor Day to allow for an additional Sabbath at the latter end of the season as well. But whenever the synagogue is opened each year, there can be no interruption of its routine. A traditional Jewish prayer quorum, or minyan, requires the presence of ten men age thirteen and older. This requirement has probably done more to guarantee the vital survival of Jewish communities than anything except the act of reproduction itself, and so it has proved for the Loon Lake Synagogue: the need for a traditional minyan has kept it alive.

The synagogue is set up to accommodate a maximum of seventy persons. Six long benches traverse the width of the room with smaller benches along the two side walls. Men are seated in the front half, a long table dividing them from the women who are positioned similarly in back. This arrangement represents one of innumerable compromises without which the congregation could not have been founded, and without which it could not last. Very traditional visitors regret the absence of a genuine *mehitsah* a partitioning curtain or wall to separate the men's from the women's section. For them the table hardly seems division enough. In contrast, members accustomed to Conservative or Reform synagogue practice, where mixed congregational seating is taken for granted and women are counted as members of the minyan, chafe at a physical arrangement they associate with second-class citizenship for women.

Mehitsah has probably been the most contentious issue in the Loon Lake congregation, as it has been generally in synagogue life since the nineteenth century, when the German Reform movement began to bring Jewish practice into closer approximation of the Christian norm. Probably for that very reason, those who came to be known as Orthodox insisted that separation of the sexes was crucial to maintaining the "sanctity of the synagogue." But within Orthodoxy, too, opinions vary as to the need for an actual or merely symbolic partition, which means that perpetual negotiation sustains a shifting status quo.

Several years ago the president of the congregation, polling all the members in turn, came by to ask my help with a "delicate situation." His very devout brother-in-law was paying a rare visit and would not pray in the synagogue that Sabbath unless some genuine *mehitsah* were erected. For this occasion only, the president was proposing to attach to the table a section of wooden latticework, which he would remove the following day. Was I prepared to go along with this plan?

Although my own preference happens to be for separate seating, at first I balked at the idea that someone could interfere with the established "custom of the place," which had been arrived at only after much debate and, once interfered with, would surely open itself to challenge once again. In objecting to the visitor's insistence on a stricter interpretation of the "letter of the law," I was also thinking of how it might offend a member family that had already done its share of compromise from the other direction on the spectrum. One of the women in this family serves as cantor of a large Conservative congregation near Washington, D.C.; at Loon Lake, only her husband, not she, is permitted to lead the services.

Yet when the president consulted her, she too ultimately accepted his proposal. I have always felt grateful to the family and to this woman in particular, whose cheerful spirit of participation allows us to experience the harmony of the Sabbath. She probably realizes, as do I, that without the imperatives of Orthodoxy, the congregation would have folded many years ago. For his part, the president promised us that, the week after his relative's visit, he would consign the latticework to a bonfire that the whole community would be invited to witness in assurance that this was a one-time exception.

. . .

This anomalous Jewish congregation is merely the latest incarnation of an earlier maverick institution in the same location. Our village of Loon Lake (one of several places so named in New York State) dates from 1878, when Ferdinand and Mary H. H. Chase opened a lodge on the shore of one of the loveliest bodies of water in the Adirondacks, determined to create the region's finest resort. The spot they chose was not far from a station house on the direct route of the New York Central Railroad from New York to Montreal and a branch of the Delaware and Hudson Railroad line from New York to Lake Placid. Special railroad cars on this run were outfitted for wealthy travelers and their retinue of servants. Though the area was recommended for tubercular patients—President Benjamin Harrison's consumptive wife stayed there for a time—the Chases had in mind a much grander concept than providing a service for people who wanted to convalesce among their own kind.

According to all reports, Mary Chase, who was known as The Mrs., was the driving force of this larger project from around the time of her husband's death in 1917. At first the Chases had occupied a small house on a promontory overlooking the length of the lake; later they built on this spot a hotel with two annexes that could feed their many hundreds of guests. Elsewhere around the lake, they constructed cottages for those desiring a greater measure of privacy than a hotel could provide, but the cottages were without kitchens, so all meals were taken on the American plan in the hotel's dining rooms. The same held true for those guests who were permitted to build their own cottages on the property, with Mrs. Chase having right of first refusal if they decided to sell. The Mrs. was apparently as adept at business as she was at attracting an exclusive clientele.

In its heyday, the resort included an eighteen-hole golf course, stables, a gas station, a grand beach, tennis courts, boating facilities, and more than four thousand acres of surrounding forestland. The cottage named "President" hosted, in addition to the Harrisons, Presidents Grover Cleveland, William McKinley, and Theodore Roosevelt. Though the term *exclusive* generally implied that no Jews would have been welcome, it seems that the Chases were pleased to host Guggenheims, Lehmans, and Irving Berlin, along with the J. P. Morgans, the Vanderbilts, and Theodore Dreiser. Affordability was the democratizing standard of admission. A local resident who worked at the hotel for eight years in the 1920s was still starry-eyed many years later in recalling that "the magnificence of Loon Lake [Resort] can never be overstated. . . . There was a separate kitchen for soups and vegetables, another for meat, salad, sandwiches, and coffee, cereal, and baked goods." Guests who wanted to circumvent the Prohibition laws managed to get their supply.

Traces of the old splendor were still much in view when I visited there for the first time in the summer of 1961, though signs of neglect were already noticeable in what had once been the public places. The tennis court was overgrown, the stables were collapsing, and the ruins of several burned-out buildings were happy hunting grounds for curious youngsters. But the history of the place was fresh in people's minds. The peak years had been the 1920s, when the resort accommodated almost eight hundred guests; the crash of 1929 was followed by the bankruptcy and death of its visionary owner. There followed a long period of receivership before the place was purchased in 1946 by the Andron family, who opened Loon Lake as the only kosher hotel in the Adirondacks. Mrs. Chase's separate kitchens were now divided according to the requirements of separating dairy from meat. The new clientele, from both sides of the Canadian border, gave rise to a number of matrimonial matches between religiously observant families from New York and Montreal.

Then, in September 1956, a fire destroyed Loon Lake Hotel and with it the resort that depended on its kitchens. A public auction was

held the following year; most of the cottages were bought up by lo-
cals and Orthodox Jews who had frequented the kosher hotel. Those
properties that failed to sell at auction went to a real-estate consor-
tium. It included a Jewish woman named Irene Miller who, though
not religiously observant herself, proposed to the new Jewish owners
that they chip in to buy a former hunting lodge for their common
use as the Loon Lake Synagogue they had set up in makeshift prem-
ises. Taking up her suggestion, they opened the building in 1961,
retrieving some prayer books and the reading table from the defunct
hotel and bringing a Torah scroll from a synagogue in New York.
Loon Lake had traded one model of "distinctiveness" for another.

The early problems facing the Loon Lake shul were the opposite of
those that confront it today. According to their press release, the
original founders were "a vacationing rabbi, a physician, and a select
group of professional engineers, teachers, lawyers, and businessmen,
all steeped in traditional observance, and well versed in theological
teachings." That some of these illustrious Jews were related to one
another by birth or marriage strengthened their sense of community
while also creating the potential for dynastic rivalries. For a function-
ing congregation, the presence of so many knowledgeable Jews was
both a rare blessing and a source of perpetual friction.

At Sabbath morning services, the central event is the weekly read-
ing from the Pentateuch and the *haftarah*, a section from one of the
Prophets. The *gabbai*, the congregation's lay leader, calls one man to
"rise up" to the Torah (*aliyah*) for each of the seven passages into
which the reading is divided, plus one more for the reading from the
Prophets. Those called up are selected at the discretion of the *gabbai*,
subject only to a strict criterion that is hierarchically controlled: the
first *aliyah* is given to an individual who is a descendant of Kohanim,
those from the tribe of Levi who formed the Temple priesthood in

antiquity; the second to a Levite descended from those charged with certain ritual functions. The remaining six go to descendants of the other Israelite tribes.

The Loon Lake Synagogue had a resident family of Kohanim, plenty of fluid Torah readers, and a cohort of boys of bar-mitzvah age who liked to take their turns leading the two other main parts of the service. This would seem to have provided honors enough to go around. Yet not all honors are felt to be alike. Prominent within their urban year-round congregations, these men were acutely aware of the subtleties of public recognition. At various points during the summer, moreover, people would be marking the forthcoming marriage of a child, the birth of a grandchild, the anniversary of the death of a parent or sibling, or some other rite of passage or exceptional event similarly requiring recognition. Meanwhile, there was competition among the women, who took turns providing food for the receptions following the Sabbath morning service. These mini-meals brought the community together in a wonderfully festive mood but also occasioned rivalries that became toxic when they dovetailed with the rivalries of husbands.

In sum, the same values that made Jewish observance so vital to the lives of these people not only heightened the prestige members ascribed to synagogue recognition but also inflated their sense of injury at any slight—to the point where even the wording and placement of plaques commemorating the dead or honoring the living became a matter of hot contention. "I've . . . come to the conclusion that I should resign from the Loon Lake Jewish Center," reads a 1962 letter to the president after one such altercation. It ends: "Nevertheless, as befits the beautiful Jewish custom of forgiveness, I wish you and your family and all others in our Loon Lake group a happy and healthy New Year."

In his guide to Jewish religion, the late Rabbi Louis Jacobs points out that the synagogue is not only where the Jew communes with

God but also "a place wide open to the daily concerns of its members. A complete division between the sacred and the secular was never attempted." This congruence between the secular and the sacred is exceptionally tight in the tiny Loon Lake community, where proprietary concerns spill over from one area to the other. Since the synagogue-attending Jews were the most organized group at Loon Lake in the period following the public auction, they formed the original nucleus of the Loon Lake Homeowners' Association, arranging for such common tasks as garbage collection and cleaning the public beach. There was even a short-lived attempt to start a small day camp for the children. But far from generating greater harmony, this interaction provoked multiple disputes, including between siblings. The early years were marked by arguments that escalated into lawsuits over property markers and rights of way. A house we rented one summer had a decal over the window overlooking the next property that read "Loathe thy neighbor."

But the intensity of those early years yielded to Time—the governing force of all congregations—which registered its toll at the beginning of every new season in the loss of some of those who had described themselves as "steeped in traditional observance, and well versed in theological teachings." As the first generation of homeowners began slipping away, widows and children began to put their houses up for sale. The buyers were not necessarily Jews and, if Jews, not necessarily synagogue-goers. The day approached when there was no certainty that a minyan could be assembled. Unless some efforts were made to enlarge the pool of male congregants, the synagogue would cease to function.

From a sociological perspective, those unsteady years were the most interesting, forcing every Loon Lake Jewish family to define itself and to be defined by the others. There were services when only eight or nine men showed up. Delegations would then have to go looking or (as long as it was before the onset of Sabbath) phoning for the necessary bodies to make up the ten. Some infrequent attendees enjoyed "coming to the rescue" to fill out the prayer quorum; others took the occasion to emphasize their antagonism to religion in general and to this one in particular. Some irregular attendees like my husband began regulating their Loon Lake schedules according to the synagogue's needs. Thus were the requirements of Judaism felt existentially and on an ongoing basis.

Finally, and although the formation of the Loon Lake Jewish Center was a collaborative effort, I should mention two individuals to whom it owes much for its continued existence. The first is Samuel Gewurz, the youngest son of one of the founding families, who undertook to recruit a new synagogue population when he saw the old one eroding. The only one of his siblings to continue frequenting Loon Lake, Sammy and his wife, Brenda, inherited an extra house from his parents and began renting it out selectively to regular synagogue-goers from their native Montreal. When they built a new home, they applied Mrs. Chase's commercial principle to a religious purpose by selling their old one on the informal provision that the new owner attend services or else sell the house back to them. The Gewurz and other families hosted religiously observant friends from their home communities who were charmed by the place—and by the synagogue—and who bought local properties when they went up for sale or built new homes on the few empty lots. New members of the community quickly realized that they had become the guarantors of synagogue life, and several have assumed the responsibilities required to sustain it.

Similarly, although the Loon Lake congregation has never had an official rabbi, one of its mainstays has been Wilfred Shuchat, emeritus rabbi of Montreal's Shaar Hashomayim synagogue, who met his wife, Miriam, at the Androns' hotel, bought a house at the auction, and has been vacationing at Loon Lake ever since. Some of the sweetest and most painful moments in the life of the shul are associated with this passionately modest man and his family. He was one of the stalwart readers from the Torah until impeded by a loss of sight, but to this day he continues teaching sections from the Mishnah's *Ethics of the Fathers* toward the close of the Sabbath. When one of the daughters of the family died as a young wife and mother, the congregation named the house adjacent to the synagogue in her memory. The small-town quality of Loon Lake fosters an intimacy among synagogue members that extends through the rest of the year. Those who associate vacationing with shucking off communal interaction are not candidates for Loon Lake's congregation.

The archives of the Saranac Lake library treat Loon Lake as a place of fallen glory. A 1974 essay typically observes that, despite rumors of impending developments, "except for a cottage colony, nothing outstanding has developed." Indeed, no one driving in season past the few cottages on Route 26 and catching sight of the sign "Loon Lake Jewish Center" could imagine the glamour once associated with the place. The consortium that now owns most of the former Chase estate recently refused to renew the lease on the golf course, which is quickly becoming overgrown. A few brave souls who bought the smaller of the hotel annexes appear to have given up their plans for redevelopment. A tiny functioning inn on the property closed in 2008. A tall stone chimney in the woods, a pair of stone pillars at the entry to a driveway, and a few crumbling stairs of the grand descent to the lake are the only remaining markers of Mrs. Chase's empire.

In some sense, the glory days of the Loon Lake Synagogue are also past, as the generation of European-trained rabbis and learned Jews has died out, leaving humbler laymen to conduct the service. Yet when the Loon Lake Jewish Center celebrated its fiftieth anniversary in 2008, it seemed to be gaining rather than losing strength. The otherwise regrettable demise of the golf course may have helped in this by discouraging the kinds of buyers who are primarily interested in the sport, and the otherwise lamentable lack of regional development that keeps prices from rising too steeply has also made it easier to recruit new families suited to the shul. Only by drawing in religiously compatible families one at a time has the synagogue avoided the fissures that a larger, more eclectic membership would create. An influx of Jews either more or less religiously observant would make it that much harder to maintain the delicate balance.

The experience of the Loon Lake Synagogue suggests that the freedoms of America provide unparalleled opportunity for new initiatives—but few safeguards against their failure. When the reign of Mrs. Chase was ended by the Depression, Loon Lake became a haven for observant Jews who could now reach it by automobile. They created an independent and self-sustaining congregation that managed to hold together people from New York, New Jersey, Pennsylvania, Massachusetts, Washington, D.C., Ontario, and Quebec. Without defining their affiliation, they created a model of "modern Orthodoxy" that reflects the tensions inherent in the term.

Like America, traditional Judaism is based on the premise that freedom must be tamed by civilizing imperatives and that only adherence to such imperatives makes for genuine freedom. Certainly, only such adherence to imperatives has sustained *this* congregation, with the added proviso of a continual negotiation between tradition and adaptation, between the lenient and the strict. This maverick congregation may claim its own small place in local history as an example of tenacity, creativity, and freedom in the American grain—so long, that is, as it can manage, like America itself, to keep its balance.

PHILIP YANCEY

What Art Can and Can't Do

FROM *First Things*

DURING FLIRTATIONS WITH EXISTENTIALISM IN MY YOUTH, I CAME TO love the mysterious Book of Ecclesiastes, with its ambiguities and exquisite sense of the rhythms of life. In the years since, I have moved well beyond existential despair, but many times I have returned to Ecclesiastes and breathed a prayer of thanks that God saw fit to include such unbleached realism in Holy Scripture. During the Festival of Tents, Jewish families read the entire book aloud, a practice I would recommend to certain groups of happy-face Christians today.

In time, I noticed that the last chapter of Ecclesiastes contains words directed toward people in my own profession of writing: "He pondered and searched out and set in order many proverbs. The Teacher searched to find just the right words." Clearly, the Teacher of long ago knew something of the laborious process I go through each time I approach my computer today.

Then, in a sentence packed with mixed metaphors, the Teacher concludes, "The words of the wise are like goads, their collected sayings like firmly embedded nails—given by one Shepherd." In typical contrapuntal style he adds this tweak: "Be warned, my son, of anything in addition to them. Of making many books there is no end, and much study wearies the body." The Teacher speaks truth. For writers, I have learned, there is a time to be a goad and a time to be a firmly embedded nail.

A goad, such as farmers use on oxen and jockeys on horses, prods to action. Goads cause enough discomfort to get animals—or people—to do something they otherwise might not do. Over the centuries, human history has seen many examples of the creative arts used as goads, and these goads often rattle those in power. According to the late Russian dissident Andrei Sinyavsky, "Every self-respecting writer of any significance is a saboteur, and, as he surveys the horizon wondering what to write about, more often than not he will choose some forbidden topic."

After General Pinochet seized control in Chile, his minions broke the bones in the hands of Víctor Jara, whose guitar playing had kindled the hopes of the poor. That goad the authoritarian leader could not tolerate, and Jara was eventually shot and killed. Similarly, paintings like Picasso's *Guernica* have gotten under the skin of dictatorial regimes. ("Did you do that?" a Fascist soldier asked Picasso reproachfully, pointing to the painting. "No, you did," Picasso replied.)

The Prophets of the Bible similarly served as goads. Boiled down, their magnificent poetry reduces to a one-line message: Repent, change your ways, or judgment will come. Harriet Beecher Stowe, a radical Christian, sought to communicate the abolitionist message to many who had blocked their ears to sermons and jeremiads. She wrote a novel instead, *Uncle Tom's Cabin*, that sold two hundred thousand copies in its first year and, as much as any other force, goaded a nation toward change.

Not long ago we lived through perhaps the most momentous change in modern history. Within the span of one year, six hundred million people gained freedom, with hardly a shot being fired. How did it happen? It will take historians years to sort out all the reasons behind the fall of Communism. As one who lived through the 1960s—a decade when barricades went up in the streets of Paris, when leftists were bombing public buildings in America, and when every intellectual worth his salt was coming down on the side of revolution—I trace the fault line of change back to a lone Russian, his courage hardened to steel in the gulag, who dared proclaim, "It is a lie." The massive documentation assembled by Solzhenitsyn bore witness to a different truth.

Many Christians in the creative arts today strive to be goads, striking the flank of society. I applaud them and sometimes join them. There is a time to be a goad, and, many examples show, we should not underestimate the effect of the arts in bringing about change.

At the same time, I have increasingly come to see the limitations of a goading art. The Prophets take up so many pages of the Old Testament because, by and large, they were spectacularly ineffective. There was Nathan, of course, who through the sheer power of story struck King David to the heart. And there was Jonah, the reluctant goad who, much to his own dismay, brought all Nineveh to its knees. But few of the other prophets had much impact on Israel. Jeremiah 36 records an all-too-typical response: The offended king simply cut up and burned Jeremiah's scroll.

Aleksandr Solzhenitsyn often paid tribute to his colleagues who died unknown in the gulag, their works taken to the grave with them, buried in tundra caches that will never be discovered. Six hundred million may have found a new measure of freedom in 1989, but one billion Chinese experienced a crackdown. Sometimes goads have little effect.

In the United States today, I wonder how much difference Christians are making through the arts. All the words pouring forth in our magazines and books, for example—are they influencing the culture at large? Do we not end up goading mostly one another?

One reason we make so little difference, I believe, is that the Church, like government, prefers propaganda to goads. The same Church that commissioned Michelangelo to paint the Sistine Chapel later hired a man called "the Trouserer" to clothe the nude figures. In modern times, we impose limits on our artists, and, as we do so, we draw walls around our subculture. There is an account in Solzhenitsyn's memoir *The Oak and the Calf* about the brief period when even the Communist government of the Soviet Union acknowledged the genius of Solzhenitsyn's work. The communists thought (fatally, as it turned out) he might be a goad they could control. Write moral and uplifting literature, they admonished him; be sure to exclude all "pessimism, denigration, surreptitious sniping."

I laughed aloud when I first read that scene. The advice Solzhenitsyn got from the Communists bears striking resemblance to what I sometimes hear from evangelical publishers. Every power, whether Christian or secular, desires moral, uplifting literature—as long as they get to define what constitutes moral and uplifting.

We cannot expect art always to educate and inspire as well as to portray. In the words of Alan Paton, literature "will illuminate the road, but it will not lead the way with a lamp. It will expose the crevasse, but not provide the bridge. It will lance the boil, but not purify the blood. It cannot be expected to do more than this; and if we ask it to do more, we are asking too much."

Keats said that literature sometimes demands of us Negative Capability: the ability to accept multiplicity, mystery, and doubt without reaching out for the illusory comforts of certainty and fact. Faith, too, demands a kind of Negative Capability, and that does not always sit well with many of the folk who distribute Christian art and many of the folk who consume it. For this reason, among others, some necessary goads never find their target. Like the works of Solzhenitsyn's anonymous comrades, they remain buried in the tundra.

There is a time to be a goad, and a time to be a firmly embedded nail. A goad prods to immediate action, but a firmly embedded nail settles deeper, as an indelible marker of what T. S. Eliot called "the permanent things."

Toward the end of his life, Paul Gauguin painted a huge triptych pulling together all his styles of art. In an extraordinarily unsubtle move, he scrawled across the painting, "Who are we? Why are we here? Where are we going?" That triptych, now hanging in the Museum of Fine Arts, Boston, poses a grand summation of Gauguin's work and a grand summation of the questions to which modernity has no answer. Soon after completing the work, Gauguin attempted suicide.

Civilization once looked to art as the means of passing on wisdom from one generation to the next. The act of writing was invented, after all, to convey the sacred: Permanent things must be passed on in a permanent way, hence the hieroglyphs on Egyptian tombs. But a civilization that no longer believes in permanent things, one that holds to no objective truths, resorts to deconstruction, not construction.

The editor of the *New Yorker*, David Remnick, recently contrasted modern writers in Russia with the tradition of the Great Russian Writer: such figures as Gogol, Tolstoy, and even Solzhenitsyn, who represented both sagacity and idealism. Nowadays the liberated writers, free to join the decadent chorus of modernity, are deliberately destroying that tradition, brick by brick. One recent story begins with a mythic scene familiar to all Russians, an old man describing the Nazi siege of Leningrad to a young boy. The story ends, though, with the old man raping the young boy. No convention, no memory is safe from assault.

As such voices as T. S. Eliot, Walker Percy, and Flannery O'Connor have reminded us, the modern world must look to Christians, who stand virtually alone in seeing the need for (or even believing in) firmly embedded nails. On the modern landscape of a decaying Western civilization, Christians still cling to a view that ascribes meaning and worth to individual human beings. The novelist Reynolds Price once remarked that there is a single sentence that, above all, people crave from stories: *The Maker of all thing loves and wants me.* Christians still believe in that story.

Perhaps the existence of art—its inherent, permanent-seeming worth, as well as its echo of original Creation—can be a pointer to a grand artist, a rumor of transcendence. Five hundred years ago, the Renaissance scholar Pico della Mirandola delivered his famous "Oration on the Dignity of Man," which defined the role of humanity in creation. After God had created the animals, all the essential roles had been filled, but "the Divine Artificer still longed for some creature which might comprehend the meaning of so vast an achievement, which might be moved with love at its beauty and smitten with awe at its grandeur." To contemplate and appreciate all the rest, to reflect on meaning, to share in the power and exuberance of creativity, to revere and to hallow—these were the roles reserved for the species made in God's image.

When I look back on my own conversion, I cannot credit a gospel tract or an altar call or an exposition of John 3:16. I had encountered these things many times over in childhood and had learned to mistrust them. Rather, nature, classical music, and romantic love formed the channel of grace that awakened my senses to perception of God. Through that channel I came to believe first in a good world and then in a good God. It is a terrible thing to feel gratitude and have no one to thank, to feel awe and have no one to worship. Gradually, prompted by beauty and by art, I returned to the cast-off faith of my childhood.

"The Catholic writer," said Flannery O'Connor, "insofar as he has the mind of the Church, will feel life from the standpoint of the central Christian mystery: that it has, for all its horror, been found by God to be worth dying for." Modern humanity does not perceive the world as worth God's dying for. We Christians must demonstrate it.

I have a hunch that, as history looks back on the twentieth century, the most chaotic of all centuries, certain Christian artists will be remembered simply because they hammered in a few firmly embed-ded nails. Creation is beautiful and good, and humanity upholds God's image within it; creation is fallen, evil, corrupt; creation can be, and will be, restored—that triune intuition of Christian faith provides a template of meaning that at least attempts an answer to Gauguin's questions. Who else is even offering one?

Note the clues to this triune intuition in Vincent van Gogh's re-vealing letter to his brother Theo: "I feel more and more that we must not judge of God from this world, it's just a study that didn't come off. What can you do with a study that has gone wrong?—if you are fond of the artist, you do not find much to criticize—you hold your tongue. But you have a right to ask for something better. . . . The study is ruined in so many ways. It is only a master who can make such a blunder, and perhaps that is the best consola-tion we can have out of it, since in that case we have a right to hope that we'll see the same creative hand get even with itself." Christians believe, of course, that the master was not the one who blundered, and yet Van Gogh's instincts are deeply Christian (he was, after all, a lapsed minister). This world bears the stamp of genius, the stain of ruin, and the promise of restoration.

Fray Luis Ponce de León, one of the literary masters during Spain's Golden Age, barely survived the Inquisition. Having offended the authorities by translating the Song of Songs into Spanish and criticiz-ing the text of the Vulgate, he was dragged from his classroom in the midst of a lecture at the university in Salamanca. Four years of prison and torture followed. Then hysteria faded, and the stooped, nearly broken professor was allowed to return to his classroom. He shuffled in, opened his notes, and began his lecture with a phrase that became legendary in Spain: *Como decíamos ayer*—"As we were saying yester-day," he began, and continued his lecture where he had left off before the interruption.

Those words can be heard in Russia today. A regime that tried harder than any other to kill off God instead ended up committing suicide. I believe, truly believe, that sometime in the future, as civilization continues to collapse into an intellectual and moral vacuum, other voices will take up Fray Luis' refrain: "As we were saying yesterday."

What writers from our century will endure? Surely the poets T. S. Eliot and W. H. Auden will make the list, both informed by Christian sensibility. Solzhenitsyn no doubt will, albeit more for the raw force of his words than for their craft. Perhaps J. R. R. Tolkien will also be read a century from now, his invention of another world still shedding light on this one.

Of those artists, Eliot makes an interesting study. Faced with the political crises of Communism and Nazism, for twenty years he wrote little poetry, concerning himself instead with more urgent matters such as politics, economics, and pragmatic schemes to improve society. In such works as *The Idea of a Christian Society, After Strange Gods,* and *Notes Towards the Definition of Culture*, he turned away from firmly embedded nails and toward goads. Yet who reads those works today? Eliot's poetry easily outlasted his well-intentioned ideas. Can we learn a lesson from Eliot? Perhaps the best way to achieve the values we approve is not to talk about them all the time, or to try to legislate them, but rather to create literature and art in which they are placed as firmly embedded nails.

There is a time to be a goad and a time to be a nail. Lest aspiring writers get too inflated with notions of their significance, however, the Book of Ecclesiastes adds with a sigh, "Of making many books there is no end, and much study wearies the body."

In the final analysis, the sharpest goads and the sturdiest nails merely add to the burdensome accumulation of human creation. I have that sense every time I enter a bookstore and scan through the dozens of new titles that have appeared in the previous week. The self-help section promises me a hundred new ways to save my marriage, thin my thighs, succeed in business—if these work, why are there so many divorces, fat thighs, and business failures?

Of making many books there is no end. As a person who makes a living at writing, I confess that regularly—every five minutes or so—I must battle artistic pride. All art is an act of arrogance. As I write this sentence, I have the chutzpah to believe it will be worth your time to read it. I, a person you have probably never met, hereby demand your attention. Listen to me, please, without the possibility of reciprocation. Subject yourself to my words and thoughts.

Just as I begin to slip into my seat of authority and believe the jacket copy the publishers write about me, Ecclesiastes brings me back to earth. I am a drone, cranking out yet another book to bend the shelves of libraries and bookstores.

In the Gospel of John we find the only scene from the Bible that shows Jesus in the act of writing. Jesus left us relatively few words—a person could memorize them all—and he spoke with such economy and precision that each can be seen as a goad and a nail. Only once, though, did Jesus write, as far as we know. It came at the tense moment when Pharisees brought to him a woman caught in the act of adultery, demanding that Jesus pronounce the death penalty. Jesus stooped and drew figures in the sand.

The Irish poet Seamus Heaney finds in that scene an allegory for poetry: "The drawing of those characters [in the sand] is like poetry, a break with the usual life but not an absconding from it. Poetry, like the writing, is arbitrary and marks time in every possible sense of that phrase. It does not say to the accusing crowd or to the helpless accused, 'Now a solution will take place,' it does not propose to be instrumental or effective. Instead, in the rift between what is going to happen and whatever we would wish to happen, poetry holds attention for a space, functions not as distraction but as pure concentration, a focus where our power to concentrate is concentrated back on ourselves."

For both poetry and prose, there is a time to spur to action, and a time to instruct with wisdom—and also a time merely to fill spaces of attention. Jesus, who had participated in the design of twenty thousand abstract designs on butterflies and half a million species of beetles, left no lasting works of art for us to admire from his sojourn on earth. He chose as his medium not plates of gold or rolls of papyrus, which could be preserved by the Church and revered as icons, but rather a palette of Palestinian sand. The next rainstorm that came along obliterated every trace of Jesus' only written words.

Jesus had come primarily to change lives, to write his words on the hearts of his followers. Following in those footsteps, the apostle Paul would later say to the Corinthians, "You yourselves are our letter, written on our hearts, known and read by everybody." Both Jesus and Paul knew that only one thing will survive into eternity from this planet: the souls of individual human beings. We deceive ourselves with delusory talk about the permanence of art: Of the seven wonders of the ancient world, six did not survive into the Middle Ages.

The Czech novelist Milan Kundera once said that he always objects to the cliché that "a life is like a work of art." Art is precisely unlike life, imposing an order that life does not have. He made an exception, however, for the dissident playwright Václav Havel, who went on to become president of the Czech Republic after the fall of the Communist regime. Havel's life, said Kundera, was ordered and structured, just like art.

Kundera's comment about Havel should be true of every Christian. As I sit at home and grapple with adjectives and adverbs, my wife works as a chaplain on the night shift at a hospice. Tonight she will probably see someone die. She will break the news to the family, listen to their grief, offer words of comfort. She will touch their souls. Humbly, ashamedly, I confess that before such acts my own profession shrinks into insignificance: I am, as Seamus Heaney noted, scribbling in the sand—filling spaces, marking time. Art nourishes the soul in wonderful ways, and may be an essential part of our humanity, and yet it represents one offering among many, perhaps higher, forms of service. In modern society, we elevate art because we have dethroned so much else.

In full awareness of its limited role, though, I am convinced that we need art now, perhaps more than we ever have—the kind of art that humbly fills spaces in our lives. Movies and television and video games are currently fashioning images far worse and more horrifying than the world we live in. Compared to any other time in history, we moderns scream and shout at each other. Listen to the music on any Top 40 station. Visit a museum of contemporary art. The world today contains no subtlety, no silence, no spaces.

For those of us who labor in the arts and who believe in transcendence, here is a place to start. Some are called to be prophetic goads, and some giants may hammer in firmly embedded nails. But the rest of us can aspire, with no tinge of shame, to scribbling in the sand. Spaces need filling. The father of cellist Yo-Yo Ma spent World War II in Paris, where he lived alone in a garret throughout the German occupation. In order to restore sanity to his world, he would memorize violin pieces by Bach during the day and then at night, during blackout, he would play them alone in the dark. The sounds made by the reverberating strings held out the promise of order and hope and beauty. Later his son, Yo-Yo, took up the father's advice to play a Bach suite from memory every night before going to bed. Yo-Yo Ma says, "This isn't practicing, it's contemplating. You're alone with your soul."

I know of a woman whose neighbor learned he was going blind. As his sight began to fail, the man booked a plane to Amsterdam and spent a week in the Van Gogh Museum. He wanted these images to soak into his brain as his last visual memories.

I will never forget one encounter with art's power. I was visiting Rome, and I wanted to fill my time with the treasures offered by the churches and museums. Well before dawn the first day, I took a bus to the Tiber and stood on the bridge colonnaded with Bernini's angels, watching the sun rise, glinting orange off the still surface of the water. Quietly I walked the few blocks to St. Peter's. I strolled its vast spaces long before most tourists arrived, at a time so silent that each of my steps echoed off its graceful walls. Except for a few faithful nuns kneeling in prayer, I was alone.

After a while I climbed stairs to the roof, where I could examine the statues and look out over the plaza. I saw a long line snaking outside in the plaza and, assuming them to be tourists, I congratulated myself on having beat the madding crowd. They were not tourists, however, but a choir of two hundred bused in from Germany. As they filed past, I went back inside and stood on the balcony of the dome designed by Michelangelo. Beneath me, the choir formed a large circle under the dome and began to sing a capella. Some of the words were in Latin, some in German—and inside that dome with its perfect acoustics, I was suspended in their music. I had the feeling that if I lifted my arms the medium itself would support me.

Michelangelo once confessed that his work had crowded out his own faith. As his life drew to a close, he penned these lines:

> So now, from this mad passion
> which made me take art for an idol and a king
> I have learnt the burden of error that it bore. . . .
> The world's frivolities have robbed me of the time
> That I was given for reflecting upon God.

Perhaps. But Michelangelo and others like him have through their labors—sometimes as goads, sometimes as nails, sometimes as scribblers in the sand—helped turn us from the world's frivolities and given us time for such reflection. My other memories of Italy involve pollution, long lines, traffic gridlock, and snarling motorbikes. But for that one moment inside St. Peter's, I had inhabited a glorious space not on earth, a moment of time not in time. Art had done its work.

Contributors' Notes

Coleman Barks is professor emeritus at the University of Georgia. He has published seven books of his own poetry, along with *Essential Rumi*, *Rumi: The Big Red Book*, and numerous other works that bring into American free verse, in collaboration with scholars of the Persian language, the poetry of the great thirteenth-century mystic Jelaluddin Rumi.

Rick Bass is the author of twenty-five books of fiction and nonfiction, including, most recently, a novel, *Nashville Chrome*. He lives in Yaak and Missoula, Montana, with his wife and daughters, and is a board member of the Yaak Valley Forest Council (www.yaakvalley.org).

Joseph Bottum is the editor of *First Things*.

Alice Lok Cahana is an artist who lives in Houston, Texas.

Joel E. Cohen, author of *How Many People Can the Earth Support?*, is the Abby Rockefeller Mauzé Professor of Populations at the Rockefeller University and Columbia University in New York and a member of the National Academy of Sciences in applied mathematics. He was a MacArthur Fellow.

Billy Collins's ninth collection of poems is *Horoscopes for the Dead*. He is a Distinguished Professor at Lehman College (CUNY) and a Distinguished Fellow at the Winter Park Institute of Rollins College.

Robert Cording teaches English and creative writing at College of the Holy Cross, where he is the Barrett Professor of Creative Writing. He has published six collections of poems, most recently *Walking with Ruskin*.

Paul J. Griffiths has held the Warren Chair of Catholic Theology at Duke Divinity School since 2008. Before that, he held academic positions at the University of Illinois, the University of Chicago, and the University of Notre Dame. He is the author of nine books, most recently *Intellectual Appetite: A Theological Grammar*. He was received into the Catholic Church in Chicago during Advent, 1996.

Zenshin Michael Haederle is a Rinzai Zen monk, writer, and teacher living in New Mexico. His work has appeared in *Miller-McCune, The Los Angeles Times, Reader's Digest, People, The New York Times, AARP Bulletin Today, Shambhala Sun, Tricycle: The Buddhist Review,* and many other publications.

Edward Hoagland's many books include *Hoagland on Nature: Essays, Compass Points: How I Lived,* and *Tigers & Ice: Essays on Life and Nature.*

Nancy Honicker lives in Paris, France, where she teaches at the University of Paris 8. She has published essays and fiction in many reviews in Europe and the United States and writes a monthly column about her life in France for the Times-Shamrock Newspaper Group of Scranton, Pennsylvania.

Robert D. Kaplan is a national correspondent for *The Atlantic*. His many books include *Imperial Grunts: The American Military on the Ground*, *Eastward to Tartary: Travels in the Balkans, the Middle East, and the Caucasus*, and *The Coming Anarchy: Shattering the Dreams of the Post Cold War*.

Jesse Kellerman is the bestselling author of *The Executor*, *The Genius*, *Trouble*, and *Sunstroke*. He also holds a master of fine arts in theater. He has won several awards for his writing, including the Princess Grace Award, given to America's most promising young playwright. He lives with his wife and son in California.

Bruce Lawrie lives in Scotts Valley, California. A father of two handicapped children and a cancer survivor, he writes about the beautiful catastrophe of life here on earth during this particular slice of eternity. For more, see www.beautiful-catastrophe.com.

Philip Levine's many books of poetry include *Breath*, *The Mercy*, *The Simple Truth* (Pulitzer Prize for Poetry, 1995), and *What Work Is* (National Book Award for Poetry, 1991).

Barry Lopez is the author of thirteen works of fiction and nonfiction and the recipient of the National Book Award and other honors. He wrote the introduction to *The Best Spiritual Writing 2005*. For more, see www.barrylopez.com.

Robert Miola is the Gerard Manley Hopkins Professor of English and Lecturer in Classics at Loyola University Maryland. A graduate of Fordham University, he has written widely on ancient and early modern writers, especially Shakespeare.

Seyyed Hossein Nasr is the University Professor of Islamic Studies at George Washington University and the author of many books, including *Man and Nature: The Spiritual Crisis of Modern Man*, *Religion and the Order of Nature*, and *Knowledge and the Sacred*.

Marilyn Nelson's books include *Carver: A Life in Poems* and *A Wreath for Emmett Till*. Her honors include a Guggenheim fellowship and three honorary doctorates. The former Poet Laureate of Connecticut, she is the founder/director of Soul Mountain Retreat.

Melissa Range's first book of poems, *Horse and Rider*, won the 2010 Walt McDonald Prize in Poetry from Texas Tech University Press. She is currently pursuing her PhD in English and creative writing at the University of Missouri.

Philip Schultz is the author of several books of poetry, including *The God of Loneliness, Failure* (Pulitzer Prize for Poetry, 2008), *Living in the Past*, and *The Holy Worm of Praise*. He is also the founder and director of the Writer's Studio in New York.

Anita Sullivan is a poet, gardener, translator, birdwatcher, rock art enthusiast, and piano tuner, whose NPR broadcasts, essays, and poems have reached a wide audience. She has published two essay collections and two poetry chapbooks, and recently earned an MFA in Poetry from Pacific Lutheran University. She lives in Eugene, Oregon, with her husband, piano historian Edwin Good.

Terry Teachout is the drama critic of *The Wall Street Journal* and the chief culture critic of *Commentary*. His books include *Pops: A Life of Louis Armstrong, The Skeptic: A Life of H. L. Mencken*, and *A Terry Teachout Reader*.

Richard Wilbur's books include *Collected Poems 1943–2004* and many others. He has twice been awarded the Pulitzer Prize for Poetry, and in 1994 he received the National Medal of Arts. He served as Poet Laureate of the United States from 1987–1988.

Robert Louis Wilken is the William R. Kenan, Jr., Professor of the History of Christianity Emeritus at the University of Virginia.

His most recent book is *The Spirit of Early Christian Thought: Seeking the Face of God.*

Nancy Willard is the author of two novels, *Things Invisible to See* and *Sister Water*, and twelve books of poetry, including *In the Salt Marsh*. Her most recent book, *The Left-Handed Story*, is a collection of essays on writing. She has been awarded grants from the National Endowment for the Arts in both fiction and poetry, and her book *A Visit to William Blake's Inn: Poems for Innocent and Experienced Travelers*, was awarded the Newbery Medal. She teaches in the English Department at Vassar College.

C. K. Williams's most recent book of poems, *Wait*, was published in May of 2010, as was a prose study, *On Whitman*. He is a member of the American Academy of Arts and Letters and teaches in the Creative Writing Program at Princeton University.

Christian Wiman's latest book is *Every Riven Thing*. He lives in Chicago, where he edits *Poetry*.

Ruth R. Wisse is the Martin Peretz Professor of Yiddish Literature and Comparative Literature at Harvard University. Previously she taught at McGill University, where she helped to establish the Jewish Studies Program. Her books include *The Modern Jewish Canon* and a political study, *Jews and Power*.

Philip Yancey, a journalist by profession, has written more than twenty books, including such bestsellers as *The Jesus I Never Knew*, *What's So Amazing About Grace*, and *Prayer: Does It Make Any Difference?*

Philip Zaleski is the editor of the Best Spiritual Writing series and the author of many books, among them *The Recollected Heart, Gifts of the Spirit,* and *Prayer: A History* (with Carol Zaleski). He is a research associate at Smith College.

Other Notable Spiritual Writing of the Year

Dick Allen, "Taoism: A Primer," *The Georgia Review*, Fall.

Gary A. Anderson, "Does the Promise Still Hold?," *Christian Century*, January 13.

Fred Bahnson, "Martyr's Mirror," *The Sun*, June.

Mike Barrett, "Searching for Radical Faith," *Christianity Today*, February.

Stephen Batchelor, "Tibet: Fifty Years of Exile," *Tricycle*, Summer.

Brian Doyle, "The Order by Which People Are Admitted to Heaven," *Notre Dame Magazine*, Autumn.

Ann Conway, "The Rosary," *Image*, Summer.

John Herlihy, "Elixir of the Heart," *Sophia*, Summer.

Andrew Hudgins, "Suddenly Adults," *The Gettysburg Review*, Spring.

Katie Kresser, "Night Vision," *Image*, Spring.

Mark I. Pinsky, "The Greening of Jesus," *Harvard Divinity Bulletin*, Winter.

Maggie Robbins, "Without a Prayer," *The New York Times Magazine*, May 3.

Michael Schulman, "The Chapel on the Moon," *Believer*, June.

Sally Thomas, "Shadows in Amsterdam," *First Things*, May.

Charles Taliaferro and Jil Evans, "The Origin of Aesthetics," *Touchstone*, November.

Charles Wright, "Yellow Wings," *Harvard Divinity Bulletin*, Winter.

Franz Wright, "Learning to Read," *The New Yorker*, January 19.

Sara Zarr, "Who Is My Mother, Who Are My Brothers?" *Image*, Spring.

Grateful acknowledgment is made for permission
to reprint the following copyrighted works:

"Starting Out from Ted Hughes's Letters" by Coleman Barks. First appeared in *The Georgia Review*, Fall 2009. Copyright © Coleman Barks, 2009. Reprinted by permission of the author.

"The Return" by Rick Bass. First appeared in *Orion*, May/June 2009. Copyright © Rick Bass, 2009. Reprinted by permission of the author.

"Words of Nectar and Cyanide" by Joseph Bottum. First appeared in *First Things*, May 2009. Reprinted by permission of *First Things*.

"Words Are Not Enough" by Alice Lok Cahana. First appeared in *Portland*, Autumn 2009. Copyright © Alice Lok Cahana, 2009. Reprinted by permission of the author.

"A Mindful Beauty" by Joel E. Cohen. First appeared in *The American Scholar*, Autumn 2009. Copyright © Joel E. Cohen, 2009. Reprinted by permission of the author.

"Grave" by Billy Collins. First appeared in *The Atlantic*, September 2009. Reprinted by permission of the author.

"Czeslaw Milosz's Glasses" from *Walking With Ruskin* by Robert Cording. First appeared in *The Southern Review*, Spring 2009. Reprinted by permission of CavanKerry Press, Ltd.

"Turning Points" by Paul J. Griffiths. First appeared in *The Christian Century*, November 3, 2009. Reprinted by permission of *The Christian Century*.

"Sesshin with Sasaki Roshi" by Michael Haederle. First appeared in *Shambhala Sun*, January 2009. Reprinted by permission of the author.